# Captured by Canada:

## Alive in Algonquin

by
Skeeter Lee

# Acknowledgements

First and foremost, a massive hug and kiss to my wife who supported me as I struggled through the writing and editing process. I am in her debt for allowing me to escape to the woods when I needed to find tranquility.

I would like to thank all the campers and students with whom I worked over the past five decades. You taught me so much about how people learn and how teenagers rise to overcome challenges. I apologize to some of you for my stubbornness and lack of understanding early in my career. Your successes as adults have made me proud.

None of the characters in Captured by Canada – Alive in Algonquin are based on a specific individual. However, some may think they see a little of themselves. This is normal. While I tried to avoid stereotypes, there are universal character traits. While each person is unique, we do share certain kinds of behaviors.

Specific thanks to:
Dan Elish for his initial guidance and thoughtful developmental editing.

Liz Shay for her copy editing, forcing me to clarify my ideas into precise words on the page.

The many beta-readers over the years for your observations and keen insights. Your comments give this book added depth.

# Table of Contents

# Chapter 1
## Arrival

Tom's grandmother was driving too fast over the worst road Tom had ever seen. His head bounced off the roof as the car lurched over the ruts and dust swirled behind them. As their car rounded a sharp turn, a rusted road grader rolled toward them, throwing up its own dust cloud.

"Damn!" yelled his grandmother.

Their car heaved to the left and skidded to a stop inside a bush. The two clouds merged to create a kind of spooky stillness. As Tom's heartbeat slowed, he wondered if this was what it would be like inside of a sandstorm.

His grandmother's snarl broke the silence. "The silly boys' camp always waited until the last minute." She struggled to open her door.

As if by itself, Tom's door flew open and a gray-haired man grabbed his arm.

"You okay?"

"Yes."

The man helped Tom to the road. His strong hands were grimy, but his smile was kind.

From the other side of the car, his grandmother muttered, "This damn brush! I think I ripped my skirt!"

Tom's rescuer scurried to his grandmother and helped her stomp through the branches.

Once she was standing in the road, she pulled the

leaves from her short dark hair. She smiled benevolently at her rescuer. "Thank you. I was driving too fast. I'm sure I scared you. I'm so sorry."

"Didn't expect anyone today. Camp opens tomorrow."

The man stood awkwardly, obviously uncomfortable.

Hesitantly, he asked, "Can I see if I can get the car onto the road?"

His grandmother's face broke into one of her *'you'd be my best friend for life'* smiles. He'd seen her use this look before, and he knew she'd get her way.

"That would be so kind. I'm know that you have so much to do. I'm so sorry." She turned to Tom. "Go stand out of the way."

He walked a dozen steps down the potholed road. The dust was settling and sunbeams splashed through the green leaves. He was definitely no longer in New York City.

Coming to Camp Catamount had been a lifelong dream, but now that he was minutes from arrival, he wondered if he'd made a terrible mistake. He knew almost nothing about what happened at a tripping camp. To say he was apprehensive was an understatement.

Tom's eyes surveyed the surrounding forest. Except for the bushes along the sides of the road, the forest floor was not cluttered. Tom thought he could walk among the trees almost as smoothly as he could have ambled through the groves of Central Park. But the Canadian trees were far larger than those in Central Park and they towered majestically. He hadn't been in the deep woods since his father's accident. There was a sense of mystery there, but at the same time, he felt oddly at ease.

A sharp grinding sound shot through the quiet and the car heaved backwards. Tom moved further away so he couldn't be blamed for anything.

So far, the summer of 1980 had been a disaster. Two of

his teachers had reworded the essay questions on their final exams and he'd failed both subjects. After pleas from his mother and threats from his grandparents, the school had changed the F's to D's. But it had been too late. The boarding schools had rejected him.

Not being accepted into high school had changed everything. In the original plan, Tom, his mother, and stepfather would have been in Paris visiting his step-grandparents right now. After a month in France, they'd planned to go to Moscow for the 1980 Summer Olympics. After that, they were to travel to his mother's new home in Delhi, India. Then, in early September, he would have flown back to the US to live in a dorm at his new school.

The closing of the car door brought Tom back to the present. The gray-haired man was peering under the car.

"There's a big rock behind the front wheel. I'll get the shovel out of the grader. "

"Oh, thank you so much," charmed his grandmother. She walked to Tom and smiled. "Welcome to the North."

He didn't know what to say, so he said nothing.

She continued, "I miss the smell of the northern forest. It's clean and fresh. In many ways, I wish I was coming back."

Carrying a small shovel, the man walked to the car. Tom noted he was wearing a faded blue Camp Catamount t-shirt.

"I'll see if I can give him a hand, but I doubt it." Her face blossomed into her special smile. "In the old days, they were so competent. They could do anything."

"Can I help?" asked Tom.

"No," she said as she turned back to the car. "Sometimes staying out of the way is the best thing. He'll get us back on the road, and then it's only another three or four minutes to the Lodge."

In the quiet, Tom realized that the woods had come alive. Bird calls echoed from the canopy. Across the road, two chipmunks scurried from rock to rock as if they were playing tag.

Tom's childhood fantasy had been to come to Camp Catamount, following in both his father and grandfather's footsteps. As a young boy, he'd listened to their adventurous tales about the North, but after his father's death, his mother had refused to talk about Tom spending time in the woods. While she had been comfortable with his explorations around the city, she had even been concerned about his ramblings in Central Park.

After his academic failures, Tom had been aware of the conversations between his mother and grandparents regarding his future. While he'd been left out of the discussions, he'd known that his opinions would have had little impact on whatever was decided.

Before his mother left for Kennedy Airport eleven days ago, she'd signed guardianship papers, leaving him in his grandparents' care. Even though she was crying as she got into the cab, he'd sensed that she was relieved to have someone else take over so that she could move on to her new life.

During dinner that evening, Tom's grandparents had presented the idea of a month at Catamount. Tom had been excited but apprehensive. He'd begged for a day to think. Then, just before lunch on the following day, his grandfather's car had been demolished by a dump truck.

Tom and his grandmother spent the next two days outside the Intensive Care Unit. Once his grandfather was out of danger, they began planning for his recovery. Moving a hospital bed into the living room of their small apartment meant that his new US home, the guest room, had been piled with excess furniture.

Getting out of the way began to make sense. When Tom agreed to go to camp, his grandmother was visibly relieved.

After his grandfather moved back into the apartment, it became very clear that his nurse was giving the orders. Her hostility toward Tom's attempts to be helpful reinforced his feeling that he'd made a good decision to attend Catamount. The afternoon before his departure, however, he frankly missed his mother's insistence on careful planning as he watched his grandmother hurriedly stuffing his clothes into two over-sized canvas duffels.

Tom enjoyed the flight to Toronto. The drive from the airport had taken them from an eight-lane expressway to an endless two-lane road that wound through smaller and smaller towns. Except for the unfamiliar names on signs, the city and the suburbs looked like those in New York. In several places, Tom had seen signs saying, "Boycott the Olympic Boycott." His grandmother had assured him that most Canadians supported the US-led decision to withdraw from the Moscow Olympics over the Russian invasion of Afghanistan. Tom hoped that she was right.

During the last hour, the small villages had seemed to be farther apart and the quality of the pavement deteriorated. Even so, his grandmother continued to drive well above the speed limit. Tom was relieved when he saw a sign for the Trans-Canadian Highway, but once they'd turned onto the highway, he was surprised that it was just another two-lane road. It was well-maintained, but in the ten minutes that they drove on it, only two cars and one tractor trailer passed them going in the opposite direction.

As the car slowed and turned onto a rutted dirt road, Tom's grandmother pointed to a weathered sign with blue lettering. "The boys still haven't done anything with their sign. I wonder how many new campers will miss the entrance."

Exiting a national highway directly onto a dirt road

was a first for Tom. He wondered what other kinds of transitions would be facing him in Canada.

The sound of spinning tires brought Tom back to the immediate. The car rocked forwards and lurched backwards, shooting back onto the road. His grandmother waved for him to come back to the car.

"Thank you so much," she repeated to the man. "It was all my fault. I'm so sorry. I'll tell the office how helpful you were."

"You're welcome," the man said with a smile. "Let me back the grader to a turn out. That way, you can get around me without any problem."

"That would be wonderful. You've been so caring. It's good to see Catamount still has its strong values."

As he walked to his machine, Tom saw the man beaming proudly.

"Tom, back into the car. The camp is just ahead."

On the newly-leveled road, she drove more slowly and seemed to wrestle with the steering as the car slid in the turns.

"Damn fresh gravel," grumbled his grandmother. "They should have done this days ago so it could pack down. This road will be a mess tomorrow."

Trying to lighten the mood, Tom said, "At least there's no traffic."

"Thank God for small favors." She smiled. "I wonder what's changed in center camp. It's been more than 20 years."

A few minutes later, the car exited the forest and drove past two well-maintained sports fields, one lined for soccer and the other for football. At the far end, a shaded dirt parking lot was crowded with six trailers piled with canoes. His grandmother stopped the car at the top of a steep hill, beeped the horn, and inched down a narrow lane. After a sharp turn, they exited the trees. In front of them, beyond a wide expanse of grass, crisp sparkles danced off the water.

His grandmother pulled the car onto the freshly cut lawn and turned off the motor. They exited the car and looked around. After experiencing the road, Tom was relieved to see the buildings seemed to be well-maintained.

Finally, in a quiet voice, his grandmother said, "Nothing has changed."

Tom didn't know whether this was good or bad, so he waited.

A smile appeared on her lips. She pointed to the massive dark wooden structure overlooking the bay. "That's the Lodge."

She waved her hand. "This area is called the Main Yard."

The green field sloped down to brown weathered docks.

"That's the Canoe Dock," she said, pointing to the left side of the bay.

Blue, gold, and silver canoes were stacked on the wide boards. At the far end, an elevated walkway continued to a forest of colored poles hung on a series of lines.

Tom's grandmother waved her hand to the other side. "That's the Waterfront."

An H-shaped swim area sported a blue diving board and a tower with a yellow slide. Beyond it, a dozen or more white sailboats floated in narrow slips.

"It's good to be back." She took a deep breath and stood taller than normal.

"You'll love it at Catamount," his grandmother said. "It's a special place."

"And what if I hate it?" Tom whispered.

"We've talked about that. I'll speak with the Director."

"You promise?"

"Yes. But I doubt that you'll let me forget."

Taking a deep breath, she said, "Thomas, let's get

going. I have a plane to catch tomorrow morning. I need to get back to your grandfather."

The Lodge's wide staircase invited them to climb up to its shaded porch.

"Yes, Gema. Should I bring my stuff?"

She paused, lost in thought. His grandmother had become quieter as they approached the camp, and he was having difficulty reading her. Was she pleased to be here, or did she want be on her way?

He knew that her memories were conflicted. Early in their drive, she'd talked about the good times. Her recollections of her days as a camper and counselor were filled with joy. She had become pensive and then silent when he asked about his father's years at Catamount. And now their almost-accident with the road grader had pushed her into her *'I'm in-charge'* mood.

Finally, she said, "No, we need to see where you'll be sleeping tonight and what cabin you'll be in. Let's go to the office first."

Tom followed his grandmother up the wide stairway.

From a rocking chair on the expansive porch, a young man in a blue shirt jumped up. "May I help you, ma'am?"

"No, thank you. I know my way to the office, assuming it's in the same place. To the right of the kitchen?"

"Yes, ma'am. Welcome to Camp Catamount."

Tom was comforted that his grandmother knew her way around the camp headquarters. He scurried to keep up as she marched across the large dining hall. She was in one of her moods.

A light-filled doorway welcomed them.

His grandmother stopped abruptly and her eyes widened. Her voice uncertain, she said, "Earnie?"

"Barbara, we've been expecting you. You haven't changed since the last time I saw you."

His grandmother said nothing. Tom had never seen her so still.

Behind the desk, a blue-shirted older man smiled. His green eyes and white teeth sparkled from his lined, tanned face. The man jumped up and motioned her to one of the four chairs. He pointed Tom toward another. He sat and slid his chair close to his grandmother.

"How's Charlie doing now that he's home?"

"How did you know about the accident?" his grandmother asked quietly. "It was last week. As we tried to sort out things for Tom, he told me he'd talked with the Director. Camp had an open bunk, and everything was set."

"The Catamount network." The man smiled. "Someone hears something and tells someone. Before long, everyone knows."

Tom's grandmother shook her head. "Speaking of accidents, the man on the road grader was such a big help. I was driving too fast and ended up in a bush. Please thank him for helping us back on the road. He was so kind."

"I'll thank him. Leo's a good man. He's been with us for decades. He works wonders with the fields and the vehicles." Earnie grinned. "You never did know the meaning of slow. Speaking of older men, what's Charlie's prognosis?"

"He's got a long recovery ahead of him. He's already begun his physical therapy. His left wrist and his left leg were broken. Luckily, his heart seems to be fine. Did you hear about his heart attack?"

"He mentioned it to me the last time we spoke, but he said everything was fine."

This was news to Tom. His childhood feelings about not being told about his father's failing health unexpectedly flooded back.

"That's Charlie. Always the optimist. He was lucky

we were in London. The doctors said he recovered nicely. We decided we were tired of living overseas, so he retired. In April, we moved back to New York."

"Except for camp, I've retired too, kind of. I know Charlie will work on getting back his strength." said Earnie. "You seemed surprised to see me?"

"Charlie said nothing about you being at Catamount. He just said that he'd talked to the Director and found a place for Thomas." His grandmother sighed, and her shoulders dropped slightly. "The last couple of weeks have been so crazy."

"I guess he wanted to surprise you."

Tom's grandmother huffed and sat up straight. "You talked with him, and he didn't tell me? That's just like him. He can be such a brat when it comes to surprises."

"I guess that means he hasn't changed much. He always was a trickster." Earnie swiveled his chair and extended his hand to Tom. "I'm Earnie McMannius. Welcome to Camp Catamount."

"I'm Tom Woodruff. Pleased to meet you, sir."

Firmly, Tom shook Earnie's hand and looked him square in the eyes. Earnie's smile was welcoming. Earnie's handshake was firm, and Tom sensed he was physically fit despite having a stomach that inched over his belt. His short gray hair and his weathered face spoke of wisdom earned through years of experience.

"Your grandfather and I paddled together when we were young. Later, I guided your dad through some whitewater on the Dumoine. Then, for a few years, he worked for me."

Earnie paused.

Tom knew what was coming.

"I'm sorry about your father. He was a good man. I know his death must have been tough for you."

"It was." Hoping to change the subject, Tom asked, "Are you by any chance the Mac Man my grandfather talked about?"

"I'm the same. Few know me by that name anymore. Now, I'm Earnie, the Senior Guide. I'm in charge of everything having to do with any kind of camp trip."

"Grandfather told me you once saved his life."

"Your grandfather saved my life as well." Earnie grinned. "We made a talented team back in the day."

"They were a pair of crazies," Tom's grandmother said. "Earnie was, and may still be, your grandfather's best friend. They tripped together as campers. Then, as adults, they paddled together in the far North."

"Yes, we did. If I remember, Barbara, you had a big part in one of those trips."

"Did you do a northern trip?" Tom peered at his grandmother. "I know you met Grandfather at camp."

"I did a few canoe trips when I was younger."

"You never said a word when Grandfather and Dad talked about the North."

"I didn't want to interrupt their tales or correct any details." Tom's grandmother smiled. "Sometimes, they exaggerated a little."

"Sometimes, a story takes on a life of its own," said Earnie as he turned back to Tom's grandmother. "Now, tell me more about Charlie and what he's facing in rehab."

Tom's grandmother launched into the details of the accident and his grandfather's injuries. He was disappointed not to hear more stories about his grandparents. On the other hand, the grown-up conversation was allowing him to examine his surroundings.

As the two adults talked, Tom looked around. On one wall, there were large maps of Canada, Ontario, Quebec, and Algonquin Park. On another, smaller sections of individual maps were tacked together to create a long, wide stretch of the Ottawa River. From what he'd seen outside, the river appeared to be a big lake. The map was dotted with pins of various colors. Tom guessed that the bigger blue pin was the camp. He was puzzled by the empty bookshelves covering the wall behind the desk.

Looking out the large window, Tom gazed at an open-sided building with a sign saying Trip Shack. He guessed that was where the equipment was kept.

Tom had long dreamed about paddling in the North. When he was little, he'd thought that his first wilderness trip would be with his father. After his father had died, he'd hoped for his grandfather.

Now that he was in Canada with a group of strangers, the Northwoods seemed both mysterious and exciting. Could he survive the wilderness? While he knew that his mother's fears about outdoor adventures were overblown, he'd hadn't slept in a tent since he was a boy.

"Tom."

He snapped back to the conversation.

"You'll be a Scout in Eagle's Roost," said Earnie. "It's at the far end of the Cadet section. I'll get to know you, because when the Scouts are in camp, I bunk with them."

Tom knew he should respond, but he didn't know what to say. After a too long pause, he mumbled, "Does that mean you paddle with us?"

"Probably not on your river trip; maybe your service trip. These details are still being worked out."

"The Scouts do the Dumoine River, don't they?" Tom hoped to confirm what he'd been told.

"Yes, they do. What did your grandfather tell you about the river?"

"He said that it was the biggest challenge of his life, and he was lucky to make it out alive."

Earnie chuckled. "Your grandfather always did like telling tales. My guess is, whatever he told you, it's an exaggeration. The river is not as dangerous as its reputation. Understand?"

Tom paused, again, unsure of what to say. The easiest was, "Yes, sir."

"Good. Your counselors are Jack Atherholt and Rio Brunner. At the moment, they are paddling with the Director and the rest of the staff. I got the short straw and had to stay back to answer the phones and greet any early arrivals."

Tom's grandmother interjected, "Isn't Eagle's Roost way out at the end of the point? That's a long way to carry Tom's gear."

"Barbara, you have an excellent memory. The answer is yes. But, if you think it would be easier, we could paddle?"

"Could we? That would be delightful." Tom's grandmother almost jumped out of her seat. Her face beamed. "I'd love to paddle. I'll have to change, though. Can I use the Boat House?"

Her eagerness surprised Tom. He'd known that his grandmother had gone to a Canadian camp where she'd met his grandfather. But she'd never talked about canoeing in the same way that his father and grandfather had. When Tom was little, he vaguely remembered her in the front of a canoe, but that was years ago. For that matter, he hadn't been in a canoe since his father's accident years ago. What, if anything, would he remember?

"Of course we can paddle. There's no one around, so using the Boat House will be fine. Shall we get started?"

Earnie stood up.

"Please sit down," Tom's grandmother said. "There's one more thing."

"Yes, I know. The escape plan."

Tom stiffened. How did Earnie know?

"Tom, you're not the only boy who's been uneasy about coming to Catamount. And there's one other new boy in the Scouts, so you're not the only new person."

This made Tom feel better.

"Here's how the *I-want-to-go-home* plan works. Tom, you give camp two weeks. That includes a trip. If you're miserable and can't stand being here, we will not keep you. On the morning after the Circus, which is two weeks from now, you'll go to the Nurse for sick call. You'll have stomach pains. We'll take you to a doctor. You'll have appendicitis. After the operation, you'll have to go home. Understand?"

"Yes, sir." Tom swallowed.

"No one else will know except for the Nurse, and then, only if you show up. You ask her to see me. She'll talk to me, and the rest happens. Does this seem workable?"

Tom looked at his grandmother.

"He'll be fine." She smiled. "Catamount will work its magic."

"Tom, what do you think?" Earnie asked.

"I'm good. Thank you, sir. I'll give camp a try. I hope it works."

"It should. Remember that I'm Earnie, not 'sir.'"

"Yes, Earnie."

"Now, Tom, let's get your belongings. Your grandmother will meet us down at the Canoe Dock. After she changes, she can find paddles and lifejackets in the Boat House."

The three walked out a side door. Tom's duffel bags filled the back seat of the car. As Tom struggled with one, Earnie slid the other out of the far door and threw it up across his shoulders. His grandmother grabbed her travel bag and walked down the grass.

"Glad that you don't have a big locker trunk. They're a pain to carry," said Earnie.

Tom struggled to get the bulky duffel onto his shoulder. Earnie trotted ahead, catching up to his grandmother. She seemed to be dancing down the hill. He was glad to see her in such high spirits.

14

After his duffel fell a second time, Tom dragged it the last ten feet to beside his other bag, three lifejackets, and paddles. He turned and saw someone come out of the Boat House carrying a yellow canoe with blue stripes in its middle. Tom's jaw dropped when his grandmother flipped the boat down onto the dock. Her smile was bright. He hadn't seen her in a t-shirt and shorts in years.

"MacManny, after all of these years, I can still carry a canoe," she called. Let's see if I remember how to paddle."

Tom's grandmother slipped the yellow canoe into the water and held it next to the dock with a paddle. After dropping a faded blue lifejacket into the canoe, she slid into the seat and pushed away from the dock. She kneeled and rocked the canoe onto its side so the lower hand on her paddle was close to the water. The tilted canoe looked unstable, but his grandmother seemed at ease.

Tom was stunned that she looked so comfortable. He'd never remembered seeing his grandmother paddle by herself. With a sweep of her paddle, the canoe skimmed away from the dock. She looked as relaxed as if she were walking her little dog in Central Park.

Earnie came up behind him. "Tom, you seem to have brought a lot for camp."

"The day before we left, Grandmother crammed everything on the clothing list into the duffels."

"I'm not surprised. She always was last-minute. Didn't your mother help before she left?"

"No. In fact, she doesn't know I'm here. She would not approve. Anyway, she would have been useless. She would have wanted me to be stylish."

"I guess that your mom's not a camper?"

That was not the question Tom was expecting.

"No, she's not. Dad used to say that her idea of roughing it was a Holiday Inn rather than the Ritz."

"I understand. Let's load your duffels into the center

of the canoe and see if we can catch your grandmother. When were you last in a canoe?"

"Not since before Dad died." Tom felt tears welling. He wiped his eyes and took a deep breath. "I'm not sure I remember anything."

Earnie smiled. "It'll come back. I bet that your dad and grandfather had you in a canoe before you could walk."

"I think Grandfather said something about that before we left."

"Tom, let's put a boat in the water."

From the canoe racks, the two carried a canoe to the lake. Earnie stuffed the duffels into the center.

"Can you swim?"

"Yes. For three years, I was on the swim team at the Y."

"What strokes did you swim?'

"100 crawl and 100 breaststroke."

Earnie threw lifejackets in the front and rear of the canoe and handed Tom a paddle.

"With those strokes, you can swim, so no lifejacket for now. When conditions call for it, moving water and foul weather, we wear them. You have to pass the swim test, though."

Tom grimaced.

"So does everyone else. Safety first. The Plebes and Middies always wear jackets. Every summer, the Cadets and Scouts must swim 200 meters without stopping. Only then can they paddle without a jacket in calm conditions. So, here's a paddle. I guessed on its size. Now, let's catch your grandmother. I'll hold the canoe while you get in."

Tom sat on the dock and eased himself onto the bow seat. He didn't feel stable, so he grasped the wooden edge of the dock. The canoe rocked as Earnie got into the stern.

"You can let go."

After pushing away from the dock, without thinking, Tom slid to his knees and felt more secure. He dug his paddle into the water and pulled hard. He concentrated, trying to remember what his father and grandfather had taught him. It didn't take long for Tom's arms and back to begin to ache. He was grateful when Earnie called to switch sides. Tom swung the paddle to his left without missing a stroke.

"Well done," said Earnie. "You remember something about paddling."

Tom smiled.

The two began to catch up to his grandmother, but she disappeared around a point of land. As they rounded a granite outcropping, Tom saw his grandmother drifting ahead of them.

"Relax. Don't paddle any more. We'll raft up with your grandmother."

Earnie eased their canoe next to his grandmother, so it stopped precisely as the two gunwales kissed. Tom was impressed at Earnie's skill. His grandmother grabbed their boat, and Tom pushed up onto the seat. He straightened his knees and stretched his muscles.

Tom's grandmother smiled at Earnie. "Took you long enough."

"You had a head start. Tom's paddling is impressive. I believe that his dad and his grandfather taught him something. He went to his knees like an experienced tripper."

Tom smiled, feeling that camp might be okay.

As the canoes drifted into a second bay, Earnie pointed. "This is Cabin Cove. Directly across is Scout Point. Your cabin, Eagle's Roost, is in the woods behind that first small dock. Down a path to the right are the washhouse and shower building. The larger dock near the bridge is used by the Cadets. They are the campers a year or two younger than you. On this side of the cove are the Middie and Plebe sections. The Plebes are the youngest and live the closest to the point. This is the Plebe dock here, and the Middie dock is down by the bridge. Have I been clear?"

"Yes, sir," said Tom.

"I'm Earnie. Remember, there's no 'sir.' We're at camp."

"Okay, Earnie."

"Shall we go see Tom's cabin?" asked Earnie.

Tom's grandmother said, "Let me be the first to the dock."

"Always the adventurer," said Earnie.

"I think I've been here before."

Tom's grandmother smiled as her canoe pulled away.

"Give her a minute," said Earnie. "If you're kneeling, you might want to slide your lifejacket under your knees. Otherwise, they get very sore this early in the summer."

"Thanks."

Tom slid the lifejacket under his knees.

"Let's go," said Earnie.

With effort, Tom pulled on his paddle.

"No need for speed. We're not going that far," said Earnie.

When Tom's grandmother reached the Scout dock, she exited gracefully and pulled her canoe out of the water. Then she steadied their canoe as the two unloaded the duffels. Afterwards, she and Earnie lifted the canoe up onto the little dock.

"Barbara, go up to Eagle's Roost. Tom and I will get his gear."

Earnie swung one of the duffels onto his shoulders and said, "Tom, follow me."

Tom tried lifting his duffel by its strap but stumbled. Earnie eased his duffel down to the ground.

"Tom, let me show you how to get a load up on your shoulders. With the weight high on your body, you'll find it a lot easier to carry."

Tom felt awkward.

"First, pull the duffel up onto a bent knee. Then, jerk the load up onto your shoulders as you twist under it. Watch."

Earnie made the lift seem simple.

"Now, your turn."

After a second try, and with Earnie's help, Tom had the duffel resting on his shoulders.

"Good job. It takes practice. Now, follow me."

Earnie trotted up a narrow path.

Tom found the load didn't seem so heavy once it was high on his shoulders. He walked up the trail and came to a large clearing. Tom's grandmother was holding the cabin door open, and he walked inside. Earnie eased his duffel to the wooden floor and then helped Tom lower his load.

"Welcome to Scout Point. This is Eagle's Roost." Earnie smiled. "It's your home when you're in camp."

"The cabin hasn't changed since William was in it." Tom's grandmother blinked and wiped her eyes.

Earnie said, "They're built to last."

Tom examined the rectangular wooden structure. Its angled roof line gave it a ski chalet appearance. Each end had a door and two large, screened windows that extended almost from floor to ceiling. The beds ran perpendicular to the walls, and Tom thought it looked like a hospital ward from a World War II movie. Seeing that there were no bunk beds, Tom realized that he had wasted time agonizing over a possible choice of top or bottom. He was surprised that there were no mattresses on the bunks; the sleeping surface was a piece of canvas slung between 2 x 4's.

As if she was reading his mind, his grandmother said, "The bunks are comfortable once you get used to them. Back in my day, we had the same set-up at Otterslide. I'm pleased to see that it hasn't changed. Where is your bunk, Earnie?"

"I'm at the far end, closest to the point and the firepit, but it's the farthest from the washroom and the showers. It's cooler when it's hot because any breezes blow off the water. The two counselors have taken their bunks at this end. They like being near the showers. Tom, you're the first camper. Make your choice."

Tom considered his options. He guessed that being as far away as possible from the counselors would be the popular place. He didn't really care about the bathroom and having an ally nearby would be good.

"I'll go across from you," said Tom. He pulled his duffel bag onto his knee and swung it up onto his shoulders.

"You're a quick learner." Earnie hoisted the other one. "I'm glad to have a neighbor for the night."

Tom dropped his duffel next to his bed.

"Pull out your sleeping bag and get out a flashlight. We won't be back here until after dark," Earnie explained. "Do you have something to put under your sleeping bag?"

"I think so."

"We packed two wool blankets," stated Tom's grandmother, using one of her tones. "It gets cold up here."

"Yes, it can, especially in late August and up North," said Earnie. "But, for now, Tom, you only need one."

Tom opened one of the duffels and pulled out his sleeping bag, a small pillow, and his sleep clothes. His grandmother had done what his father had taught him - pack as though the first thing that you do in a new place will be to sleep. As he dug down around the interior for a wool blanket, his clothing spilled out. Tom heard his grandmother groan. Tom relaxed a little when she didn't make her usual comment about him being messy.

"Don't forget a flashlight," said Earnie.

Tom opened the other duffel. When he threw a giant

neon-orange lifejacket onto his bunk, his daypack fell to the floor. From its front pocket, Tom pulled a small flashlight and pocketed it in his shorts.

"Now, this is a lifejacket!" Earnie held up the orange mass of foam. "This would float an elephant."

Tom turned bright red.

"Barbara, take this home with you," Earnie threw the lifejacket to Tom's grandmother. "We'll get Tom a tripping jacket from the Boat House. He has to paddle and float."

"Okay," Tom's grandmother huffed. "It's the only lifejacket we had. It was his father's for offshore oil rigs. Whitewater lifejackets aren't on every shelf in New York City. If it wasn't appropriate, I had confidence that Catamount would sort it out."

"I understand your dilemma. Take the lifejacket. You don't want to embarrass your grandson."

Thus commanded, Tom's grandmother grabbed the oversized mass and walked to the door. She turned and used her own command voice. "Tom, don't leave a mess. Put your clothing back in your duffel. We'll meet you down on the dock."

"Being organized is a good thing," said Earnie as he exited the cabin.

After Tom stuffed everything into the duffels, he slid them under his bed. A cool breeze flowed through the cabin. The blue-green water reflected the azure blue of the sky. The view was much better than the grayish red brick wall six feet outside his bedroom window in New York - a big positive for camp.

As Tom walked back to the dock, he heard his grandmother say, "I'll consider staying the night, but that makes for a long drive tomorrow."

"If you stay, you can chat with George and the Director at dinner. You know that you miss being at camp." Earnie grinned.

"It would be great if you'd stay," Tom said enthusiastically. Having her at the camp made his first night less foreboding.

"You can call the airline from the office and get a later flight," Earnie offered. "I think they fly hourly to and from New York."

"We'll see," said his grandmother.

"Tom, you need to find your way on land to the Main Yard," said Earnie. "Go up to the clearing, turn right, and follow the path towards the head of the cove. You'll go past the washroom and the showers. Stay on the main path through the Cadet section, cross the bridge, and then follow the trail along the shoreline until you get to the Middie Dock. Turn left and take the wide path up over the ridge. You'll come down into the Main Yard. We'll meet you there or on the Canoe Dock. Be sure to look behind you as you walk so you have landmarks to use when you go back to the cabin. It's different in the dark. You don't want to get lost. Any questions?"

"Yes, sir. I mean no. I'll meet you in the center of camp, Earnie."

Tom felt his temper stir and took a breath. He had wanted to say: 'I can find my way through the woods of Central Park at night. Do you think I'm an idiot?' But he took a breath and stayed calm.

"See you soon." His grandmother pushed her canoe from the dock.

"Be watchful," Earnie said as his paddle bit into the water.

Paddling side by side, the two canoes looked like skaters gliding on a frozen pond. So much for a quick getaway. Tom was pleased that his grandmother seemed happy. She'd had a couple of rough weeks. He guessed that she'd stay the night.

Tom launched himself down the path, almost jogging. If he was slow to arrive, his grandmother might bark at him and bring up how he was always late. Then she'd comment on how he could never find his belongings. He'd heard her speech on his shortcomings hundreds of times.

Pausing at the bridge, he saw the two canoes further out than he expected. The boats seemed to be playing a game of cat and mouse.

Following the wide path was no problem. The walk took a while.

When Tom strode into the Main Yard, it was quiet, yet not peaceful. Everything seemed to be waiting, and it made him a little uncomfortable. He walked across the grass and stood on the Canoe Dock.

His grandmother and Earnie's canoes were headed into Boat Bay. Well behind them, a flotilla of canoes dotted the southern horizon. The two boats paused for a moment, and Earnie's took the lead. It sped up and headed straight for the Canoe Dock. Tom was sure it was going to crash. In a single second, as if by magic, the canoe turned on a right angle and stopped parallel to the dock as if it had a brake.

Earnie smiled up at Tom. "That's a landing. Let's see if your grandmother can do one."

His grandmother's canoe accelerated, perpendicular to the dock. The boat appeared to be crashing. At the last moment, as the canoe spun, something happened. The boat snapped upside down.

As Earnie scrambled on the dock, he yelled, "Tom, hold my canoe!"

From the water, a voice laughed. "No need for panic. I'm fine."

With the waterline at her shoulders, his grandmother was standing on the bottom, holding her paddle above her head. "The old instincts are still there." She grinned. "I didn't lose my paddle. Catch!"

She threw her paddle to Earnie and pushed up one

end of the swamped canoe so he could pull it out of the lake. Tom was dumbstruck. He'd expected his grandmother to be angry and upset, but she appeared almost excited about her near-disaster.

After she climbed up the ladder onto the dock, she said, "My landing started perfectly, but I lost it. Not surprising since I haven't soloed since we got married!"

Tom was surprised that she didn't demand a towel. As she brushed her wet hair away from her eyes, she smiled. "I guess I need some practice."

"It was an excellent attempt," said Earnie.

"Let's get this canoe back inside and see if I can find something to dry off with."

As the adults hoisted the canoe, Tom asked, "What should I do?"

"Wait," said his grandmother. "We'll be out in a minute or two. Tom, you just saw a perfect example of why you should always be prepared for your boat to flip." She laughed. "Imagine what a mess I'd be if I hadn't changed."

Tom sat on the dock with his feet dangling in the canoe. The canoes that had been far away began to arrive and unload. No one paid any attention to him.

When Earnie and his grandmother walked back into the sunshine, an older man barked, "Who was using the Commodore's canoe? Earnie, what in the blazes are you doing? You know that no one is supposed to use it unless he's won the Director's Challenge."

"It's my fault." Tom's grandmother walked over with hand extended. "I'm Barbara Woodruff. A few years ago, my husband, Charlie Woodruff, won the Director's Challenge, and I won the Lady's Cup at Camp Otterslide. Now that the girl's camp is closed, I believe that I can use the Commodore's canoe, can't I? Unless the girl's boat, Silverstreak, is available?"

The man smiled. "I'm Clark Gillard, the Director.

Welcome to Camp Catamount. You must be Tom's mother."

As her *'You're my best friend for life'* smile beamed, they shook hands. "I'm his grandmother."

"You're Charlie's bride. Barbara Hale was your maiden name, wasn't it? My older brother talked about you and Charlie being the first camp romance. Charlie is a legend in the camp's history. Where's Tom?"

"Holding my canoe," said Earnie. "I'll get him."

Tom insisted on helping pull the canoe out of the water before he walked over.

After the Director finished introducing his grandmother to several men, he turned to Tom. "Welcome to Catamount. You must be Thomas Woodruff. I'm the owner of the camp. We're glad that you'll be with us for the month. Are you ready for adventure?"

"Nice to meet you, sir. I'm glad to be here." Tom stuck out his hand.

"No need for the 'sir.' The boys call me Director. It's nice to have an American. We haven't gotten many Yankees in the last few years. Luckily, we had space when your grandfather called me."

After a quick handshake, the Director turned to Tom's grandmother and inquired about his grandfather's health. As the adults chatted, Tom could tell that the Director was more interested in his grandmother than he was in getting to know a new camper. While his face was tanned, it didn't show ruggedness. Tom guessed the Director spent most of the summer on the camp grounds. Over the years, Tom had learned how to fade into the background around adults. This enabled him to watch, listen, figure out who was who, and plan to escape the boredom.

"Tom, I'd like to introduce your counselors."

Tom turned to Earnie.

"This is Jack Atherholt, and this is Rio Brunner."

"I'm Jack. Welcome to Catamount." The dark-haired man extended his hand. "I'm the lead counselor for the Scouts."

"Nice to meet you." As Tom shook hands, he saw that Jack was well-muscled and looked like he was an athlete. His messy, blonde hair and sharp blue eyes made his smile seem genuine and friendly. He looked relaxed and at home.

"This is Rio." Jack motioned to a shorter, wiry man. "He's the other counselor for the Scouts. He's from Switzerland. This is his first time in Canada."

Rio's dark, combed hair, white collared shirt, and clean-shaven face contrasted with Jack's scraggly whiskers and rumpled t-shirt. Tom's first impression was energy. He wondered if it was nervousness or a desire to always be doing something.

"Nice to meet you," Rio said. "Maybe, I think, I can get a picture of the two of you shaking your hands together with the Boat House and Canoe Dock in the background. The first camper of the summer." From a well-used, padded backpack, Rio pulled out a fancy camera.

"Sure." Jack grabbed Tom. "Sounds like a great picture."

As Earnie walked away, he said, "Tom, when you're done being a model, Jack will show you around the Main Yard. I'll be taking your grandmother up the guest cabin so she can change before dinner."

Rio maneuvered Jack and Tom back, forward, and sideways. When he was pleased, he snapped a photo, made an adjustment, moved the two, took a second picture, turned another knob, repositioned them, and took a third photo.

After the photo session, Jack pointed out most of the same things that his grandmother had mentioned. In addition, he pointed out the tetherball poles and explained that the Main Yard functioned as an amphitheater for all-camp events. A bell rang from the roof of the Main Lodge.

"Time for supper," said Jack. "Who are you eating with?"

"With my grandmother."

"You're welcome to eat with us."

"Tom!" the Director called. Tom walked over, shook hands with several gray-haired, middle-aged men. He was confused by their names and their titles. There were directors of everything. He hoped that he'd meet them again in a way that made it easier to distinguish between them. As the group walked to the Lodge, all the counselors nodded and smiled. Tom knew that he was with the important people.

As the people began to sit down, Tom was concerned he hadn't seen his grandmother.

"Tom, sit here at the Director's table," said Earnie. "Your grandmother will be here in a few minutes."

After grace, Tom sat next to Earnie at the far end of the table. Finally, after the meal had been served, his grandmother walked out of the office. She'd changed into a faded blue Camp Catamount t-shirt and had dried her hair into a stylish ponytail. When she announced, "I'm spending the night," Tom smiled.

The Director offered her a seat next to him at the head of the table.

The food was tasty. He wasn't sure what he'd expected, but Canadian dinner seemed a lot like supper south of the border. Throughout the meal, the adults told stories about Catamount's history. Tom learned that his grandfather had been one of the first to start as a camper and finish as a guide. Earnie's chronicles had a special way of highlighting Tom's grandfather's ingenuity. He was surprised at how many of the men had known his father. When he heard that several were disappointed about the Olympic boycott, he sat smaller.

After dinner, the administrators sipped coffee on the porch of the Lodge. Their tales of the North continued, each sounding wilder than the last. On one hand, Tom was fascinated. But he'd had enough listening. He wanted to do something.

"Who wants to go for a sunset paddle?" Earnie asked.

"That would be delightful!" said his grandmother.

Tom was overjoyed. He scrambled ahead to the Boat House and selected two paddles and lifejackets. His grandmother nodded as he handed her the equipment. Tom knew better than to interrupt when she was engrossed in conversation.

The adults paired off and carried canoes to the edge of the dock. Tom felt abandoned when he realized that his grandmother was paddling with Earnie.

"Why don't you paddle with me?" came a voice from behind.

Tom turned to a bearded man with salt-and-pepper hair.

"I'm George Lansbury, the Canoe School Director. Let's get a canoe."

At dinner, George had told a story about his dad guiding a trip and insisting on cooking raincakes in the middle of a downpour.

"I'm glad you have a paddle and lifejacket. Can you go grab mine? They're next to the right-hand door. I'll put a boat in the water."

The well-worn paddle and faded yellow lifejacket looked like they'd had many years of service. When Tom returned and handed his equipment to George, he was sitting in the stern of the canoe.

"How well do you swim?"

"I was on a swim team. Earnie said I'm okay and

didn't make me wear one when we paddled to my cabin."

"That's what I guessed. Get in the bow. I'll show you around."

The canoe rocked as Tom pushed away from the dock, and he kneeled immediately. He didn't want to be responsible for overturning. He grasped his paddle and asked, "Which side?"

"Your choice. In asking that question, I know that you've paddled before."

"Yes. When I was younger, I paddled with my dad and my grandfather."

"Sounds good. Start on your left. We'll catch up with the Director so you can get the full tour."

Seeing four canoes ahead, Tom pulled as hard as he could.

"Slow down. They're not going that fast. No need to kill yourself."

At the mouth of the bay, the canoes turned left, opposite the way that Tom had paddled to Scout Point and Cabin Cove.

"They're going to look at Otterslide."

"What's that?"

"It's your grandmother's old camp, around the next two bays upstream. It was set up like Catamount when it was built."

As Tom and George caught up, Tom heard his grandmother say, "Clark, from out here on the water, the camp looks the same as it did when I was last here."

"Yes," said the Director. "Once it closed, we continued to keep up the grounds, its docks, and the buildings. Back when Catamount was full, we'd use their Lodge for rainy day activities, but with enrollment down, we haven't used it in several years."

"That's sad," said his grandmother. "Why did it close?"

"After my sister passed away, we couldn't find

29

anyone with her drive. And, I think, girls aren't that interested in camps anymore."

"That's too bad." His grandmother smiled. "I'm not so sure about girls and camps. If Tom had been a girl, she'd be at a camp. Let's go have a look."

The five canoes paddled along the shoreline dotted with boarded-up cabins. Tom felt a stillness fall over the group.

"Let's paddle out into the middle of the river," Earnie said. "We can watch the sunset from there."

The canoes turned away from the shoreline, and Tom felt their canoe begin to slow.

"I don't know about you, but I've seen lots of sunsets," George whispered. "Do you want to go race on the slalom course?"

Tom had no idea of what a slalom course was, but he was tired of adult conversation.

"That sounds great."

George shouted, "Tom and I are going over to the slalom course."

Tom's grandmother turned and talked with Earnie.

"We'll be out here until dark," she called. "I'm staying in Guest Quarters. Tom, I'll see you at breakfast. George will take care of you."

"Okay," he responded. Tom was surprised that she was leaving him with a stranger.

"I'll get you to your cabin. Don't be annoyed at your grandmother. I've seen this behavior before. Often when former staff members come to visit, they feel at peace. They are reconnecting with powerful memories of being part of a brotherhood. They have complete confidence in everyone."

Tom said nothing but nodded. He guessed that explained his grandmother's behavior. "Let's do something exciting," said George.

The slalom course was the forest of colored poles that

Tom had seen beyond the Canoe Dock. In it, a pair of greens or yellows created a series of gates. As their canoe wove from gate to gate, George taught Tom three strokes: the draw, the cross draw, and the bow pry. The purpose of each stroke was to move the bow of the canoe to the left or right as quickly as possible. Tom was pleased that twisting and reaching with the paddle seemed natural. As they practiced, he responded more quickly to George's commands. Their canoe went from lumbering to snaking smoothly through the course.

The sun dropped below the tree line.

"That's enough for tonight. I need to stretch my legs. Tom, you learn quickly. I think you have a future as a competitive paddler."

"Thank you."

Tom smiled. Despite his tired arms and sore knees, he was excited that George recognized his progress.

As they racked the canoe, Jack and Rio walked down from the Lodge.

"Tom, it's getting dark. We'll walk back to the cabin with you." Jack turned to George. "How's he paddle?"

"Nicely for an American." George winked and smiled. "Someone taught him well when he was young. He's got excellent instincts. Tom, I imagine that I'll see you early tomorrow morning."

"Thank you." Tom was curious. "What do you mean by see me early?"

"You'll see. The sun comes up very early this time of year." George chuckled.

"And goes down late," said Jack. "Let's get going before it's completely dark and the bugs get really bad."

As Tom followed Jack and Rio, he realized that Earnie had been right. He would have had difficulty maneuvering the paths in the dark. By the end of the twenty-minute walk, the shadows were black. As they hurried into the clearing, Earnie walked up from the

Scout dock.

"Breaking the rules, are we?" Jack smiled. "You're not supposed to paddle in the dark."

"I guess so." Earnie grinned "But it's almost a full moon, so it's not that dark. And, there aren't any mosquitoes on the water."

While they'd been walking, they'd been swatting mosquitoes. Now that they'd stopped, the bugs multiplied.

"Let's get inside," said Jack.

The inside of the cabin was pitch black. The others were grateful when Tom pulled out his flashlight and lit the way to their bunks. When he discovered the cabin had no electricity, he realized that being in the North had layers of roughing it.

"Tom, Rio, let's go to the washhouse for a last pee," said Jack.

The three walked to the washhouse, and Tom was grateful for the company.

When they reentered the cabin, Jack said, "Tom, it's later than you think. It's close to 11 p.m. Time for shut eye. See you in the morning. Breakfast is at 8:00. If you wake up early, please be quiet. It's our last morning to sleep in. Dawn starts about 4:30. The sun comes up about 5:30."

"What do I do if I wake up early?"

"You can wander over to the Main Yard. Some Senior Staff get up early and drink coffee on the porch."

"Thanks. Since school ended, I've been sleeping late. You'll probably have to wake me up."

"Perhaps. Until you get used to it, most people wake up with the sun. See you in the morning."

Tom was glad that he'd put his sleep clothes at the top of his duffel. After changing, he slid into his sleeping bag. He nearly jumped out of his skin when Earnie spoke from his bunk.

32

"It'll cool down as the night goes on. You should have a sweater ready." Earnie lowered his voice to a whisper. "And if you need to pee, you can go outside at this end and step to the bushes. Be quiet with the door and don't pee in the same place every night. That way, you won't kill the plants."

Tom was sure that peeing away from the bathroom was a no-no. He appreciated the advice. He leaned out of his bunk and pulled a sweatshirt from his duffel.

The temperature was dropping. Tom snuggled into his sleeping bag. After getting up at 5 a.m., he was exhausted and excited. Catamount seemed welcoming. The adults were friendly. Earnie understood his situation. Jack and Rio were nice. George had been interested in improving his canoe skills.

As he wiggled for a comfortable position, Tom wondered what his future cabin mates would be like. He wanted a fresh start where no one knew his history.

Outside, the cry of an animal cut through the darkness. Tom bolted upright and bumped his head.

"Sorry, I forgot to warn you about the slope of the wall," said Earnie. "That call was a loon. I love their sounds. To me, it means that all is peaceful." He sighed and turned over. "Sleep well."

When Tom lay down, the canvas felt softer. Another loon call murmured over the water. A third whispered in the distance. The calls began to repeat as though friends were talking.

Earnie was right, the sounds echoed gentleness and harmony. Maybe camp would be okay. Tom closed his eyes. The day had been long, and sleep came quickly.

# Chapter 2
# Opening Morning

As the sun rose above the distant tree line, it shone directly into Tom's face. He turned over to go back to sleep but couldn't escape the glare and the cackle of the birds. Remembering that the wall had attacked him last night, he sat up slowly. Looking around the wooden cabin, Tom realized how far he was from his city apartment. Across from him, Earnie slept soundlessly and, at the far end, Jack and Rio were motionless.

The low angle of the sun meant it was early. Jack had told him he'd probably wake up about 5:30. With breakfast at 8:00, unless he could go back to sleep, he had over two hours to kill.

The morning air was cool. Pulling the warmth of his sleeping bag around him, he tried to relax, but his mind raced. Today was the opening day. The other six Scouts would arrive before dinner. He was nervous about fitting in with Canadians. Arriving a day early and learning the camp's geography gave Tom a small degree of comfort.

Grumbling and rustling, one of the counselors re-snuggled into his sleeping bag. Tom was jealous of their ability to sleep. He reviewed what he knew about them. Jack, the lead counselor, was an athlete. He had graduated from college in Toronto. He had been coming to Catamount since he was young. Rio, the assistant, was a Swiss college student. Although his English was far from perfect, Tom knew he could learn a lot by watching him ask questions and listening.

From the lake, a loud slap rang sharply. Then, a second one. A human whistle followed. Quickly and quietly, he dressed and scampered to Scout Point. George was sitting in the middle of a birchbark canoe.

"As I said yesterday, I suspected that you'd be up early. Do you want to go for a paddle?"

"Sure." Tom paused. "What about Earnie and the counselors? If I'm not there, won't they be worried?"

"It's okay. I do this early-morning paddle on most days. Last night, I told Jack that I might get you. I'm pretty sure that they'll know where you've gone. To be sure, go put this on your bunk."

George reached out with his canoe paddle. On the end was an Indian-looking pipe.

Tom grabbed it and dashed to and from the cabin.

"How do I get into the canoe without getting wet?"

"Step two meters to your right. I'll pull the canoe next to the rock."

Tom inched across the narrowing ledge. At its end, it disappeared into the crystal-clear water. The canoe glided beside the gray rock.

"Let me move to the stern and then you can get in the bow."

Without rocking the canoe, George glided to its rear.

"Get in."

As Tom stepped in, the canoe wobbled. There was no seat.

"Kneel and rest your butt against the front thwart. That's the straight piece of wood between the sides of the canoe. Slide the lifejacket under your knees. I imagine they're a little sensitive after last night."

Tom appreciated the padding.

"Last night, Earnie told me you needed a tripping lifejacket. The one under your knees is yours for the summer. It's used, but it's good. I put your initials in it."

The red nylon was faded, but Tom saw no rips or tears.

"Thanks."

"Use the paddle beside you. I found one that's a couple inches longer than the one you were using last night. It's a stout piece of ash. It's been around for a while, maybe for decades."

The paddle felt natural in Tom's hands.

"Feels good. Which side?"

"Start on your right."

Tom dug his paddle into the water. The canoe slid across the mirrored surface of the lake, and the two paddled toward the center of the river. Normally, he would have been uncomfortable with no conversation, but the tranquility of the moment created a feeling of contentment.

After a few minutes, George said, "Let's drift for a moment."

The early morning sharpened Tom's senses. Intense colors reflected off the surface of the water. White clouds bit into the blue of the sky. The green trees defined the gray rocks. The still air was magical, and he felt a peace that he hadn't experienced in months.

"Let's continue your orientation to Catamount. What questions can I answer?" George asked.

Tom hesitated, trying to think of something intelligent. He remembered that people liked to talk about themselves.

"What do you do at camp?"

"I teach boys how to paddle canoes, how to build and repair canoes, and how to think in canoes. I've been at Catamount since I was eight. Your grandfather was my first guide. During the school year, I teach at a nature center north of the city. I'm married to the camp nurse. We have two grown Catamen. They live and work in Toronto. While they love camp, they think their parents are crazy because of the time we spend here. But that's enough about me, Tom Woodruff. Tell me about yourself."

Tom collected his thoughts.

"Last week, I barely graduated from 9th grade at Hudson East River Day School in New York City. I've always wanted to come to Catamount because Dad and my grandfather went here."

"They were good people," said George. "Why is this your first summer?"

"Lots of reasons. Dad's accident and his passing. My reading problems and summer school. My mom hates the woods. Dad used to laugh and say that her idea of roughing it was traveling with one suitcase."

"I've heard that from other Catamen. Being in the woods when you're young teaches you about a simple way of living."

Tom knew what awkward question was coming.

"Where are you going to school next year?"

Tom took a breath but felt he could trust George.

"I don't know. I'm dyslexic and have trouble reading and writing. Until exams, I was on the waiting list at a couple of schools. My English and Ancient History teachers screwed me when they changed the essay questions on the final exams, so I got D's in both courses. None of the schools would take me. My grandmother is working to find me a school that can help me with my dyslexia."

Tom knew the next question.

"Where's your mother?"

"She and Pierre are on their way to India. She met him while she was working at the UN last fall. He's a French diplomat. He got transferred to India, and they left last week. They're stopping in Paris to see his family."

"It must be tough to have your mother going so far away."

"Yes and no. I miss her. But she never understood that I'm not lazy. My reading problems are real. School work takes so much time. She didn't think I was trying. My eyes get tired. My brain overloads. Sometimes I get headaches. Homework is hard to finish. Pierre didn't understand at all. When Mom got frustrated with me, he got mad and yelled."

Tom took a deep breath.

"Mom wanted me to go to a well-known boarding school so she could brag about me. She said that she didn't care where I went to school, but I knew that it was really important to her. My not being accepted anywhere threw her for a loop. The last few days before they left for France were pretty nasty."

"I'm sorry," said George. "Sounds like camp is a good place for you."

"I hope so."

The quiet of the natural world whispered peace. Seagulls flew overhead, and the cries of a loon echoed across the stillness. Tom loved the serenity. The city and its issues seemed far away. George interrupted the silence.

"It's time for you to start paddling in the stern. Let's change places."

Tom's sense of peace vanished.

"How do we do that?"

"You turn around. Slide your paddle and lifejacket in front of you and move to the center of the canoe. When you're ready, crouch down. I'll climb over you and get ready to paddle. Then you move to the back of the boat. Got it?"

"I guess so."

"Okay. Get started."

Tom turned and eased to the center of the canoe. He tensed as the canoe rocked.

"Relax. We're not going anywhere."

"I don't want to flip us."

"You won't. Canoes are more forgiving than most people think. Yes, they rock, but rarely do they roll."

Having seen his grandmother capsize, Tom didn't feel so confident. He bent as low as possible into the bottom of the canoe. The smell of the cedar planking was powerful.

"Here I come."

As a spider would dance on its webs, George scrambled over him. The canoe rocked only slightly.

"You can move now."

Tom slithered to the back of the canoe. As he turned to sit in the stern seat, he found himself staring directly at George, who was facing backwards.

"I've found that it's easier for people to see me when I demonstrate. The J-stroke is the key to keeping the canoe headed where you want. Watch both my hands and the paddle."

George pulled with his paddle.

"Watch carefully."

George took another stroke.

"Now, on your strong side, do exactly the same thing."

Tom was confused. He'd seen the paddle flip over as it moved through the water and saw it act, ever so briefly, as a rudder.

"Which is my strong side?" he asked.

"The one that's most natural."

"That's my right."

Tom attempted to turn the paddle sideways, but it didn't do what he wanted.

"Try again. This time, turn the thumb on your top hand so it faces down, toward the water. Watch mine." George's paddle slid through the water.

"Got it?"

Tom nodded. This time, the leading edge of the

paddle caught the water, and the paddle acted as a rudder. Tom beamed.

"Again." said George. "Do 10 or 12 strokes."

As the canoe moved, it circled toward the side on which he was paddling.

"You're correcting too much. Remember that you're trying to keep the canoe going in a straight line, eh?"

"I think so."

"Well, start paddling for the white cliff up on the far side. That way, the sun will be behind you."

Tom pulled, turning over his upper hand. He found that he had to balance forward power with correction. Too much power, and the canoe moved away from the side on which he was paddling. Too much correction, and the canoe slowed and turned toward the side on which he was paddling. After a few minutes of intense concentration, Tom began to feel more confident.

"Okay. You appear to have the basics." said George. "Be ready to brace while I turn around. We'll paddle together. Ready?"

"Yeah."

Tom had no idea what a brace was, but he didn't say anything.

After he was settled, George rocked the boat wildly. Tom grabbed the sides of the canoe. George's paddle slapped down on the water and the boat calmed.

George turned, smiling.

"Caught you. You grabbed the gunwales."

"You got me. I didn't know what a brace was."

"That's what I guessed. A rocking canoe is trying to maintain its balance. If you grab the gunwales the canoe becomes top heavy and flips over easily. If you keep a relaxed waist, your body will flex and the weight will stay low. A brace is when you slam your paddle flat onto the surface of the water. It steadies the rocking. Keep your hands on your paddle and keep the paddle ready whenever there's motion in a canoe. Understand?"

"I think so."

"You have a lot to learn in a short amount of time. You learn quickly because of your experience with your dad and grandfather. People will assume that you know more than you do. Asking questions is always good, eh?"

"Yes, George."

"Let's work on your tandem paddling. As the stern man, you're the boat's commander."

"Does the bowman have any responsibilities?"

"Yes. In flat water, the bowman keeps the pace, but you tell him what it should be. The bowman and the stern man should paddle at the same time. Eh?"

"I think so."

"Last night, you saw how the bowman and the stern man are a team. On flat water, you keep the canoe on a straight course. Rarely does the bowman make any correction strokes. Any questions?"

"I think that I've got it."

Tom's palms were sweating. Being in the stern was complicated, but he enjoyed being in control.

"Okay, let's paddle," said George.

Tom's J-stroke took a little more time to complete than a normal stroke, so he had George slow his pace. Then, the canoe moved off course. When Tom told George to pick up the pace, he didn't have enough time to correct. He was getting frustrated.

"Let's take a break." said George.

The canoe drifted to a stop. The day was warming, and Tom pulled off his sweatshirt. A breeze puffed, and a few small wavelets developed. A bell rang from the Lodge.

"Wake-up bell," said George. "It's time for us to head in. Let's switch positions."

This time when they moved, Tom felt at ease. While he felt comfortable being back in the bow, he missed being in charge of the boat. And his shoulders were beginning to ache.

"Can we change sides?"

"Sure."

Using different muscles felt better. A second bell rang from the Lodge.

"That's waiters' bells. I've got lots of work today. Tom, if you're interested and have time, I could use some help."

"As far as I know, I have nothing to do. I'd like to help."

"Good. We'll need to clear it with Jack."

They paddled easily for a minute.

"Now, full speed!" George commanded. "Strong forward-stroke until I tell you to cross draw."

Tom pulled hard. The canoe jumped toward the dock.

"Keep paddling. Trust me."

Tom's nerves began to fire when he could see the individual planks of the dock. At full speed, the canoe was three meters from the dock.

"Crossbow!" George shouted.

Stretching across the bow, Tom jammed his paddle into the water. Within two feet of the dock, the bow slid to the left. The canoe stopped, dead in its tracks, its side within six inches of the dock. Tom's stomach unwound.

"Nicely done. That's what teamwork is about. You need to trust your canoe mates. What we just did is called a landing."

George sat up on the dock with his feet in the canoe.

"It's something that you'll master with time and practice."

Tom committed himself to learning all that he could about paddling.

From the front porch of the Lodge, Tom heard clapping and some happy-sounding comments - "You call that a landing?" "Where's my change from a silver dollar?"

Perplexed at the catcalls, Tom lurched out of the canoe, unsteady on his feet. Standing on solid ground felt good.

"Let's see how this paddle fits you. Put the blade on the ground."

The top of the blade hit Tom's palm. The top of the grip stood at eye-level.

"It may be a little long for the bow, but it's perfect for the stern." said George. "How does it feel?"

"Seems okay."

Tom wondered at the reference to paddling in the stern. How did George know that even though he was new to camp, he wanted to be a stern man?

"I think it will work." George smiled. "You have potential as a paddler. Your instincts are good. You need to practice, a lot."

Tom beamed.

"Thanks."

He knew he'd spend as much time as possible at the Canoe Dock.

"Need a hand with the canoe?" asked another staff person.

"Sure," said George. "We need to keep this one away from the parents. They'd all want to use it. Everyone's an expert paddler, even if they haven't been in a canoe for years. All the dads want to show off for their sons."

"Where should I put my jacket and paddle?" Tom asked.

"Here, carry mine with you. Put them inside the right-hand door. With everyone coming and going, keeping track of belongings today will be a challenge."

After the two racked the birchbark canoe inside the Boat House, Tom joined them walking to the Lodge. As he listened to them joke about the landing, Tom felt included.

At the bottom of the stairs, George turned to Tom.

"Wait here in the Main Yard until the breakfast bell rings. We're going to get some coffee. The bell will ring in a couple of minutes. I'll see you inside, eh?"

"Okay. Where's my grandmother?" Tom asked.

"I'll check. My guess is that she's having coffee with Earnie and the Director."

"Can I join her? I'd love some coffee. I drink it on the way to school."

"I doubt it. Campers aren't supposed to drink coffee."

"Can you ask?"

"I'll inquire. If I'm not back in a minute or two, the answer is no."

Tom sat down on a bench to wait.

As he was putting his feet on the log footrest, an older teenager barked, "Get off the 100-point bench, newbie."

"Now, new boy!" growled another bigger boy.

"Do you mean me?" asked Tom.

"Yes, I do. You can't sit on the 100-point bench until you have 100 points. You're a new boy. You have zero points. Get off!"

"Okay. I didn't know."

"There's lots that you don't know, new boy. Watch yourself. You could find yourself in real trouble," snapped a third older boy.

"Where can I sit?"

"On the ground, newbie!"

All three laughed.

From behind Tom, an adult voice snapped, "GENTLEMEN, what's going on here?"

"Earnie, we were telling this new camper about the Catamount traditions. He was sitting on the 100-point bench. He's a new boy with no points."

"As first-year apprentices, you should be welcoming and supportive of all campers, especially the new boys," barked Earnie. "Do I make myself clear?"

"Yes, Earnie," the three chorused.

44

"Tom, come with me. Your grandmother is having coffee with the Director, who is a dear friend of hers."

Earnie stared at the apprentices.

"The Director likes to know that sons of former staff members are happily welcomed at Catamount. Doesn't he, boys?"

"Yes, Earnie," came a subdued chorus.

The three turned to Tom.

"We're sorry. Welcome to Catamount."

They shook hands with Tom and introduced themselves. Tom could tell that the three apprentices were embarrassed. He hoped that he would have nothing to do with any of them in the future.

As he hurried up the stairs behind Ernie, he wished that he was anywhere but at this stupid camp with its dumb traditions.

Ernie stopped inside the wide wooden doors and turned to Tom.

"I'm sorry that those boys were mean to you. I know that it made you feel like an outsider. I hope those three will behave like Catamen in the future. Do you accept my apology?"

"Yes, Earnie."

Tom knew that he had to say 'yes' even though he didn't really understand. He hoped he could fit in. Tom hungered for a place to belong. He wanted to be a Cataman like his father and his grandfather, but making friends had never been easy for him. Camp seemed a little like school, but very different; a unique place in a different country with very peculiar traditions.

With a steaming cup in her hand, his grandmother walked out from the office. George and the Director followed behind her.

"Good morning, Tom."

"Good morning, Gema. How did you sleep?"

"Exceptionally well. It's good to be back in the

45

Northwoods." His grandmother smiled. "George tells me you can paddle."

A loud bell rang in the ceiling above them.

"That's the bell for breakfast. Barbara and Tom, will you join me at the Director's table?"

At breakfast, his grandmother fired questions at the Director. Tom learned more about Catamount.

The Director explained, "The youngest boys, the Plebes, live in groups of ten with two full counselors. They spent most of their time in camp and do two short, two-night trips. The Middies live in groups of eight with a counselor and an assistant. They explore Algonquin Park on week-long canoe trips. The Cadets are the 13- and 14-year-old campers who complete ten-day trips in the Temagami region. The 15-year-old boys, like Tom, are Scouts and paddle for two weeks on the Dumoine River in southern Quebec."

"Does anyone still do big trips?"

"The Voyageurs are the oldest campers. Their trip is a four- to five-week expedition on a river up North. When they are in camp, they live on the Island."

"William loved his big trip on the Rupert," said Tom's grandmother. "What's changed in the camp's day-to-day program?"

"Not much. When in camp, all the boys have swim lessons every day until they pass the Advanced level," said Earnie. "Then we expect them to work on the Lifesaving medallions. Plebes and Middies paddle three mornings a week and spend two afternoons on campsite skills. The Cadets and Scouts have their choice of activities. We added sailing and rock climbing about ten years ago. They're quite popular."

"I never learned to sail. I always wanted to," said Tom's grandmother. "Tom has passed Junior Lifesaving. How does that compare to the Canadian expectations?"

Everyone at the table looked at Tom. His face turned

red.

"They're more comprehensive," George said. "Tom says he's a strong swimmer. All the Scouts work on water safety for the first few days."

Tom relaxed, knowing he wouldn't be singled out.

"Does the Junior Guide program still operate?"

"The whole leadership program has been expanded," said Earnie. "Many of the Voyageurs come back as apprentices. In July, they rotate through the activities and go on canoe trips with the Plebes and Middies, primarily to carry canoes. In August, they begin to specialize in a couple of skill areas. If they are invited, they can come back as assistants in the Guide program or a skill area."

Earnie turned to Tom.

"Do you want to be a guide like your dad and grandfather?"

Tom had no idea of what to say. Tom had heard his dad and his grandfather talk of the North and had dreamed of the adventure, but now that he was at Catamount, he was unsure. While the North was alive in the depths of his imagination, first he had to survive this summer.

"Maybe someday."

"Time for announcements," said the Director. "We need to get things moving."

The Director rang a chime. Several staff stood and detailed the opening day's activities. Tom learned that most campers would arrive after lunch. Breakfast ended with the Director reading a poem called *"If you can't go over or under, go around."* The dining room echoed louder and louder each time the refrain was repeated.

As everyone stood after dismissal, Tom's anxiety returned. His grandmother was leaving. He was the only camper in camp.

"Tom," came a booming voice from the crowd. Jack was walking over, followed by Rio.

"Can we get to know your grandmother? We didn't do more than say hello last night."

Tom made the introduction and stood back. Jack and his grandmother chatted. Again, Tom learned by listening. Jack had studied accounting at the University of Toronto. He had been at camp for ten of the last thirteen summers. In addition to running the Scout program, he was on the camp sports staff.

"Mrs. Woodruff, I've enjoyed meeting you. I assure you we'll take good care of Tom. He'll have a great time at Catamount. If you'll excuse me, I need to go to a meeting. Rio will walk you and Tom to your car."

"Jack, it's been a pleasure," said Tom's grandmother.

"Rio, when you're done at the car, please take Tom to the Canoe Dock. George has something for Tom to do this morning."

During the walk to the car, Tom learned that Rio was from a ski town in southern Switzerland. He was a third-year university student studying physics. For the coming school year, he would be an exchange student at the University of Toronto. As a young boy, he had done a lot of hiking and camping in the mountains with his grandfathers during the summers. Tom's grandmother was charmed when Rio promised to send her a picture of Tom.

"Have a safe drive to the airport. Give Gepa my best," said Tom.

As Tom hugged his grandmother, concern flooded over him. Should he be hundreds of miles away, or should he be assisting his grandmother with his grandfather's recovery? Tom forced himself to smile.

"Tell him that Catamount is great. He'll be happy to know that I paddled with George early this morning and last night on the slalom course."

"I will," promised Tom's grandmother. "Catamount is a wonderful place. You'll love it."

As his grandmother drove up the gravel road, Tom hoped that Catamount would accept him. Now, he was on his own.

"Let's go to the Canoe Dock," said Rio. "I think that there's lots of things to do there."

"Sounds good to me," said Tom.

As they walked, Tom discovered that Rio liked to talk. Rio had only been in Canada for eight days, six of which had been spent at Catamount. Rio loved photography and was thinking about studying optics and the mechanics of cameras. The details overwhelmed Tom, but he happily said, "That's interesting." Tom had learned that if he pretended to pay attention, people seemed happier, and his life was easier.

The Canoe Dock was active. Aluminum canoes were being placed near the water. Rio and Tom were told to equip each canoe with three paddles and four lifejackets. After about half an hour, a bell sounded.

"Coffee break," yelled George. "Many thanks to everyone. Counselors to your cabins. Staff to your activities. Admins to your positions."

George came over with a cup of water.

"Thanks for your help. We sure do have a lot of canoes."

"How many?" Tom asked.

"Catamount has one of the largest fleets of canoes in the world. We have 65 wood and canvas canoes, half a dozen birchbark, 35 aluminum and 20 plastic boats - either fiberglass or Royalex."

Most of the canoes on the dock were metal or plastic.

"Where are the wooden canoes?" Tom asked.

"We've learned that families don't respect the wooden canoes. We had too much repair work. Tomorrow, the tripping boats get carried up to trailers in the parking lot. All the wooden boats get carried down here. That's the first job for the apprentices."

"What do you want me to do?" Tom asked.

"This morning, you can help manage the paddles and lifejackets. After lunch, your fellow Scouts will arrive. You can help them."

Tom felt glad that he had somewhere to be and something to do. He squared his shoulders.

"George, exactly what should I be doing?"

"Most of the families want to see the cabins and meet the counselors. The easiest way to get the luggage to the Middie and Senior cabins is to paddle to Camper's Cove. Some families go in one canoe with three people. But, if there are brothers and sisters, some need two canoes. Your job is to be sure that every canoe has a lifejacket for each person. All campers and children should wear them. As it gets busy, paddles and lifejackets tend to get thrown around."

As the campers' families arrived, Tom was pleased that people saw him as a helper. He had worried that he might stand out as an American.

"Tom, can you come over here?"

George was standing with a family of six - mother and father, an older son and three daughters, one about his age, and two a bit younger.

"Tom, this is Duncan Whitmarsh. He's a Voyageur. Griffin and Annabelle are his parents. These are his sisters, Cecille, Rebecca and Margaret. They need an extra paddler going to and from the Island. I'd like you to accompany them. You'll paddle with Cecille. Get your paddle and lifejacket."

Tom shook hands with everyone. Cecille's blue eyes and her white teeth sparkled against her tan face. Her blond hair flowed down her back and bounced as she walked. She was very pretty, looked athletic, and had a nice figure.

Duncan's father, a former camper, and his wife got into the luggage boat. Duncan and his two little sisters climbed into the second. The third boat was for Tom and Cecille.

"I'll take the stern, if you don't mind?" Cecille asked in a quiet, matter-of-fact tone.

"That's fine with me."

Tom felt relieved. He wasn't sure that he was ready for stern paddling in public.

After the canoes shoved off, Griffin challenged his son and daughters to race to the Island. The two canoes sped out ahead.

"Dad's always doing that," sighed Cecille. "No need to push hard. I'm not due at Caribou until mid-afternoon."

"What's Caribou?"

"It's one of the two girls' camps in the Ottawa Valley. We are a tripping camp like Catamount. Our trips are as long as Catamount's, but we don't do whitewater rivers until we're the oldest."

Tom hoped that Cecille was a talker. With a few questions, she would keep the conversation going.

"Where is Caribou?"

"Upstream of Catamount. Downstream, below the big dam, are Timberland and Pine Bluff. Timberland is a big sports camp for boys, and Pine Bluff is the same for girls. All the camps get together for the Circus, the Lumberjack Roundup, the Fair, and the Regatta."

As she talked, Tom learned Cecille's opinions on each camp's strengths and weaknesses. She liked wilderness tripping and wasn't impressed by the high-end athletic facilities at Timberland and Pine Bluff.

"Where are you from?" asked Cecille.

"New York City."

"That must be so exciting."

"It can be. Where do you live?"

"Arnprior. It's a little town closer to Ottawa."

They questioned back and forth.

Cecille was 15, Tom's age, and had finished grade 9, like Tom. She had lived in the same house her entire life. Her parents had been high school classmates. There were only 16 people in her grade, and she had been together with them since she had started school. She planned to become a wildlife biologist. She was a Marten, the same as a Scout at Catamount. To her, it was stupid that each age group had an animal name at Caribou.

Tom found the conversation very natural. He provided only a brief biography. He tried to highlight that his father and grandfather had attended and worked at Catamount. Cecille was more interested in his father's accident and declining health, his mother's remarriage to Pierre, and his grandfather's accident.

"Sorry about your dad. I hope your grandfather gets better soon. I'm sure he'd love coming back to camp."

The other two canoes waited at the Island dock.

"Took you long enough." Duncan smiled.

"No need to rush," Cecille said with a grin.

"That's what you get for letting a girl take the stern. Cecille thinks she can paddle as well as anyone."

Their father smiled.

"She's pretty good, for a girl."

Cecille splashed at her father with her paddle. Tom couldn't read the intent of the comments. But, somehow, as a male, he felt an unspoken burden had been placed on his shoulders.

Once they had secured the canoes, everyone carried Duncan's belongings. On the Island, the boys lived in large canvas wall tents and used pit latrines. There were no showers or running water. The Voyageurs paddled over to the Lodge for many of their meals, but sometimes they stayed on the Island and cooked for themselves.

Running water and showers were essential to civilized life, so Tom was glad that he wasn't living there.

"Let's head back to the Canoe Dock," said Duncan's

father. "We need to get the girls to Caribou."

"I'll take the bow on the way back," Cecille stated. "I assume that's what you want?"

"Yes, of course."

Tom hid his apprehension. He'd only paddled in the stern this morning. He wasn't sure that he could control the canoe. But he didn't want to show any weakness, especially in front of a girl.

After the canoes pushed off, father and son were racing. As a breeze spun the bow of his canoe off course, Tom struggled to keep going straight. His upper hand and the paddle's blade weren't working together. The canoe wasn't going anywhere.

"You don't really know how to paddle in the stern, do you?" Cecille asked.

Tom could see that she was trying not to show her annoyance.

"Not really. My first time was this morning."

"It takes practice, especially in the wind. If we're going to get back to the dock before lunch, we need to change places. Do you know how to do that?"

"Yes, I did it this morning."

"Like you learned to stern? Before we do anything, tell me what's going to happen."

"Who's going to start?"

"You move first. That'll keep our weight as low as possible. You weigh more, so I'll climb over you."

"Okay," said Tom. "I'll slide my paddle forward, go over the thwart in front of me, shimmy behind the center thwart, and crouch down. Then, you'll turn around, climb over me, and drop into the stern. When you have your paddle, I'll move. You can brace if necessary."

"You seem to know what you're doing." Cecille nodded. "I'm ready. You can start."

Moving to the center, Tom flattened as low as he could.

53

"I'm ready."

"Okay, here I come." Cecille spun and scampered. "Keep your head down. I'm coming over you."

Tom dropped his head and felt Cecille's body slide above him. Her hair slid down and whispered in his ears. A wave rocked the canoe, and her body dropped onto his back. Tom blushed, realizing that a woman's body was draped over him. She scampered up, whirled, and grabbed her paddle.

"Now, stay low, get into the bow, and start paddling. We've drifted farther than we should have."

Tom scrambled into the bow and grabbed his paddle. Feeling foolish, he pulled as hard as he could.

"No need to kill yourself. I know that you are embarrassed and that you didn't want to admit that you couldn't paddle. At our outdoor-ed trips, I've seen this over and over. Boys can be so stubborn."

Tom relaxed a little. He knew that he should say something.

"How long have you been paddling?"

"I've been in canoes since before I could walk. My dad works for the Ministry of Natural Resources. He used to take Mom, Duncan, and me on survey treks. He taught Duncan and me how to paddle as soon as we could sit on a canoe seat. When I got to camp, I knew all the basics and could do most of the advanced skills. I was the youngest camper to earn the Advanced Level 2 badge. Last summer, I would have gotten my Level 3 except that I wasn't strong enough to complete the wind triangle. Now, I need to start from the beginning. But I have to wait for the right wind."

Tom enjoyed hearing her talk. She was a wealth of information. He had so many questions, and she seemed so friendly.

"When did you start going to camp?"

"Five summers ago. That was the first year that Dad

was the Forestry Fire Chief. To support families like ours, the Ministry and the summer camps cooperate. Otherwise, our family could never be able to afford all of us. The private camps are expensive, so the Ministry helps. The camps have scholarship programs funded by their alumni. Did you know that the Prime Minister was a canoe instructor at Catamount?"

"No." Tom paused. "This is a stupid question, but what's a Prime Minister? Is it like our President?"

They talked about the political differences between Canada and the US. Tom was amazed at how much Cecille knew about the US and how little he knew about Canada. As they reached the edge of the dock, a bell rang.

"That's for lunch. Of course, you and the family will stay for lunch." George turned to the little girls. "Are you hungry? Lunch is sloppy joes. That used to be your dad's favorite. We'll sit at my table."

The little girls giggled enthusiastically. As they walked into the Lodge, Tom could see a lot more people would be eating lunch. George led his group to a table near the office. Duncan begged to join his Voyageurs friends. Tom and Cecille sat across from each other at the end of the table. A chime clanged. Silence fell. The Director said grace. As he finished, a stampede of boys raced toward the kitchen.

A loud voice bellowed above the crowd.

"Stop! Behave like gentlemen!"

Earnie blocked the IN entrance to the kitchen.

"Please go sit down. We'll call waiters by section."

Boys scrambled back to tables.

"I'll be the waitress." Cecille looked at George. "Assuming that you do it the same way as Caribou?"

"It's the same. Thank you, we'll be one of the last tables called."

Tom was confused, so Cecille explained.

"Each table has a waiter who goes to the kitchen,

always through the IN door. She carries the food to the table. At the end of the meal, the waiters take the empty platters back to the kitchen and carry the scraped dishes to the dish room. That's on the far side of the kitchen. After dismissal, the waiter wipes down the table. Each cabin has a table and the waiter's job rotates through the cabin."

"Staff tables," shouted Earnie.

Cecille sprang up.

Tom watched, intrigued. He'd never been in a dining hall with so many people. At Hudson East River, each student brought his own brown bag lunch. Each age group had eaten in the school gym, sitting at long folding tables.

Cecille returned carrying a large metal tray filled with platters. George served a plate to each person - a sloppy joe sandwich, a few French fries, a pile of green salad, and a brownie.

While they ate, Cecille continued describing the details of life at camp. All campers had a job every day. Besides having waiters, each cabin had a washer who worked in the dish room and a sweeper who swept the dining room. Other chores required work around the cabin or center camp.

While Tom was pleased to have learned about camp life, the details were overwhelming. He struggled to find another question.

After an awkward pause, Cecille asked, "Have you always lived in New York?"

"We moved to the city after my father was hurt in the car accident. Before that, we were in Houston and Saudi Arabia, but I don't really remember either of those places. After Dad passed, Mom and I lived in a small two-bedroom apartment on West 77th Street. It felt smaller when Pierre, her new husband, moved in. He's a French diplomat, so they are moving to his new post in India.

After camp, I'm living with my grandparents in their city apartment. How long have you lived in your house?"

"As long as I can remember. We have a three-bedroom house. Maybe you can say that it has four because Duncan's room is in the basement. He and Dad built his space three years ago. I have my own room, and the girls share theirs. Where are you going to high school?"

Tom hesitated. He didn't want to disclose his problems, but he felt that he couldn't avoid it. Because she'd be at a different camp, he felt safer sharing.

"I'm not sure. The school I was going to ended in ninth grade. I have reading problems and writing takes me a long time. School is hard for me. I almost failed two courses, so no high schools would take me."

"That's a bummer."

"On the bright side, two weeks ago, I did graduate. My grandmother's looking for a program for me. Where do you go to school?"

"I go to Arnprior Consolidated School. It starts in kindergarten and goes through grade 10. Then, I'll go to Western, which is closer to Ottawa near where my dad works."

"What's his job?"

Tom hoped that she'd have a long answer.

She did. Her dad managed forest fire control for the entire province. He traveled much of July, August, and September. While she didn't like the time that he was away from the family, she was pleased because his job meant that she could go to camp. She was thinking about studying the Arctic at university so she could travel up North as part of her courses. She loved wolves and polar bears.

"Cecille, it's time to clear."

Tom was eager for her to finish clearing their table. Being part of an active Canadian family seemed more exciting than his life as an only child of a single mother confined to a small apartment. He had more questions. As she sat, the chime rang. Silence fell instantly. Most of the announcements made little sense to Tom.

After dismissal, everyone walked to the porch. Jack and Rio appeared.

"Who's this lovely young lady?" Jack asked.

"I'm Cecille Whitmarsh, Duncan's sister. He's a Voyageur this summer."

"Duncan knows me. I'm Jack Atherholt. I'm Tom's counselor. Your brother's a pretty talented baseball player. We'll miss him at the Lumberjack Round-Up. Which camp are you headed to?"

"Caribou. I'll be a Marten."

"Outstanding. Martens are tough animals. Your lead counselor will be Mary Rose McHerren."

"How do you know that?"

"We're good friends."

"Boyfriend-girlfriend friends?"

"You never know." Jack winked at Tom. "I saw you two paddling back from the island. You make a good team. Were you practicing for the Lumberjack Round-Up?"

"You never know."

Cecille turned red.

"Tom, be a gentleman and say goodbye. Meet us down at the Canoe Dock. We have a job this afternoon."

As the two counselors walked away, Jack whispered to Rio. Both turned and grinned.

"It was nice to meet you." Tom stuck out his hand, knowing his mother would be proud of his politeness. "I enjoyed paddling with you. Thank you so much for filling me in on what happens at camp."

"I liked meeting you. Thanks for paddling with me." Cecille smiled and squeezed Tom's hand, hard. "Would you like to be camp pen-pals? You can get my address from Jack. I like answering your questions and I'd like to know more about New York City."

"Sure." Tom dropped her hand as though it was a flaming ember. "I guess that would be nice."

He grasped for words.

"I'd like to know more about the forests."

He could feel his face blushing and he froze.

"Cecille! We need to go," called her mother.

Cecille turned away and then turned back.

"I look forward to seeing you at the Circus. Have a good afternoon."

She spun and danced away. Her ponytail waved alluringly like the ones in Central Park.

"Have a good start to camp," mumbled Tom.

Cecille had been so welcoming. Writing letters would be okay. Maybe they could become good friends. He'd never had a girlfriend in the city. It would be crazy to have one in a different country.

In front of him, in the Main Yard, cars were parking everywhere - on the sides of the hill and inside the amphitheater. Boys and their parents were unpacking trunks, duffels, pillows, blankets, lifejackets, and canoe paddles.

# Chapter 3
## Scouts Assemble

Tom wound his way to the Canoe Dock, dodging between parked cars and angling between families. The minute he arrived, Jack said, "Get your paddle and lifejacket. You and Rio are on luggage patrol."

Rio was struggling to keep the gunwales of a loaded canoe from scraping against the dock. The six locker trunks in the boat were stacked side-by-side and looked like they might tumble into the water.

"Tom, you're paddling in the bow," Jack ordered. "Rio, you're in the stern. I know that you've just started paddling, but you've got more experience than Tom. With this breeze, no one wants to paddle to the cabins. Since everyone is walking, George and I are organizing cargo canoes. Take these locker trunks to the Middie Dock and come back right away for another load. Rio, let me hold the boat."

While Rio pulled on his lifejacket and tightened it, Jack steadied the canoe. As he pushed them off, he smiled. "Good luck. The trunks are more stable than they look. If you're not back by dinner, we'll send a search party."

The canoe rocked in the waves but was surprisingly stable. While they paddled, Tom learned more about Rio. He had come to Canada to study and improve his English. He'd come to Catamount to experience the great North. As a staff member, he had been forced to paddle in the stern on the three-night staff canoe trip, because paddling in the stern was what the staff did. Rio didn't understand the prestige of the role. In his opinion, paddling was a partnership, and both paddlers were essential.

"Steering the canoe is the more powerful position. That's why it's seen as more important," said Tom.

A burst of wind swung the canoe off course. Tom thought Rio struggled more than was necessary to get them back on track.

"What does your family do in Switzerland?"

"My father runs the lifts for the skiers at the local resort. My mother manages the household. My two younger sisters are ski racers. They are winning a lot. This is exciting for my family, but I am at university."

"Did you race?"

"Yes. I was on the team. But not so good as my sisters. Everyone in town is racers," Rio said as they approached the Middie Dock.

Unloading went quickly, and they headed back. Tom wanted Rio to keep talking. "Where are you in college?"

Rio ran with the question. He attended university in Bern and chose Canada because he had an uncle who lived in Toronto. His grandfathers were carpenters in a custom woodworking shop and, as a boy, Rio had loved going into the mountains with them. Rio said that they'd never traveled outside Switzerland and would be amazed to see so much water.

"Now, Tom, I am talking a lot. I hear that you are from New York City. For what reason did your grandmother bring you to Camp Catamount?"

Tom explained the complications of his mother's remarrying and moving to India. He tried to think of a question, but Rio spoke first.

"Is not New York City a dangerous place?"

"Not really. You need to be careful, especially after dark in some places."

"Is your safety not imperiled when you walk about Central Park?"

"No. I walk across it going to and from school every day."

As Tom answered Rio's endless questions, he tried to convince him that New York was not crawling with drug addicts and crazed killers. Rio seemed to think that American city life was a combination of the *Columbo* and *Barney Miller* TV shows.

Rio continued to have difficulty keeping their canoe on track during their second cargo run. The boat weaved to the left and right as he tried to negotiate the heavy breeze.

When they finally arrived back at the Canoe Dock, Jack introduced Tom to two Scouts who had just arrived - Lloyd and Borden. Lloyd was taller than Tom with neck-length blondish hair. Borden was shorter with a jet-black buzz-cut. He looked strong and solidly built.

Both boys were overjoyed when their parents didn't want to see the Scout cabin. Their goodbyes were quick.

"Tom, you and Rio load Lloyd's belongings into your boat," Jack ordered. "We'll get a canoe for Lloyd and Borden."

Borden's stuff went into the middle of the second boat.

"Take their things to the cabin and come back. Stay close together. Be quick. There's more to ferry and the other Scouts will be arriving."

Conversation flowed between the two canoes. Borden remarked on how much Lloyd had grown in the past year.

"I grew almost a foot. I've become clumsy, but it makes my basketball coach happy," said Lloyd with a shrug. "How was your hockey season?"

"Okay. I didn't play as much as I'd hoped."

Both boys had been at Catamount for five years and Rio asked them multiple questions about their experiences with camp life. At the cabin, he and Tom held the canoes while the two carried their belongings to the cabin.

"Thank you for being quick," said Rio. "We must be getting back."

As they paddled, Rio continued to interrogate the two campers. When Rio learned that Borden's father was First Nations, and that his paternal grandparents lived in the bush during the warmer months, he peppered Borden with questions. Much of what Rio asked showed that he believed that 'Indians' still lived in teepees and 'cowboys' still wore six-shooters. Tom was impressed with Borden's ability to answer Rio's questions without sarcasm.

When they returned to the Canoe Dock, Tom saw Earnie and Jack chatting with another boy.

"This is Rishard Hairreson," said Jack.

"It's Ric," said the boy.

Borden and Lloyd knew Ric from previous summers and they immediately launched into a discussion about his football season.

"Let's get Ric's stuff to the cabin," interjected Jack. "Tom, you can move into the middle of Borden and Lloyd's boat. Ric can paddle in front of Rio with his trunk and his fishing rod."

Being sent to the middle stung, but Tom understood. He was the new guy. As they paddled, he listened. The three joked about Ric's love of fishing and his dislike of bugs.

Again, Tom and Rio managed the canoes while the others carried Ric's belongings to the cabin. On the return trip, Rio asked a series of questions about Canadian government and Tom quietly appreciated learning about Canada and its provinces as they paddled.

As they arrived back at the dock, a black Cadillac drove across the grass to the edge of the water. Out piled two large men and their sons.

"Earnie, good to see you again!" roared the large, gray-haired man.

"Camp looks good," yelled the second, a smaller man with a sharp nose. "Wish I could stay, but the world of high finance calls."

Earnie reminded the men that they had to check in at the office.

"Shaine, get two canoes," barked the large man.

"Yes, Dad," responded the tall athletic-looking blonde as he supervised the unloading of the Cadillac and the commandeering of the canoes.

While the fathers lingered on the porch chatting with the Director, everyone else waited with the canoes. Surrounded by conversation about the Maple Leafs, the Canadiens, the Blue Jays, the Astros, the Argos, and the Alouettes, Tom felt like the odd man out. He didn't follow hockey and was a Mets and Jets fan.

"I thought they said that they wanted to get out of here as quickly as possible," muttered the second boy, Chet, pushing back his unruly curls.

"You know my dad," said Shaine. "If he thinks he can impress people, he'll talk them to death."

As the Main Yard began to fill with laughing and shouting campers, Tom listened to his cabin mates catch up on their school year and joke about previous summers. Other than being at camp, they seemed to have little in common.

Tom noticed a small car driving down the road toward the Lodge. A thin woman and a tall, skinny boy got out. Earnie greeted them, called to Jack, and the four walked up the broad stairway to the office.

Campers and counselors milled about. Tom became aware of a collective hunger and realized that he was famished.

Earnie and the mother walked to the car. Jack and the boy joined the waiting Scouts.

64

"This is Ack Smythe. He's new to Catamount. We need to get his stuff out of their car before dinner."

The dinner bell rang. The world froze for half a second. Then the herd in the Main Yard thundered up the wide staircase.

"My guess is we're not paddling," said Shaine. "But you never know with my dad."

"Wait for your fathers. If you don't paddle, unload the canoes."

Jack turned to the others. "We're sitting at the Scout table in the back left. Rio will show you. Borden, Lloyd, you are waiter and washer. We'll be in after we get Ack's stuff. Who wants to help?"

Tom volunteered.

"I'm Tom. I'm also new."

At the car, Ack opened the trunk and wrestled with a well-worn, oversized leather suitcase. From the backseat, he pulled a canoe paddle and a yellow lifejacket.

"Tom, help Ack take his stuff down to the Canoe Dock. We'll paddle it over after dinner." Jack said.

Tom grabbed one of the rounded ends. Ack manhandled the other side. They waddled awkwardly.

"I'm from New York City."

"I'm from Scotland, or was."

Tom stumbled, and everything bounced to the ground.

"I'm sorry," Tom mumbled.

"Don't worry. There's nothing in the suitcase except clothes. I've been carrying this piece of shit for a week. It has a mind of its own."

The two boys lifted together and shuffled toward the dock.

"Why are you here?" Ack asked.

"My grandparents. It's a long story. Both my dad and grandfather went here. My mom is moving to India."

As they eased Ack's stuff onto the dock, the horn of

the Cadillac blared.

"I guess we're not taking our stuff to the cabin," said Chet.

"My dad always schmoozes too long," said Shaine. "I'm sure that he's charmed the Director, though. That's good for us."

"Stop standing around. Unload the boats," Jack yelled. "Pull the canoes onto the dock."

The horn trumpeted again. The two ran for goodbyes. Tom heard the men joke about having a restaurant dinner rather than eating camp food. With tires spinning and gravel flying, the vehicle roared away. The two boys ran to the Lodge.

Ack and Tom walked with Jack to his mother's car.

"You're welcome to stay for dinner," Jack offered. "The food is quite good. We always have a guest or two."

"Thank you, but no," said Ack's mother. "I need to get on the road. It's a long drive back to Burlington."

Ack and his mother exchanged an embrace. As the little car puttered up the road, Tom saw a flash of sadness on Ack's face.

"Time to eat," said Jack.

The Dining Room was dizzying. There were more people eating and talking loudly in one place than Tom had ever seen. Tom and Ack sat at the end of the Scout table and talked under the din.

"Where do you live now?" asked Tom.

"I'm not sure. We lived in Scotland until six days ago. We're staying with my grandparents in Burlington until my mom finds a job and a place for us to live."

Tom thought he heard the soft lilt of a Scottish burr in Ack's voice. "Where's Burlington? This is my first time in Canada."

"Burlington is on Lake Ontario, west of Toronto. It must be exciting to live in New York. Not like where we lived in Scotland. It was nowheresville. We lived with my grandfather in a little village called Drumoak, about half an hour outside Aberdeen."

"I hate to be stupid, but where's Aberdeen?"

Tom felt better asking rather than answering questions.

"Don't worry. No one outside of the UK has any idea."

"Sorry."

"No problem. We're not going back. We moved to Canada permanently."

"How come?"

"My grandfather died. My father kicked us out of the family house as soon as I finished school."

Before Tom could express sympathy, Ric interrupted, "Do you follow the Leafs or the Canadiens?"

"Who are they?" asked Ack.

"They're hockey teams. The Canadiens are the best. What teams do you follow?"

As Ack explained his recent arrival in Canada, Tom saw that his fellow Scouts didn't grasp the significance of Ack's move. Tom sensed that Ack might be seeking a fresh start from recent troubles, but dinner conversation was not the time to hear the complete story. Exchanging a glance without words, Tom and Ack agreed to focus on the group conversation.

The table chatted about the various teams and their rivalries. Shaine appeared to be the group's leader. He led the conversation from pro sports to successes during the past school year, and to previous summers' excitements. As Tom listened, he again felt the uncertainty of being in a different country with an unknown culture.

Announcements followed the meal. The Director gave a welcoming speech. Tom had heard similar "Let's be good and do our best" speeches from his school principals. It surprised him that both campers and staff recited the Catamount motto with gusto - *Adventure, Brotherhood and Courage.*

After the speech, everyone filed outside.

At the Canoe Dock, Jack said, "As Scouts, we have the privilege of paddling everywhere. After we take everyone's luggage to the cabin, we're going for our first real paddle."

Shaine held up a shiny paddle and a bright blue lifejacket, both obviously brand new. "The best you can have. Better equipment makes for better paddling. Bring on the Dumoine."

"I agree." Chet held up an identical paddle and lifejacket. "Wait until you see how much water I can pull with this."

"Get your belongings into the canoes," said Jack. "With seven Scouts, you have two doubles and one three-man boat. Rio and I will take Ack's suitcase,"

While Jack and Rio were putting their canoe in the water, Shaine assigned paddling groups. Chet sat in Shaine's bow. Borden paddled in front of Lloyd. Ric was in the stern with Ack in the bow and Tom in the center.

"Until tomorrow's swim test, everyone wears lifejackets," said Jack.

"That sucks," complained Shaine. "We can all swim, except for the new guys."

"You know the rules. Safety first," said Jack.

"Whatever," mumbled Shaine under his breath.

Ack pulled on his bright yellow lifejacket. "I hope this doesn't make me look too conspicuous."

Tom was grateful that his wouldn't draw any attention.

"Look, it's fucking Big Bird!" shouted Shaine. "We'll never lose you, newbie!"

"You look like a giant fucking canary," said Chet.

"More like a yellow, safety-shit, fucking flamingo," said Shaine. "I hear it screaming, *save me, save me!*"

"NO swearing! You know it's against camp rules," Jack snapped. "Watch the wise cracks. We're a team. We all have strengths and weaknesses. EH?"

The silence indicated that Jack had been heard.

"Now for the evening's plan. After we take everyone's stuff to the cabin, we'll paddle across the river. We have a meeting with the Director at our firepit at 8:30. Any questions?"

There were none.

With limited conversation, the four canoes paddled to Scout Point in a swirling breeze. Shaine and Chet rushed to the cabin to claim empty bunks. They chose the ones closest to the bathroom. The others carried their gear. The only open bunk was next to Tom.

"Welcome to life in the North," said Tom. "The canvas feels better than it looks."

"I hope so," said Ack. "It'll be good to be in one place for a while."

"Time to paddle. Get down the canoes," Jack yelled. "Let's see what you remember."

Staying close together, the four boats paddled toward the opposite shore. When the breeze allowed, the boys bantered about whose sports season had been the most successful. Not having anything to contribute, Tom was silent.

At the midpoint, Jack ordered the canoes to raft together.

"Boys, welcome to being a Scout at Catamount. This a major step for all of you. We will spend more time on the water than we will at camp. The Dumoine River is our ultimate challenge. The rapids are wild, and the portages are demanding. To be successful, we will become a smoothly functioning team. No one is Superman. Each of us has strengths and, also, limitations. We need to help each other, as brothers."

Jack paused for effect. Tom guessed that Jack had rehearsed this talk several times.

"At all times, Rio and I are here to support you - on

the water, on the fields, at the campsite, on stage, and in all activities. We are teammates and fellow travelers. Together, we compete to win, and we work together to succeed."

Jack took a deep breath. Tom tried not to roll his eyes. Jack was not an eloquent speaker.

"As most of you know, as Scouts, we step back in time when we are out of camp. This is deliberate, so we can appreciate the traditional skills of the native peoples and the fur traders who came before us. We must always be ready for whatever comes our way so..."

Jack paused.

Tom sensed something was coming. He was not alone. All the boys tensed.

Jack yelled, "First boat to the opposite shore gets a point. Then, switch positions so that each boat has a new stern paddler. Then the first boat back to Rio and me gets an additional point. GO!"

The canoes pushed apart. A sprint ensued. The shore looked far away to Tom. Arms and backs began to tire. Tom's canoe was second to Shaine's. The third canoe was losing distance.

"Do we have a plan to change places?" Tom asked

"No," Ric and Ack said.

"Ack, how well do you paddle in the stern?"

"Never done it."

"Tom and I will switch," said Ric.

"Okay," said Tom. He was hesitant to take over the stern.

In front of them, Shaine's canoe stopped ten feet from the shore. The two paddlers moved at the same time and the canoe rocked wildly. Shaine dropped his paddle into the water.

Tom's canoe glided to a stop for the exchange. Ric crouched and Tom slid over him.

As soon as he was in position, Tom yelled.

"Ack, pull hard on your right."

Tom pried on the left as hard as he could. The canoe started to spin.

"Now, both of you, forward as hard as you can."

Glancing over his shoulder, Tom saw that Shaine's boat was beginning its turn. The third canoe was drifting toward the shore.

"We need to paddle steadily and not get too tired. Let's change sides every 30 seconds - Okay?"

"That makes perfect sense," Ack said. "That way, we use the muscles on both sides - good thinking."

"I like it," said Ric.

"Change sides! NOW!"

Behind him, Tom heard Shaine shouting at Chet. Switching sides enabled Tom's canoe to keep up its speed, and the three reached Jack first. Shaine's boat finished about thirty seconds later. The third canoe was several minutes behind. Its paddlers seemed relaxed. Tom and the other four groaned about sore muscles.

Jack and Rio were smiling. Jack said, "Tom, Ric, and Ack, a nice paddle. You pushed hard. Boys, what did we just learn about group paddling?"

"Nothing," snapped Shaine. "Ric's boat switched sides as they paddled. Everyone knows that's a shithead way to perform."

"It's tradition, asshole!" Ric said. "There aren't any rules about that."

"It's fucking Boy Scout to switch sides. We all know that Americans don't appreciate the North. They expect us to follow them in everything. They do stupid things all the time, and we all know it - don't we?"

Shaine glared defiantly at Tom.

Tom was shaken at the attack. He hadn't heard this kind of talk at Catamount.

"NO cursing!" Jack yelled. "You know the rules. Next foul language earns an extra job. ANY QUESTIONS?"

The stillness was immense.

"Scouts, we ARE a team." Jack said. "And we need to learn from one another."

Turning to Borden and Lloyd, he asked, "Boys, what did you learn today?"

"There was no way that we could compete with Shaine's and Ric's boats. They had the stronger paddlers." Lloyd said. "We chose to have a relaxed paddle. Now we're not exhausted. If necessary, we could continue for miles."

Lloyd dipped his paddle into the water and pulled.

"But you lost and don't get any points," Shaine snapped.

"Who cares about the stupid points?" said Lloyd "Those are for the younger campers -unless you're trying to be the July BAC."

"Somebody has to win it," Shaine said.

"The Best All-round Camper is not a competition. It's earned because of success and behavior in all areas of camp life. It's chosen by the entire staff," interjected Jack.

He glanced at his watch. "We have an appointment with the Director at 8:30. Let's head for our dock. In silence."

The four canoes paddled to the Scout Dock where another canoe sat off to the side.

"Put our canoes on the rack." said Jack. "Leave your paddles and lifejackets under them."

The Director and Earnie were waiting for them around their fire pit. The Director motioned for them to sit on the logs.

"Good evening, Scouts," he said. "Catamount has three critical ideals, *Adventure, Brotherhood and Courage.* These are the core of everything that we do."

For the second time in one day, Tom felt that he'd heard this speech before. In a small group, he knew he had to look like he was paying attention.

"Catamount turns young men into leaders. We base our programs on years of traditions. We balance competition and exploration. The in-camp activities and the trips complement each other. As Scouts, we expect you to set the example for sportsmanship and positive leadership in everything that you do."

Tom had been right; he'd heard this talk before. He wasn't sure how much longer he could pretend to be interested.

"For much of July session, you will be the oldest boys in camp. You will lead the camp at the Circus and in the Lumberjack Roundup. As you remember, last summer, we finished behind Pine Bluff, again. I hope this year that Catamount can win. The first step towards winning the McGill Cup for the Ottawa Valley camp championship is the Lumberjack Roundup."

The Director looked carefully at each boy.

"We are counting on your leadership."

"Remember you are not alone," said Earnie. "We're always available to listen and help in any of your endeavors. We are like the fur traders of old, bound together for discovery and glory."

Tom took a deep breath. They had made camp sound a lot like school. At least he wouldn't have to read, write, or study. And being outside was definitely better than sitting in a stuffy classroom.

"We brought the makings for s'mores. Before we head out to the Island, I want to do one more thing. I need your help in remembering your names. During the winter, I learned this name game at a workshop. Please tell me your first name and an animal that starts with the same letter. I'm Clark, the cougar."

The Director looked at Jack.

"I'm Jack, the jumping jaguar."

"Wonderful," said the Director.

"I'm Rio, the restless and rambunctious Rhesus."

"Three and then four word-descriptions. But don't feel the need to compete. Let's go around. Try to come up with a unique animal. Borden, you're first."

"I'm Borden, a brown bear."

Chet was sitting next to Borden. "I'm Chet, the clever cheetah who climbs into the canopy to catch chipmunks."

"Seven! So inventive. I love it," said the Director. "Next."

Shaine cocked his head.

"I'm Shaine, a sharp shark-like scorpion who slithers through slippery swamps and sinuous sands."

"Very creative," said the Director. "I love the sound of the letters. That was eight. Inspiring."

"I'm Ric, a rambunctious rhino."

"I'm Lloyd, the llama who leaps like a lion."

Tom had done this exercise before on an outdoor education trip and had an answer.

"I'm Tom, a timber wolf."

"I'm Ack, an amazing, ambidextrous antelope who ambles awkwardly over ants who avoid angry anteaters, aggressive aardvarks, and adventurous armadillos."

Ack smiled and sat straighter.

"Delightful," said the Director. "That's twelve. I wondered who can be the most ingenious. I can't wait to hear what you have created, especially later in the summer."

The Director and Earnie stood.

"Have a good fire," said the Director.

"That was awesome, Ack," said Earnie.

They walked toward the Scout dock.

"Ric and Borden, can you start a small fire?" Jack handed them a box of matches. "There's kindling, tinder, and firewood under the cabin."

As the other boys sat around the fire pit, the two made quick work of igniting the twigs and branches. Tom hadn't built a fire in years, so he watched carefully. The wood blazed in the deepening twilight.

"The Director's game was stupid," said Shaine. "He must think we're little kids. He knows us old-timers."

The Scouts' faces shimmered in the flames. The silence was awkward. Tom guessed that no one would attempt this exercise again.

"Can we make s'mores now?" Chet asked.

"Not yet," Jack said. "We have things to do. Hopefully, the breeze and the fire will keep the bugs at bay. After we do introductions, we'll make s'mores. Then, we'll review the job wheel and tomorrow's schedule. I'll start. Rio will go second. We'll continue around the circle."

Realizing that he would be second to last, Tom relaxed a little.

"I'm Jack Atherholt. I've been coming to Catamount since I was 8 years old. I did my Voyageur trip on the Missinaibi. I only did one year of the Apprentice Program because my knee got blown out playing football. I'm fine now, but the full recovery took a couple of years and messed up my sports in high school. I wasn't at camp last summer because I was working for an accounting firm in the city. In May, I finished at U of T. I have an older sister and a younger brother. He's a Cataman, but this summer, he's out west doing a geology field study. I look forward to paddling with each of you. This is Rio Brunner. He's from Switzerland."

Jack seemed both knowledgeable and approachable. He looked like an athlete, muscular and lithe. He did seem jaguar-like. Tom guessed that Jack was unsure of his future, which made him feel some kinship.

"Hello. I am Raffinelle Brunner. Please do call me Rio. I am a three-year physics student at the Bern University of Engineering and Science. I grow up in a small ski town in the mountains of south Switzerland. I have two young sisters. When I was young, I spent time camping in the mountains with my grandfathers who are woodworkers. I am at Catamount to perfect my English and learn about Canada. I was in a canoe for the first time six days ago. I like to take photographs. Can we gather over here so I can take a picture of our first night together with the fire and the cabin in the background?"

Tom had learned nothing new about Rio. As Rio arranged everyone for a picture, Tom sensed that Jack was already tired of being a photographic model. He wondered what had made Rio select a rhesus monkey as his animal.

"Borden, your turn," said Jack.

"Hi. I'm Borden McKinien. This is my fifth year at Catamount. I live in Sturgeon Falls. I have a younger sister who is a pain. In the fall, I run cross-country. I play hockey and, in the spring, lacrosse."

Borden seemed solid. He did look a little bear-like.

"I'm Chet Mossiere. I'm an old timer. My dad went here. I have a younger sister who is a prima donna. I live in Toronto and go to North York Academy where I play football and baseball. I'm a receiver and a cornerback. I play second base, next to this jerk."

Chet smiled at Shaine. He looked at Shaine every time he made a comment.

"I'm Shaine Cavendish, the third. I live in Toronto with my father. My parents are divorced. I have an older brother at university and an older sister who lives with my mom. Thankfully, I don't live with them. I go to North York. My father went there. I was the starting quarterback on the JV football team, the point-guard on the freshman basketball team, and the shortstop on the JV baseball team. My dad was on the Catamount staff for years. He was the head coach when Catamount last won the McGill Cup. We're going to win it this year, eh?"

Everyone responded with a quiet 'yeah.'

"And to start, we're going to beat Pine Bluff at the

Lumberjack Roundup. Right?" said Shaine.

Another collective 'yes.'

"Do we mean it? How loud can we be? Beat Pine Bluff!"

A loud 'Beat Pine Bluff' chorused over Cabin Cove. Tom thought, *I bet that your dad's a jerk, just like you are.* It was clear Shaine considered himself the Scouts' leader.

"That's enough of that," said Jack. "Ric, continue."

"I'm Rishard Hairreson. Call me Ric. I'm from Montreal. I play football and hockey. In the spring, I'm a catcher on the baseball team."

Tom couldn't read Ric. He was a big person. When paddling, he'd pulled hard. He had moved slowly but surely as they had changed positions. He seemed friendly but quiet.

"Lloyd, you're up," said Jack.

"I'm Lloyd Bradley. I'm from Ottawa. I play soccer, basketball, and baseball. I've got an older brother who's at university and an older sister in grade 13. This is my fourth year at Catamount."

Lloyd was tall, thin, and relaxed. He looked like a hippie with his long, light-colored hair.

It was Tom's turn. He kept it simple. "I'm Tom Woodruff. I live in New York City. In the fall, I run cross-country. In the winter, I wrestle. In the spring, I play lacrosse. This is my first summer at camp."

"That's obvious," Shaine said. "An American and a city boy! Can't wait until he meets a moose. You're no timber wolf; more like a titmouse."

"Shaine, you're not being brotherly," snapped Jack.

Shaine whined an insincere, "Sorry."

Ack spoke up.

"I'm Alexander Smythe. Call me Ack. This is my first time at camp. I used to live in Scotland, but my mother and I moved to Burlington last week. I run track, long distances. I play volleyball and shinty."

"What's shinty?" asked Chet.

"It's like the Irish sport, hurling. It's a traditional Scottish game. We play with sticks on a soccer pitch. It's a very physical game."

"I saw hurling on *Wide World of Sports*," said Lloyd. "That's cool. You clobber people with sticks."

Playing shinty made an impression with the other Scouts. Ack had been friendly at dinner. Tom was pleased that he had the bunk next to him.

"Thanks. It's s'mores time," said Jack. "Rio and I already cut marshmallow sticks."

Ack and Tom shared a stick. Each ate two s'mores. Tom watched in amazement as Ric consumed six.

When all the sweets had been eaten, Jack said, "Let's take a pee break. Come back ASAP."

Neither Tom nor Ack moved. The others headed to the washroom.

As they sat quietly, Tom asked, "Why were you living in Scotland?"

"My mom met my dad at university, St. Andrews. He's Scottish. They got married. He works in the oil industry."

"How come you had to move to Canada? You said that your grandfather passed away."

"It's a long story. The short version is that my mom is Canadian. Mom and Dad divorced about five years ago. Mom was close to my dad's father and was helping Grandfa manage the family house and grounds. As his health declined, she became his caretaker."

"That must have been tough," Tom said. "How long was he sick?"

"He was bedridden for about a year. Grandfa and my dad didn't get along. My dad hated the fact that my mom was the family manager. Grandfa passed in late May."

Ack took a deep breath and stared into the fire.

Tom felt a wave of guilt. Was he abandoning his

grandparents? Maybe he had made a bad decision. Thank God he had an escape plan.

Ack continued, "As soon as Grandfa was buried, my dad told Mom that she no longer was needed. School was ending for me. We packed up and flew to Toronto. While I'm at camp, Mom is living with her parents in Burlington. She'll find a job and then a place for us to live."

"That's a lot of craziness. How'd you get to Catamount?"

"My mom's father came here when he was a boy. He offered to pay, and they had space. It's better than sitting in an apartment in a city. I'd rather be outside. I hope the woods are like being in the heather."

"What the heather?"

"It's the open spaces of northern Scotland. We don't have many trees but lots of open hills without many people. I like being outdoors. How did you get to camp from New York City?"

"Similar long story. My dad died. Mom remarried to a French diplomat. They're moving to India. My grandfather was a camper and a counselor at Catamount. He met my grandmother here."

Tom stopped as Jack and the others took their seats on the logs around the fire.

"Now for the daily routine," said Jack. "I'm making a job-wheel with seven jobs. It will start with Borden as the waiter for tomorrow. It will go around the circle as you are sitting now. I'll post it tomorrow."

When Jack said he would put up a physical wheel, Tom stopped paying attention. He was trying to analyze the other Scouts, their friendships, and potential allegiances.

"Any questions?" Jack asked.

While Tom had many, he kept quiet and mumbled 'no' with the group.

Jack cleared his throat.

"Tomorrow starts your experience as a Catamount Scout. As I said earlier, this is a special summer. It's very different from being a Senior camper. Before our service trip, the mornings are scheduled. During the afternoon sessions, you can choose where you want to learn and earn points. After the service trip, we'll have only a few days to prep for our Dumoine adventure. Much of the time will be trip prep. We'll spend two weeks on the river and have only a day or two before the Lumberjack Roundup and the Banquet. Now, what needs clarification?"

Not wanting to look foolish, Tom listened. The initial inquiries focused on the Dumoine. After saying the Dumoine had been Jack's favorite trip as a camper, he deferred answering specific questions, saying that they needed to focus on the immediate. Shaine asked questions about the Lumberjack Round-Up. The questions ended with concerns about points and tests.

Many of the returning boys hoped to reach the 600-point level. This would allow them to sit on the Lodge porch before meals. Each activity awarded points by passing tests. They started with the simple and ended with the expert.

Each camper got a point per day assuming his cabin passed inspection. When you were on a trip, you earned a second point per day. Staff members could award points for special tasks or good behavior. If you were on a winning team at any of the special days, your team or cabin earned extra points. At 100 points, you could sit on the log railing above the bench in front of the Lodge.

As he listened, Tom figured out that all the returning Scouts had accumulated over 400 points. He figured that just being at camp would earn him 45: 28 for each day plus 17 for trip days. One hundred didn't seem too far.

Night had fallen. A breeze whispered softly through

the trees. Moonlight sparkled on the river's ripples.

Jack looked at his watch.

"Tomorrow morning, we're tackling the ropes course. The breeze was keeping the bugs away, but it's beginning to fade. Now, for two extra points, what are the basic needs of all people? Talk to your neighbor and develop an answer. You have a minute."

Tom and Ack prepared an answer.

"Ready!" Jack said.

Silence fell. Tom thought he heard the hum of mosquitoes rising from the forest around them. It was time to move inside.

"I have a number behind my back from 1 to 5. Whoever guesses correctly goes first. If their answer is wrong, we'll go around the circle to the left."

Seven hands went up.

Jack turned to his left.

"We'll start with Borden."

"5."

"Wrong."

"3," said Chet.

"Incorrect."

"4," said Shaine.

"Correct. What is your answer?"

"Water, clothing, and shelter." Shaine paused for effect. "And clean air to breathe."

"Very nice, Shaine, but you're missing one. Anyone have anything to add?"

The silence was profound. Tom slapped at a mosquito on his forearm.

"Sleep," Jack said. "Sleep is the most critical. You can go without water for three or four days and without food for more than a week. In the summer, in most places, clothing and shelter are not critical, unless you're in bad bug country. But, without sleep, you begin to go crazy after 36 to 48 hours. After three days, you can't function at all."

Jack's explanation brought silence.

"So, what does this mean?"

"Lights out," Ric said.

"And quiet in ten minutes," added Jack. "Get ready for bed quickly. It's late. I'll make sure that the fire is out."

Tom hustled to the bathroom with his kit. He was last in line.

As he entered the cabin, Shaine said, "Shut the door, stupid. We don't want any bugs in here."

Tom lay quietly on top of his sleeping bag. The returning campers whispered with first-day excitement.

The night cooled. He crawled inside his sleeping bag. His mind whirled. So much had happened. Paddling with George. Meeting Cecille. His cabin mates. Some seemed nice, others were questionable. The animal names had been weird. He wondered who would act like their animal. The unspoken camp expectations. The daily jobs. The point system. Where could he easily pass tests? The unknowns of the Dumoine. Would he stay or would he get sick?

"No more whispering!" snapped Jack.

"Time for sleep," Rio barked.

For a long time, Jack pleaded and threatened. As an observer, Tom found the situation amusing.

Earnie walked into the cabin and got into his bunk. The quiet lasted for a moment or two before the twittering started.

"If I hear another sound, that person will sleep on the floor next to me," Earnie bellowed.

The calls of the loons filled the silence. Overall, the day had been better than Tom had expected. The canvas formed comfortably to him. In the quiet, Tom relaxed.

# Chapter 4
# Ropes Jump Rocks

The whispering awakened Tom. It was very early and he groaned silently. If he'd been back in the city, he'd be in dreamland because he was used to background noise. Sleeping in a cabin in the woods magnified sounds.

The boys' whispers became voices.

"If you're awake, get dressed and go outside," Jack barked. "Do something quiet in the open area away from the cabin."

Shaine, Chet, Ric, and Lloyd dressed and went outside. After tossing and turning, Tom followed.

Ric was drawing a very large circle in the ground with a small stick.

"Want to play?"

"Sure. What are we playing?"

"Land."

"I don't know what that is."

"Everybody in Canada knows how, "Shaine said defiantly. "It's like Risk. You conquer the world. It's very American."

"That sounds frighteningly American. But, since I've never played, can someone explain the rules?"

"Sure," said Chet. "The world is inside the circle that Ric drew. He'll divide the Land into five pie-shaped areas. To start, we each stand in our areas. Ric starts with the stick and throws it onto someone else's land. As soon as it leaves his hand, everybody runs away. If the stick falls on your land, you grab it and yell 'Land.' Everybody freezes. You choose your target. Then, you can take one giant step towards that person, and you try to hit your victim with the stick."

"Throwing underhand," Lloyd said.

"Of course!" said Chet. "The target can dodge without moving his pivot foot, like in basketball. If you hit your victim, you take some of his land. If you miss, he takes some of your land. Got it?"

"I think so."

"You'll figure it out. Let's start," said Ric. "Everybody on their land. Ready?"

Ric made a lunge toward Lloyd. Tom ran away. Reversing himself, Ric dropped the stick on the far end of Tom's land. Tom scrambled for the stick and called, "Land." Frozen, everyone stood about 20 feet away. Chet seemed to be the closest. Tom leapt toward him and launched the stick. Chet swiveled, and the stick sailed past.

"I get to take some land," said Chet gleefully.

Chet stood on the edge of Tom's territory. Using the stick, stretching as far as he could, Chet drew a half-moon-shaped area and then re-traced it.

"Thank you," Chet handed the stick to Tom. "Now, you get to throw it."

"My pleasure."

Tom looked at his competitors and lobbed it high toward the far edge of the circle. When Ric called "land," Tom had run about 15 feet. Ric went after Chet.

The game continued. Parcels of dirt exchanged ownership. Soon, the area inside the circle no longer resembled a carefully cut pie. Being tall, having long arms, and possessing a keen balance helped as players seized territory. Tom began to understand the game's strategy. Ric and Chet made an alliance and eliminated Lloyd. Shaine and Ric allied and turned on Tom.

After Tom lost his last sliver of ground to Ric, he sat next to Lloyd. "How long do these games go on?"

"Depends," said Lloyd.

"On what?"

"Who gets lucky and who turns on who."

The sky was a clear, bright blue. A breeze stirred the leaves. Tom enjoyed the peace.

After watching for a couple of minutes, Tom asked Lloyd, "How did you get to Catamount?"

"My older brother went here. When he started a summer job, it was my turn for camp. Catamount is a good place. How did you get here from New York City? That's a long way away."

"My grandfather and my father both went here."

"Like Shaine and his crew?"

"Maybe. Except I'm the lone American and a new boy. I've never done any wilderness tripping."

"You'll be fine. Jack will take care of us. He was one of my counselors when I was a Middie. He's nice. I'm glad he's back."

A yell came from the Land arena.

"Watch," said Lloyd. "Chet's turned on Ric. He and Shaine will eliminate Ric. Then with only two, they'll go back and forth."

In the distance, a bell rang from the Lodge. In rapid succession, distinct bells rang with insistence in the Junior, Middie, and Senior sections.

Shaine and Chet agreed to a tie.

From the cabin, Jack shouted, "Time to get up. Breakfast is in 20 minutes. Remember your bathing suit. Before we leave, clean up for inspection."

Tom walked inside and straightened his bunk. The job wheel said his job for the day was the fire starter. When he asked Jack, he learned there was no need to do anything because there was plenty of wood and kindling. Ack was the Lodge sweeper, so they waited outside.

The two chatted about their former schools. Ack had attended a village school with only nine people in his grade. If he had stayed in Scotland, he would have attended a boarding school in Aberdeen because there was no local high school within a reasonable drive. Tom mentioned that he had graduated and shared the fact that he didn't know his future school plans. The two boys shared their unease about life after camp.

Ack smiled.

"My grandfather used to say, 'I choose to focus on today. I will be helpful to those around me. I will be positive and kind.'" Ack paused. "I miss him. I learned a lot from him."

"My grandfather is similar," Tom said. "He said 'The future takes care of itself. Help trim the sails and keep the wind at your back.' Whatever that means."

"My grandfather would understand."

"Down to the canoes," Jack yelled. "I'm hungry."

Quietly, the Scouts paddled in the same canoe groupings as the night before. Tom was surprised but pleased when Ric asked him to paddle in the stern and Ack agreed to sit in the middle.

During the trip to the Canoe Dock, Tom warned Ack about the 100-point bench. When Ack questioned about the quickest way to earn lots of points, Ric assured them that the starting-level tests were easy. They put their canoes among the others on the Boat House racks.

The wait in the Main Yard was brief. Breakfast was oatmeal and pancakes. It went smoothly, as Borden was an efficient waiter. Jack told them to pay no attention to the announcements as they had their own schedule for the day. While Tom and those with cabin jobs waited for the three boys who had center camp chores, they stood with Jack and watched the Voyageurs and Apprentices carry canoes. The blue wood and canvas canoes came down from the parking lot to the Canoe Dock, and the aluminum and fiberglass canoes went up to the canoe trailers.

"Why are they carrying the canoes by themselves?" asked Ack. "They look heavy."

"I agree," said Tom. "Wouldn't it be easier if two people shared the load?"

"It's the most efficient way to do a portage," said Jack. Tom was puzzled.

"On a trip, there are three people in a canoe and one person carries it on the portage. Another has the wanigan, and the third takes the pack and the paddles. This way, you should be able to complete the carry in one run."

Jack paused.

"Portaging takes practice. Given our numbers, we'll have one camper stern man on the Dumoine. He'll have to carry his boat."

Suddenly, the idea of carrying a canoe wasn't so daunting. From his days of wrestling, Tom knew that he was strong. If he wanted to be the camper stern man, he knew he had to learn a great deal in the next few days.

Once all the Scouts were together, Jack explained the day's schedule.

"We spend the morning on the ropes course. After lunch, we receive our special gifts. Then we'll do the swim test. Assuming everyone passes, we'll paddle down the Ottawa to Jump Rocks."

"What about dinner?" asked Ric.

"Today is Saturday. It's the cooks' day off. We have a cookout."

"Why are the cooks getting a day off?" asked Shaine. "Camp just started."

"The cooks have been preparing meals for the staff. They deserve a break," Jack said. "At Jump Rocks, we'll roast hot dogs over a fire. After supper, we'll head back to the cabin."

"For popcorn and s'mores?" asked Ric.

"We'll see," said Jack. "Let's head to the Ropes Course."

Tom whispered to Lloyd.

"What's the surprise?"

"It's no surprise. We get our own canoes. We get reconditioned wood and canvas boats. They are supposed to be better tripping boats."

"We used aluminum canoes for the past couple of years," Ric said. "They're heavy. I heard wooden boats are lighter."

"That's not what my brother told me," said Shaine. "He said they're heavy as lead."

"Let's go, men," said Jack, leading them into the woods behind the Lodge. "Challenges await."

Tom had enjoyed the ropes courses on his outdoor education trips at school. He guessed that most of the boys had had similar experiences.

"Who has experience on a ropes course?" Jack asked.

Every hand went up.

The group started with the Human Knot. Tom was happy when they untangled themselves quickly. A circular lap-sit followed. With experienced people, they balanced sizes easily. The All-Aboard presented an issue. No one wanted to touch anyone else for longer than absolutely necessary, but finally, they got everyone off the ground for the count of ten. At the Lava Pit and the Alligator Pond, Shaine took charge and ordered the Scouts through the challenges.

At mid-morning, they walked back to the Lodge for a water and washroom break.

As they lounged, Tom quietly asked Lloyd, "Does Shaine always tell everybody what to do?"

"Yeah. It's easier. Generally, he's right. We've learned not to cross him because he's got a temper and a mean streak."

"Okay. Thanks."

"How come you didn't come to camp before?" Borden asked.

"My mother," said Tom. "She's a city girl. She's even uncomfortable in the suburbs. She hated being at my grandparents' cabin that's an hour north of the city. While she loved my dad, she didn't like his adventurous side. She used to worry when he'd travel overseas to out-of-the-way places."

Chet sat down. "Like where?"

"The Middle East. And Africa."

"What did he do there?"

Everyone slid closer to hear Tom's response.

"He worked in the oil business. My grandfather's company manufactures and installs drilling safety equipment. Dad supervised its setup and trained the locals."

"I wonder if he knows my father," said Ack. "Does he work on the North Sea platforms?"

"Not anymore."

Tom stiffened and prepared to drop the bomb.

"How come?" asked Chet.

"He died five years ago after a nasty car accident."

An awkward silence fell over the group. Tom could tell that no one knew what to say.

"My mother didn't like the idea of a camp in the Canadian wilderness, so I've spent my summers in the city in day camps."

"Now you're at Catamount," said Jack loudly. "Time to head back to the ropes course. Scouts, you have new opportunities ahead."

The electric fence was next. Everyone had to get over a meter-high string without touching it. When Shaine started to bark commands, Jack produced a bandana.

"Shaine is blind."

Chet stepped in as the leader. Tom got the impression that he didn't have a clear sense of the challenge. To confuse matters, Shaine refused to be carried. The group was not working.

"What's happened to your teamwork?" asked Jack.

On his school trips, Tom had seen this before.

"No one is listening, so we don't have a plan that everyone understands."

"So, what should you do?"

"Develop a plan and listen to each other," said Lloyd.

"Okay. Create one. We're not moving to another challenge until everyone, including Shaine, Rio, and I are on the other side of the fence. And Rio and I can't speak."

Two new wrinkles. In previous initiatives, Jack and Rio had been safety spotters. Now, they were silent participants who were heavy.

Everyone talked at the same time. Ric wanted to lift the smaller boys over first. Lloyd wanted to get the larger boys over at the beginning.

After a few minutes, Tom looked at Ack.

"Got any ideas?"

"Yeah. We do a combination of Ric and Lloyd's ideas."

"Then let's get everyone's attention. Yell loud. Now!"

Their shout got everyone's attention. Tom found himself managing the discussion. The group agreed on Ack's plan. Things went smoothly until Shaine's turn. It took multiple arrangements of people before Shaine allowed himself to be hoisted. Finally, with Ric and Jack lifting and Chet and Rio lowering, Shaine stood on the other side of the electric fence.

In the debrief, Jack focused on the positive. After the discussion, Rio posed everyone for a series of photos while Chet, the lightest, was lifted over the string. Tom felt that, at that moment, the Scouts were finally cooperating as a team.

Jack glanced at his watch.

"That took longer than I'd hoped. The waiters' bell is going to ring sooner rather than later. Let's try the high wall. We'll stop when the bell rings. In the last five years, only one Scout group has been successful."

The 10-foot brown wooden wall rose straight out of the ground. On the back side, a ladder rose up to a platform. Tom could see why conquering it was difficult, especially for shorter or heavier people. He knew that they needed a plan. Released from his blindfold, Shaine took charge and began to order the bigger boys to form the base of a human pyramid.

"Does everyone understand what we're doing?" Tom asked.

There was a murmur of 'no.'

"We don't have any time," Shaine said. "I know that my idea will work. Tom, get up on Ric's shoulders. You're strong and agile."

It made sense for Tom to stand on Ric; he was stout and solid. Chet scrambled onto Tom's shoulders, grabbed the top edge, and pulled himself over. Shaine followed, as did Lloyd, Ack, and Borden. This left Ric standing on the ground with Tom on his shoulders.

"Now, we hold Tom while Ric climbs up his back," shouted Shaine.

As Tom locked hands from above, he looked down at Ric. "Go ahead. Jump up and grab my belt."

Ric tried. On his third attempt, he got his fingers on Tom's belt. But, as soon as their weights combined, the hands holding from above began to slip.

"I'm falling," yelled Tom.

Ric dropped to the ground. Tom jumped wide to miss landing on Ric.

"Everybody down," shouted Jack.

Once the Scouts were sitting on the ground, Jack asked, "What happened?"

"Ric didn't climb right," said Shaine.

"I tried."

"Not hard enough."

"We didn't have a plan that everyone understood." Tom felt the group looking at him. "We had the right idea. People were in the wrong order. No disrespect, Ric, but you're too big to pull yourself up. One of the tall, skinny people should be the last person on the ground, maybe Ack or Lloyd?"

"Not me," said Lloyd.

Tom turned to Ack, "How well do you climb?"

"Like a bug." Ack smiled. "I suggest that Lloyd be the person who hangs down. He's tall. I'll climb fast. Then, everyone can pull up Lloyd. What do you think?"

"Maybe," said Lloyd. "I'm heavier than I look."

"How many have belts?" asked Tom.

Five hands went up.

"What if we link them together? That way, we don't need Lloyd. Ack can grab the rope of belts. We can help pull him up. Does that make sense?"

The nodding heads chorused 'yes.'

"Who goes when?" asked Borden.

"A good point," said Tom. "Let's decide. Ric, you're the biggest and strongest, so it makes sense for you to start as the base initially. Who next?"

The group agreed on an order of climbing. Tom was surprised that Shaine said nothing.

"This will be your last attempt," said Jack. "The bell's going to ring any minute."

Tom looked around.

"Ready, Scouts. One, two, three, GO!"

Ric set the base. Lloyd became the second level. Borden, Shaine, Ric, and Tom climbed up and over. Lloyd climbed down. Ack and Lloyd set a base for Ric. He struggled to get up. With help from above, he made it. Ack took the base position. Lloyd climbed him and was pulled over. Borden lowered the belts.

"I tied a loop at the end. If you can grab it, we'll pull," yelled Borden.

Ack backed away, ran at the wall, and sprang upwards. He grabbed the rope of belts. The boys pulled. Ack got his hands on the edge and pulled himself over the top. Cheers erupted.

A bell rang from the Lodge.

"Just in time. Well done," Jack said. "You've earned lunch."

For the first time, Tom felt included in the conversation as the Scouts walked to the Main Yard. While waiting for the lunch bell, they played tetherball. The winner of each game stayed at the pole, and the challengers formed a line. Shaine won most of the games and made quick work of Tom twice. Shaine's underhanded comments about spastic Americans got laughs.

At lunch, the conversation focused on the upcoming swim test. Shaine told everyone that there was a surprise challenge. Jack refused to confirm or deny any details of the Scout-level requirements.

Despite being good in the water, Tom was apprehensive. Last summer, he'd been a volunteer lifeguard at his day camp and had taught the 4- and 5-year-olds how to swim. While he'd passed Junior Lifesaving twice, he was still uneasy about the camp requirements. The Catamount swimming test sounded harder.

While waiting for the waiter, washer, and Lodge sweeper to join them, they discussed the upcoming trip to Jump Rocks. Cooking over a fire sounded like fun, but Tom was uncomfortable with heights, and it sounded like some of the jumping levels were pretty high. Shaine bragged about his ability to dive from the rocks. Ric and Borden challenged everyone to a cannonball contest.

Once everyone was together, they walked to the Trip Shed. It was a large building with two open sides. At one end, behind a long counter, were two storerooms. One was packed with equipment, the other had shelves loaded with rows of cans and boxes of food.

As George and Earnie walked in, Jack said, "Make a circle of benches."

After they were settled, George stepped up. "Welcome. In a moment, you will be getting canoes for your exclusive use. They're for your travel to and from Scout Point and for your trips. As Scouts, you are old enough to understand the beauty, history, and practicality of the traditional wooden canoe."

"Thank God," said Shaine. "Paddling is easier than walking."

"I agree," said Chet. "Life just got a whole lot simpler."

Tom saw George smile and nod to Earnie.

"Thank you, George. Today is Saturday. Thursday morning after breakfast, you leave for Algonquin Park. Your trip will be the first to leave camp. As Scouts and then as Voyageurs, you will have your own canoes and your own equipment. You will learn the value of long-standing traditions and understand how to care for your equipment. Let's start with your canoes. Follow me."

Behind the building sat four freshly painted blue canvas-skinned canoes. Each had unique yellow striping. One had two-foot-wide yellow bands, another had three, the third had a three-foot band beneath the bow seat, and the fourth had an X under the center thwart.

"These are your new best friends. Carry them inside the Trip Shed."

"These boats are ancient," said Shaine under his breath but loud enough to be heard. "No wonder no one comes back as a Scout."

"They feel pretty light," said Lloyd.

"Wait until we use them for a while. My brother told me they get water-logged."

"We have to be careful not to scrape the canvas," said

Borden. "We don't want them to leak."

"That means daily checking and maintenance," Shaine said. "My brother said it's a drag and a waste of time."

"Thank you for your opinion," said Jack. "We use wood and canvas boats for a reason."

"Yes. This summer, you'll learn to appreciate the canoe," said George. "In past summers, you've paddled and played with the boats. You ran the aluminum canoes onto the shore without caring what happened. You threw your packs into the boats like they were shopping carts. You didn't understand the relationship between the canoe and the water."

George winked at Tom.

"Do you want to be like dumb, insensitive Americans or true Canadian craftsmen?"

The Scouts stood taller. Tom saw that the appeal to Canadian pride had worked. He nodded at George.

"Yes, some of these canoes are old. Some may be as old as your fathers or your grandfathers. They have been reconditioned and are in excellent shape. This summer, you will learn to keep them in tip-top condition. Now, let's get them down to the Scout rack on the Canoe Dock. Solo carry!"

Few of the boys had ever carried a canoe by themselves. Everyone had seen canoes being carried by the staff, but the specifics of getting a canoe up on one's shoulders was a new skill.

"Gentlemen," said Jack. "It's time to learn how to properly portage a canoe. It's all in your technique. You'll learn to love carrying a canoe."

He smiled. Going over to one of the canoes, he began to demonstrate.

"Tip the canoe so the rounded side rests on your thighs. Reach over and grab the far gunwale. Push with your leg and pull with your arms. Flip it up onto your shoulders so that the center thwart rests behind your neck. Watch."

The canoe popped onto Jack's shoulders. He took several paces. He reversed the process and rested the boat on the floor.

"At this point in the summer, wood and canvas canoes are lighter than the aluminum canoes."

"Told you," said Lloyd.

"Thank God," said Chet. "Portaging the heavy stuff is a drag."

"As the summer continues, the canvas and the wood absorb water, and the canoes get heavier."

"Told you so," Shaine muttered.

"Let's practice getting the canoes onto your shoulders," Jack said. "The technique takes practice."

"Also, there's a way that starts with two people," George said. "Watch us."

Jack held up one end of the canoe above his head. George walked underneath and stooped to wiggle his shoulders beneath the center thwart. He stood upright, and the canoe rested on his shoulders.

"To get out, you reverse the teepee," Jack said.

Jack held the boat. George walked out from below it.

"Why is it called a teepee?" asked Tom.

"Stupid question," whispered Shaine.

George glared at Shaine.

"Good question. Remember that there is no such thing as a bad question. I imagine that, if you look at the canoe being held up, it resembles a teepee. It's standard canoeing language so paddlers can communicate easily."

"Let's practice," said Jack. "Pair up."

The two new boys found themselves together. Tom mastered the lifting technique quickly. Ack's height and narrow shoulders made it more challenging.

"Time to carry the canoes down to the Canoe Dock," said George.

"I'll carry," Tom said.

"I'll teepee." Ack smiled.

"This isn't too bad."

Initially, the canoe rode smoothly on Tom's shoulders and neck. After a couple of minutes, the thwart dug into his shoulders. He heard other Scouts stop and switch carriers. In spite of his increasing discomfort, Tom was determined to walk the entire distance.

When Ack teepeed the canoe at the dock, Tom felt like the weight of the world had been lifted from his shoulders. Around him, the other carriers groaned. Some swore quietly.

Jack pointed to an empty rack in the second row at the far end.

"That is the Scout rack. Put the canoes there until we're ready for our trip to Jump Rocks."

"Why can't we have the first row?" questioned Shaine.

"That's for the Voyageurs' boats," said Jack. "They're out at the Island. They're the oldest campers at Catamount, and they've earned the privilege. Next year, it's yours. But remember, not everyone is invited to become a Voyageur."

While Jack wasn't looking directly to Shaine, Tom knew that Jack's words were aimed at him.

"Put your paddles, lifejackets, and clothes under your new canoes. Our former boats are now for instructional use."

"What are our boat groups for this afternoon?" asked Borden.

"You can figure it out," Jack said. "People will move around until the canoes are finalized for the Dumoine."

The reference to the Dumoine caught everyone's attention. Chet and Ric looked at Shaine and Lloyd. Tom suspected these two were his competition for the camper stern position.

After their equipment was stored, the Scouts walked

to the H-shaped swim dock. In a roofless room, they changed into their swim trunks and walked to the dock.

"I'm David McElwain, the Waterfront Director. The Scout lifejacket swim test is simple. Without stopping, swim 100 meters, 4 lengths. Then, float or tread water for five minutes. Finally, swim another 100 meters. You can use any stroke."

As a cloud passed in front of the sun, the air cooled. No one wanted to be the first into the water.

"Can we wait for the sun?" asked Ric.

"Sure," said David. "The water's got a chill to it."

'What's a little cold," said Shaine. "Let's go, Scouts. Time's a wasting. Follow me."

Shaine dove smoothly and surfaced, doing a powerful crawl.

From his guard time at day camp, Tom had learned that you can tell how well a person swims by watching his entry into the water and his first few strokes. Shaine was an excellent swimmer.

About halfway, Shaine yelled, "Water's fine. Come on in, wimps! I'll be finished before some of you start."

Glancing at the sky, Tom saw that the sun was emerging. He wanted to warm up before starting, and he wanted to see how well his fellow Scouts swam.

From the other end of the swim area, Shaine's cry of 'chicken' broke the deadlock and the sun's full warmth brought courage. First, Chet, Lloyd, and then Ack dove in. Their dives and first graceful strokes showed that they were strong swimmers. But all three came up sputtering.

"It's cold," Lloyd gasped.

"Very refreshing," drawled Chet breathlessly.

Borden and Ric jumped in. They surfaced immediately and began hurried strokes. Neither looked completely comfortable in the water.

"How cold is it?" Tom called.

"It's not frigid," yelled Ric.

Tom dove and surfaced, swimming the crawl. He caught up with Borden and Ric as they made the first turn. Both were keeping their heads out of the water.

"Good thinking," said Tom. "I like to see where I'm swimming."

Keeping pace with Borden and Ric, Tom breaststroked. The lengths of the swim areas passed slowly. Shaine, Chet, Lloyd, and Ack lapped the slow group.

"Come on, slowpokes," said Shaine. "We don't have all day."

"There's no rush," called Jack. "They're saving their energy for canoeing."

Jack had been watching the swimmers closely while Rio moved around the dock snapping photos.

Shortly after the slow group began their five-minute float, the other four started the final 100 meters.

After everyone finished successfully, Jack called them together.

"Good work. Rio and I will get our food and we'll meet you at the Canoe Dock. Get the canoes ready to paddle. Stay in your suits. And don't forget your dry clothes."

Once the canoes were at the edge of the dock, Shaine assigned canoe groups. He paired Tom and Ack.

"Let's see what the newbies can do together," said Shaine, grinning.

"Do we need to bring anything?" Ack asked.

"No, stupid," said Shaine. "It's a delightful, warm afternoon. We have dry clothes if we need them."

"How far is the paddle?" asked Tom.

"Not that far," Shaine snapped.

"Do we go past the cabin? If we want anything else, we could stop."

"No one needs anything."

"I'm not so sure of that," said Ack. "If this is anything

like the open heather, the wind could kick up or weather could charge in.

"Don't be an idiot. It's a perfect day."

When Jack and Rio walked into earshot, Shaine said, "Chet, Ric, and I will volunteer as the three-man canoe."

"Thanks," said Jack. "I'll take the food pack."

"Let's stop at the cabin," Shaine said. "We need to be prepared if the wind picks up or it gets cloudy."

"Good thinking," said Jack. "Glad to see someone is planning for the unexpected. Rio and I will both be in the stern. I'll take Ack in my bow. Tom can go in Rio's bow."

Tom was disappointed to be paired with Rio. He'd hoped to work on his stern paddling.

"We are ready to go off on our first adventure," said Rio, snapping photos.

"Jack, how far is the paddle?" Ack asked.

"I said it's not far," said Shaine.

"It's farther than you think, about an hour," said Jack. "We'll stop at the cabin."

At the Scout Dock, Jack said, "Go get sweaters. Some of you might want long pants and a wind breaker. If the breeze picks up, it will cool down. If it's a headwind, we might be back after dark. You may want a flashlight."

After the stop at the cabin, the four canoes paddled into the center of the Ottawa River. The band of trees on both sides looked like curbs on a highway. In front of them, the thin horizon line beaconed between the blue of the sky and the gray of the water. Initially, there was some conversation between the boats about who did not return from prior summers, but that soon stopped. Some of the paddlers chatted with their bow or stern man, but most of the canoes lapsed into extended silence.

A tailwind created small waves that pushed the canoes. Paddling with the sun on his face and the wind behind, Tom felt good. He was surprised to find that the quiet was comfortable. He tried to maintain a steady pace, but it was a challenge. With increasing frequency, Rio paused to rudder the canoe onto a straight course, and they began to lag behind.

Far ahead of them, Jack called a halt.

As soon as they reached the group, Shaine said, "Let's get going. I'm getting hungry."

"Not so fast," said Jack. "When we take a break, everyone gets a rest. We got too spread out. We'll stop every half hour, eh?"

A chorus of 'yes' signaled everyone's agreement. Shaine leaned forward and whispered to Chet, who smiled.

Once the canoes were together at the next break, Chet said, "The cruel, cunning cheetah crawled carefully and coolly to catch a concerned but careless chipmunk before it collapsed into the canopy. Twelve! Best so far."

"Tremendous," said Rio. "The Director would be impressed."

Everyone looked at Shaine, and Tom wondered how he would react to being upstaged.

Scowling, he said, "That's stupid and silly. I'm not playing, now or ever."

"Sorry," said Chet quietly but with a smile.

Tom took a deep breath and sensed that everyone else relaxed. He had never been good at word games and was glad the competition had ended.

"Let's paddle," said Jack.

After another half hour paddle, the Scouts arrived at a tall granite outcropping. Once again, Tom and Rio were the last to join the group. Above a boulder-strewn shoreline, a wide-open area appeared to have a firepit.

"Where should we land?" asked Jack.

"Right here," Shaine said. "We can jump out on the dry ground and pull the canoes up to the campsite."

"You're no longer paddling metal bathtubs," said Jack. "Will those rocky edges be good for the boats?"

Shaine seemed chagrined.

Glancing around, Tom saw that his colleagues were bewildered.

"Could we unload the canoes while standing in the water?" Tom asked. "Once the first boat is finished, there will be extra people to carry the canoes so they don't hit the rocks."

"Sounds good to me." Lloyd looked at Jack.

"It's your decision. You're Scouts, and you need to take charge." Jack looked around. "It's fine with me. Who goes first?"

The boys turned to Shaine, who looked uneasy.

Rio spoke, "For me, I suggest that the canoe with the three boys to be the very first canoe. That makes for a third person so that the carrying of that canoe will be easier."

"Excellent," said Jack. "Shaine, you'll unload first. We'll be the second boat."

"If Tom and I are the number four, I can take excellent photographs," said Rio.

"Sounds good."

"Can we take off our shoes?" asked Shaine. "Mine are brand new."

"No. We don't want to mangle any toes on the rocks," said Jack. "You should have thought about your shoes before now."

The unloading and lifting went smoothly. Jack was the only person who easily got his shoes wet. Even though Tom knew it was coming, he was surprised at his hesitancy at stepping into the water.

Once everything had been carried to the campsite, Jack supervised its organization.

"Canoes with paddles underneath go over there. Put the pack next to the fire circle."

"Can we swim now?" Shaine asked.

"No. We need to review some things."

"Can I take off my shoes so they can dry?"

"No."

"Why not?"

"We need to review what you seem to have forgotten. I hope that everyone wore your wet shoes."

"What are wet shoes?" asked Tom.

"They are your paddling shoes, probably a pair of old runners. They stay wet most of the time. Keep your other shoes dry, especially on trips. You wear them around the campsites. Any questions?"

"Can we dry our wet shoes?" Ack asked.

"When we're at Catamount. When we're on a trip, they'll stay wet most of the time. You wear them during the day."

"Will we need them at camp?" Tom asked.

"A few times. Most of the time, your feet will be dry. I'll try to remember to let you know when you'll need wet shoes."

"Thanks for today's reminder," Shaine said sarcastically. "My best shoes are soaking wet."

"I had expected a seasoned camper like yourself to remember such an important detail. Do I have to review everything?"

A silence hung over the Scouts.

"Can we try to dry our shoes now?" asked Shaine.

"No. You have to gather firewood. Remember that you should always have shoes on your feet around a campsite. We don't want any cuts or twisted toes."

Jack pointed at a trail.

"Follow that path. It goes around the Jump Rocks. Keep going. It will lead to a cove where there should be driftwood."

The trail led to a small sandy beach with lots of dry wood. On their return, each Scout carried a large armful of wood.

"Why didn't you tell us about the sandy beach?"

Shaine asked. "If we'd gone there, most of us would have been able to keep our shoes dry."

"If you remember, I asked where you wanted to land." Jack smiled. "You chose to land here. You need to take responsibility for your decisions. But now it's swim time. You can take off your footwear."

Shaine placed his shoes in the sun. Tom doubted they would dry.

"Grab a couple of lifejackets for rescue floats," Jack said. "Let's go examine the Jump Rocks."

The outcrop of gray granite rose straight from the river. Tom saw well-defined climbs to the jumping ledges. The lower platform looked to be a comfortable ten feet. A second one was another ten feet higher, and he knew that he'd be uneasy at that height. The top of the rock face was another twelve or fifteen feet higher. That wouldn't work for him.

"Who's going to go in and check the water?" Jack asked.

"Why do we need to check it?" Shaine asked. "We were here last year. It looks fine."

"Does this river freeze in the winter?" Jack smiled.

Everyone nodded.

"Has anyone seen big logs drift down the river?"

Again, everyone nodded.

"Has anyone seen jams where underwater logs get stuck?"

Again, nods.

"With this outcrop, can anyone tell me that a spring jam didn't leave underwater logs?"

Everyone shook their heads - no.

"So?" Jack looked around.

"I'll go check," said Lloyd.

Everyone watched as he waded into the water and swam over to the landing area. He did a feet-first surface dive and stayed down a long time.

"Nothing down here. I didn't touch the bottom, but I think it's safe."

"Are you positive?" asked Jack.

"Let me do a couple more dives to be sure."

Lloyd moved six feet downstream and plunged. He swam away from the rock face and did a third surface dive.

"There's nothing down there but some real cold water."

"That's what I expected, but you need to be sure," said Jack. "Now, who has the best cannonball?"

Jumping from lowest level was exhilarating. The water was chilly, but the warmth of the sun afterwards was delightful. Shaine, Ric, Chet, Lloyd, and Ack began cannonballing. The watchers declared a tie.

"I'm going to the next level," said Shaine. "Who's ready for some real excitement?"

Tom looked at Borden and hoped that he disliked heights.

"Let's stay."

"Sounds good," said Borden. "I'm not going that high."

"Feel free to be crazy, wet, and cold," Tom yelled. "We're sane, dry, and warm in the sun. Enjoy!"

The five scampered up. On Shaine's first jump, he tucked into a can-opener, and his splash was impressive. The four others jumped. Only Ack created a sizable column of water. They climbed and launched again.

As Ric exited the water, he said, "I'm done. The water is a lot colder down deeper."

"Me too," said Lloyd.

"I'm out," said Chet. "The breeze is picking up. I'm getting cold."

"Five-minute warning," said Jack. "Then we cook hot dogs."

Shaine stood with his hands on his hips at the

beginning of the climb. "I'm going to the top."

He was challenging the other jumpers.

"Okay," said Ack. "I'll follow you."

Tom was surprised that Ack accepted the challenge.

"Not me. I'm chilly," said Lloyd.

"Go ahead," said Ric. "I want to eat."

As he started to the top, Shaine grinned. "You're all wimps."

Ack scrambled up behind him. Outlined against the sky, both boys looked small. As the two looked down, Tom sensed some doubt. They backed away from the edge. A count of '1, 2, 3, GO!' rang out.

Ack sailed out from the top, by himself. In the air, Ack straightened and pulled his arms to his sides. Feet first, he hit the water straight as a board.

After he surfaced, Ack yelled, "Where are you? We agreed to go together."

"I caught my foot on a rock and lost my balance," Shaine shouted.

"Okay," Ack barked. "Come on down. The water's getting cold."

Shaine hesitated. He stepped back and, after a pause, jumped. Shaine flailed and landed off center with one of his arms extended.

"That hurt," said Jack.

"It had to," said Chet.

Ack and Shaine swam to shore. Ack was warmly received. Shaine complained about his foot and his arm. Jack and Rio acted sympathetic, but Tom wondered at their sincerity.

"I'm hungry. Time to eat," said Jack. "Who's today's fire starter?"

The group looked at each other.

"It's me." Tom was unsure of what was expected.

"Well, get going," said Jack. "Do you need any help?"

"I'll give him a hand," Borden turned to Tom. "Let's

go get some tinder and kindling."

Tom followed Borden to a grove of pine trees. Borden started to break off the thin dead branches near the trunk.

"I'll get the tinder. You get a handful of pencil-width dead branches. Break them off the pine trees. The stuff on the ground may be damp."

As Tom gathered the twigs, he had vague memories of doing the same thing with his father and grandfather.

Back at the campsite, Tom was glad to see that the others had broken and stacked the wood. Borden placed the tinder bundle in the middle of the rock circle and showed Tom how to place the kindling twigs on top.

Jack handed Tom two matches.

"Have at it, fire starter."

Tom struck a match and carefully placed it at the base of the tinder. The little pine branches welcomed the flame. Soon, a blaze was roaring.

"I got extra hot dogs," said Jack. "There are five apiece. But I could only get three buns for each of us."

While the fire burned to coals, Borden and Ric set out the hot dogs, buns, and fixings. Lloyd and Ack cut green hot dog sticks.

Tom was full after three dogs. Ric and Borden were happy to take Tom's extras.

Once everyone finished eating, Jack said, "We need to get moving. We don't want to be on the water after dark."

To load the canoes, they reversed the process of their arrival.

Shaine tried to keep his feet dry. But Jack was insistent that, as the stern man, Shaine hold the canoe while Ric and Chet climbed in.

The evening sky was cloudless. As they started to paddle, the breeze calmed. Soon, no air was moving. Tom was happy that Rio was able to keep the canoe straight and they stayed with the other boats. The hour and a half paddle passed smoothly. Tom was pleased that Rio changed sides regularly. As the sun approached the tree line, a fresh coolness rose from the water.

Full darkness was close when they reached the Scout dock. Being careful not to scrape the canvas, the boys carried their canoes to the racks. The air was warmer on land and the mosquitoes swarmed. As Tom swatted, he was convinced that Jack inspected their placement of paddles and lifejackets slowly so the bugs could feast.

When they clambered into the murky interior of their cabin, Tom was a hero for remembering his flashlight. His beam made everyone's search for their own light easier.

As they prepared for bed, Tom said, "Ack, that was a pretty smooth jump. How'd you do it?"

Ack whispered, "Promise not to tell?"

"Sure"

"I had practice."

"What?"

"Back in Scotland. In order to go to a deep-sea station with my dad, they made me take a safety course. Part of it was learning how to jump from the drilling platform into the water. The training pool had a ten-meter platform with an elevator. The water was heated. You had to keep your legs together and hold on to your lifejacket. Luckily, I did it correctly the first jump, and, using the lift, I did it five times."

"That sounds cool, but heights aren't for me."

"Don't tell anyone. They think I'm a superstar. I guessed that Shaine was going to chicken out. I wanted to show him up."

"Your secret is safe with me."

"Lights out in five," Jack yelled.

Once everyone was in their sleeping bag, Jack offered to read a story about the North. From a short list of titles, the decision was swift. Jack began reading *To Build a Fire*.

Having studied the story at school, Tom was excited to hear it again. He was frustrated with the way Jack insisted on quiet and absolute darkness. Every time someone talked or turned on a flashlight, he stopped reading.

After numerous pauses, the Scouts listened, silently and blackly.

Tom tried to listen, but his mind whirled. The day had been better than he had expected. Most of his cabin mates were nice. Some of their "Canadianisms" made them different than his New York friends, but overall, their lives were pretty similar to American's.

On the ropes course, Tom marveled at how much several of his cabin mates had acted like their animals. Ric had stood solidly like a rhino. Chet had clambered like a cheetah. Monkey-like Rio had danced around with his camera. Shaine's verbal barbs had snapped sharply. For some reason, Shaine disliked him. Ack's family situation was almost as confused as Tom's. He hoped they would become friends.

The longer Jack read, the softer his voice sounded. The words drifted through the darkness. Following the story became a struggle as Tom drifted off to sleep.

# Chapter 5
# Diamond No Match

When the sun rose above the eastern horizon, it shone directly on Tom's face. There were no sounds within the cabin. He wondered how far Jack had read in *To Build a Fire*. Tom couldn't believe that he'd fallen asleep so quickly last night. He rotated 180 degrees to get his head out of the sun, but sleep would not come again.

For a few minutes, Tom wiggled. Then, silently, he dressed and tip-toed to the campfire ring. He wondered what the day would bring.

The first day had passed without significant problems, although he wondered what more he could do to fit in with the Canadians. He was not a great athlete. He could run, but not super-fast. He had stamina. Verbally, he was not quick. He took time to choose his words. He preferred to listen, then talk.

Friday and yesterday had included both good and unpleasant experiences. Paddling with Cecille on Friday had been fun. Yesterday's rope course had been good. Paddling with Rio had been a drag. Shaine appeared to be manipulative, unkind, and used to getting his way.

On balance, camp was much better than summer school. Tom pulled his sweatshirt around him. Camp was cooler than the pavements of Manhattan. Chirping birds danced from tree to tree calling cheerily.

Earnie sat down beside him, surprising Tom out of his reverie.

"The wake-up bell will ring in about fifteen minutes. I like the peace of the early morning. The world is fresh. The sunlight is crisp."

"Yes, it's tranquil. Not like the city where everything echoes off the concrete." Keeping his voice down, Tom asked. "I have a question that's kind of personal."

"That's fine. Ask, but I may or not answer it."

"Why are you in a cabin? I thought that the senior staff had their own cabins around the Lodge."

"I used to." Earnie drew a long breath. "When my wife was alive, we lived in center camp. She passed away about a year and a half ago. Last summer, I stayed in our cabin, but there were too many memories."

Earnie paused.

"Catamount has a hold on me. I thought about not coming back, but I'm committed to camp and to young people. I've seen camp do great things for hundreds of boys over the years. I'm not being boastful, but I know canoeing and tripping. I appreciate the North and know its power."

Earnie looked at the river.

"I know that I can't do this forever, but I hope that living in a cabin will keep me more involved. And the nights and the mornings aren't quite so lonely."

Tom didn't know how to respond. He guessed that he'd heard something that Earnie shared with only a few people.

In an attempt to continue the conversation, Tom said, "I have another question."

"Okay."

"What do you do during the school year?"

"I used to teach physical education at a middle school in Toronto. When my wife got sick, I retired. Now, I substitute teach in the winter and spend the fall and the spring at Catamount."

"What happens then?"

"Maintenance. We repair buildings and rebuild canoes. It's peaceful."

"Oh." Tom searched for anything to continue their dialogue. He heard a splash. "Do you think George will be paddling this morning?"

"Probably not. It's Sunday, and he was out later than normal. Yesterday was our day off, so we went to Ottawa for dinner with some of the other senior staff. We returned later than we'd planned."

Tom couldn't figure out what to say.

After a too-long silence, Earnie asked, "Tom, may I read your mind?"

"Sure, be my guest."

"Right now, you're not sure about camp. Being here is better than being in a classroom in the city. The last few days had parts that were good, parts that were awkward, and some things that were a little scary. You are the new boy. You see how comfortable the others are with one another and with Catamount and you wonder if they will ever accept you."

Tom's eyes widened.

"Acceptance will take time. Everyone has his own strengths and his own swamps. We all have talents and weaknesses. Even your granddad."

Tom leaned forward.

"He paddled like a man possessed and portaged with the best of them but, initially, he couldn't cook to save his soul. He couldn't read a map. He never knew where we were. Over time, he learned. We developed our pluses and worked on our minuses. The trail challenges you. You grow and just when you think you have it all mastered, something happens that forces you to reassess."

Tom was surprised to hear about his grandfather's lack of map-reading skills. That might have been why his grandfather had been so insistent that Tom learn to read a map and use a compass.

In the distance, a bell rang at the Lodge. In rapid succession, distinct bells rang with more insistence in the Junior, Middie, and Senior sections.

"Time to get up." Jack shouted, "Breakfast is in 30 minutes, and I doubt that you'll be back here until after dinner. Be sure to bring your bathing suit and a towel. You'll be swimming."

"Do we need wet shoes?" Lloyd asked.

"No, but remember that canoes aren't always stable."

Tom went back into the cabin and straightened his bunk. In last night's confusion, he'd forgotten to hang his bathing suit and towel on the clothesline. The thought of getting into a damp swimsuit was not appealing, but as he looked around, he realized he was not alone. Only Borden and Lloyd had hung their stuff.

As the Scouts put their canoes into the water, Jack told Tom and Ack that he needed to talk with Rio. The two of them would paddle together in their own canoe.

"Bow or stern?" Tom asked Ack.

"Bow," said Ack. "I don't know how to steer. I'd never been in a canoe before yesterday."

"I started learning the stern yesterday. I just hope I can keep us going straight."

On the way to the Canoe Dock, Tom was encouraged that his ability to guide the canoe felt more natural. He and Ack formed a graceful team.

As they landed, the waiters' bell rang.

"I'm the waiter." said Ack. "I've got to go set up. I don't have a clue of what I'm supposed to do."

"Go! I'll manage the canoe."

"I'll give you a hand." Borden stepped over.

Together, they racked the canoe and walked to the Lodge.

During breakfast, Tom watched Ack, knowing that tomorrow he'd be the waiter. The individual tasks seemed logical. The only thing that worried Tom was carrying the big metal tray to and from the kitchen.

At announcements, Tom learned that Sunday started with chapel at the amphitheater. Inside, he groaned. He'd sat through endless chapels at school and felt someone droning on about a Bible story was not relevant to him.

After dismissal, Jack gathered the Scouts. "After chapel, we'll do three things: some canoe instruction, a brief session in the Trip Shed, and a softball game against the Voyageurs. Any questions?"

There were none.

Immediately, Shaine began to assign positions and plot game strategy. Neither Tom's nor Ack's names were mentioned.

After sweeping the back section of the dining hall, Tom walked out onto the front porch and waited with the rest of the camp for the completion of the Lodge and groundskeeping chores. At the base of the amphitheater sat a table and a piano. Near the top, the Scouts sat on one side, the Voyageurs on the other. The view over Boat Bay was peaceful.

As Tom sat with his cabinmates, Jack distributed well-used songbooks. The service was shorter than Tom expected. He was familiar with the songs at the beginning and at the end, but he did not sing. He had been told repeatedly that he couldn't carry a tune. When a Voyageur read, *If You Can't Go Over or Under, Go Around*, the refrain echoed loudly. At the end, everyone recited a poem, *My Creed of the Out-of-Doors*. Tom was surprised that most of the Scouts and Voyageurs recited it from memory.

After Jack returned the songbooks, the Scouts walked to the Canoe Dock where George met them.

"Pair up. Jack will paddle with me. Tom, partner with Rio."

Tom was disappointed.

"The American needs a babysitter," Shaine whispered.

Tom's face reddened, but he chose not to respond.

"Chet, with me." Shaine continued in a full voice. "Ric with Lloyd. Ack with Borden."

Tom saw Jack and George grimace.

Once on the water, everyone rafted together.

"I know that most of you can paddle reasonably well. In whitewater on the Dumoine, you and your paddling partners will need to be precise and ready for anything. To demonstrate, we're going to have a competition. Who can tell me what happens in a Diamond Drill?"

"Your canoe goes around the four colored buoys that are in a diamond shape in the middle of Boat Bay," Lloyd explained.

"Thank you. Now, who can give us specifics?"

Borden volunteered.

"From the starting line between the two green buoys, you paddle out to the red buoy and go around it, keeping the buoy on the canoe's left. Then, you paddle to the yellow buoy, keeping it on the canoe's right. From there, you cut across to the orange buoy, going around it to the left. Then, it's back to the red buoy. You keep it on the canoe's right, and finally, you paddle back to the finish line between the green buoys."

"As Middies, we learned this to pass our tandem canoe test," Shaine said. "What's the big deal? Everybody can do it in their sleep, except the newbies."

"Thanks for your observation," snapped George. "I'm glad that you know how to do it. Perhaps you'd like to race us?"

"I would, but it's not fair. You have Jack in your bow."

"I agree. What if Jack was blindfolded?"

"In that case, sure." Shaine smiled at his bowman, Chet. "I think we could compete."

Tom sensed that Shaine was being set up.

"And, what if all of us did it at the same time? Would that make it even fairer for everyone?"

"Yes," said Shaine eagerly.

Tom guessed the hook was set.

"Okay," said George. "Rio will be the starter, so he can't compete. Since Ack doesn't know the drill, he and Borden can watch. Three canoes will race. Is that okay?"

"Of course." Shaine grinned from ear to ear.

"Okay," said George. "Now, who remembers the multi-boat ground rules?"

"I do," said Borden. "No ramming. No pushing off with your paddle. The inside canoe has right-of-way around the buoy unless the lead canoe is halfway around."

"You're correct. Anything need clarification?"

"Don't they do this kind of race at the Lumberjack Roundup and at the final Regatta in August?" Ric asked.

"Of course, they do," Shaine snapped.

"Not all the time at the Lumberjack," said Jack. "Always at the Regatta."

"That's what I meant," said Shaine.

"Any more questions about this race?" George asked.

The specific order of the buoys confused Tom, but he didn't want to give Shaine an opportunity for another insult. He'd figure it out by watching.

Jack tied a bandana over his eyes.

The three canoes maneuvered to the starting line.

"Are we ready?" asked George.

The paddlers answered 'yes.'

George nodded to Rio.

"Ready. On my GO."

Rio paused.

"Everybody ready. 1, 2, 3 - GO!"

The three canoes sped toward the red buoy. George and Jack slipped behind the two camper canoes to the inside position. The camper canoes overshot the buoy.

Jack leaned out with his paddle and stabbed into the water. The bow turned sharply. George slid the canoe around the buoy. For all practical purposes, the race was over. George and Jack cut precise turns around the remaining buoys and finished well ahead of the camper boats.

When the canoes rafted, George asked, "What did we just learn?"

There was an awkward silence.

"Maybe, sometimes," Ric said, "there are traps we don't recognize right away."

"Yeah," said Chet. "You set us up. I think you knew Jack was comfortable with your commands. He didn't need to see. You knew we would race out as fast as we could and that we'd be out of position for the first buoy."

"What do you think, Shaine?" asked George.

"You set us up. Can we do it again? This time, we'll definitely beat you."

"Not now," said Jack. "How does this relate to our Dumoine trip?"

There was another awkward silence. Tom saw a lot of "I don't know" on his fellow Scouts' faces.

"Rivers change all the time," said Jack. "You have to be ready for anything and everything. What if you're in the middle of a driving rainstorm? What happens if your canoe gets turned around in a rapid, and you're going down backwards?"

Jack had made his point.

"Each of you can paddle in nice weather on lakes when everything is peaceful," said George. "On your previous trips, you've been in places where people have been nearby. While the Park and Temagami are wild areas, the Dumoine is remote, no roads. Your fellow paddlers are the only resources that you have. If you need help, you have to get to the end of the river. Understand?"

Tom and his fellow Scouts nodded. He had a lot to

learn before the Dumoine. He sensed that some of his cabin mates had been humbled. Others maybe not, especially Shaine and Chet.

"Let's switch positions in the canoes," said George. "I know that some of you don't feel comfortable in the stern. That's okay. Just paddle peacefully through the Diamond Drill and see how it feels."

Under his breath, but loud enough to be heard, Shaine said, "This is stupid. Chet's happy to be a bowman. I'm going to be the camper stern man, no question."

"Let's rearrange the boats. Rio will join Borden," said George. "Borden, go to the bow. Rio needs stern time."

Tom and Ack found themselves together.

"Ack, you take the stern," George said.

Tom was disappointed not to be in the stern, but he knew that Ack needed to learn.

Once they settled on new canoe groups, George said, "With everyone paddling, you'll get strung out. Pay attention to the right-of-way rules."

Tom concentrated on his strokes. As he tried to help keep the canoe on course, he accidentally splashed Ack.

"Thanks for wetting me down." Ack smiled. "It's good to know that I can count on you to keep me cool."

"You're welcome. Now, can you figure out how to keep us going where we're supposed to?"

"I'm trying. This steering while paddling isn't easy."

"Would you mind if I made a suggestion or two?"

"Sure."

Tom tried to teach Ack the techniques George had taught him. After a few minutes of practicing, they could maneuver without too many extra zigs and zags.

"Scouts, head to the Canoe Dock," Jack shouted.

As Tom and Ack paddled by, George said, "Nice job. Both of you have potential as paddlers."

When the Scouts racked their canoes, Shaine made a quiet comment about Chet being a chipmunk that brought a laugh from several of the boys.

"I guess that me not for stern or command." said Chet. "Me too small, too stupid. Me do what me told."

While Chet's words got a laugh, Tom wondered how he felt inside.

While the Scouts walked up to the Trip Shed, Shaine shared his observations of who could and could not paddle in the stern. Again, Tom was not surprised when neither he nor Ack was mentioned.

Earnie's overview of wanigans, food packing, menus, and planning fascinated Tom.

"This is boring. We've known this for years," Shaine whispered.

"Now, an introduction to your NEW tents," snapped Earnie.

The Scouts sat at attention.

"This summer, you're not using the nylon self-supporting tents. To go along with your classic canoes, you will use traditional light-weight canvas tents, without floors or aluminum poles."

"What do you mean?" Shaine said.

"Watch!" said Earnie.

Just outside the Trip Shed, Earnie and Jack rigged a square teepee-like tent. First, with a thin branch as the center pole, and a second time using a rope strung between two trees, so the tent's peak didn't need a center pole.

"We're going back to the Stone Age," Shaine whispered. "Next, they'll tell us we have to hunt our own food."

"I've done that," Borden said.

Tom was pleased to see that Shaine had no comeback.

"Any questions?" asked Earnie.

A silence hung.

"We're due at the softball field," Jack said.

"Now, we can do something important." said Shaine.

"This is our first practice for the Lumberjack Roundup. We need to beat Pine Bluff."

Turning to Tom and Ack, he asked, "Do either of you know how to play?"

Tom didn't know what to say. He'd played softball in PE class but knew that he wasn't very good.

"No, Mr. Cavendish, sir." Ack saluted with an exaggerated snap of his wrist. "We don't do no softball in Scotland. We too feebleminded. We just hit a little tiny ball with a big stick and run down a field while the other players try to hit us with their sticks."

Everyone grinned. Shaine said nothing.

The softball game did not go well. Tom knew right away that they were in trouble. Most of the Voyageurs were good athletes. To equalize numbers, Jack and Rio played.

At the start, Shaine pitched. After the Voyageurs scored six runs, Jack took over.

Tom didn't touch the ball in the field. When he batted, he didn't strike out but hit into easy outs. Ack ran like a gazelle and made a spectacular catch. At the plate, he hit a triple and a home run.

When the waiters' bell rang, the Voyageurs led 16-8. The teams shook hands and meandered down to the Main Yard.

At lunch, Shaine complained loudly about the game being unfair. The other Scouts sat hushed.

"Who can tell me what happens on a canoe trip?" Ack asked.

The Scouts talked generously, eager to get back on the water. The trips had been a blast. They loved the excitement of exploration. The guides and the counselors prepared the food, organized the campsites, and portaged the canoes. The campers carried the packs and the wanigans. The boys had set up their tents and washed the dishes. As he listened, Tom learned that Shaine and

Chet were the least effective cleaners.

When lunch ended, Jack said, "No rest hour today. We have a special treat. Then we have a full afternoon."

"You said we had free afternoons," said Shaine.

"That starts tomorrow."

It surprised Tom that this plan met with a mixed reaction. Some boys had been looking forward to down time while others were eager for excitement.

As they approached the Canoe Dock, George was chatting with an older white-haired man. The man stepped back from the dock's edge. George pushed a canoe out into the water. The man ran and leapt into the moving canoe. Picking up a paddle, he effortlessly spun the canoe in a tight circle. With the flick of his paddle, the canoe slid parallel to the dock and its paddler introduced himself.

"Good afternoon, boys. I'm Omer Stringer."

Tom was mesmerized.

Omer began an explanation about the relationship between a canoe and its paddler. He demonstrated landings, sideways maneuvering, and pirouettes. It was fascinating. When the bell rang for the afternoon activities, he invited them to come back if they had time before dinner. Tom was determined to work with Omer.

As they walked away, Shaine said under his breath, "This is girly stuff. Real men paddle in straight lines and carry packs over portages. They don't dance with their canoe."

"By the time Omer was my age, he'd done more miles on the trail than you, your brother, your sister, and your father have done in your lifetimes," Jack said.

Shaine said nothing.

At the canoe repair shop, the Scouts learned how to patch the canoe's canvas skins using Ambroid glue or duct tape. After working on a small tear, Tom learned that a successful repair required a combination of speed, precision, and patience.

"Time for Bronze class." said Jack. "We'll put on our bathing suits at the Swim Shed."

As they changed, Shaine said, "The old canoes are a drag. My dad said we should use plastic boats that can't break."

"Shaine, a word or two," said Jack. "Everyone else head out to the dock."

When Shaine re-joined the Scouts on the Swim Dock, he was quiet.

As the boys listened to instruction, Tom overheard him whispering to Ric.

"Jack doesn't know what he's talking about. He can't threaten me. My dad and the Director are good friends. I almost wish I hadn't come. But it's better than a fishing expedition up north. I'd hate being trapped with my father and his friends for ten days."

The Bronze Medallion was like the Junior Lifesaving courses that Tom had taken. Safety was the emphasis. The Scouts were in and out of the water as victims. The rescuers threw life rings and extended paddles. As they practiced, Tom realized he was one of the better swimmers. While the sun was strong, the water was chilly. A breeze sprang up and he was thankful when they finished. He was cold and tired of smiling for Rio's photos.

The boys hung their wet bathing suits on the Swim Shed clothesline. Everyone warmed as Jack marched them up the hill to campcraft.

"Welcome back to campcraft. I'm Kent Booraem. I know that, as experienced Catamount campers, you know lots about fires and cooking, eh?"

The boys grumbled a weak 'yes.'

"Jack, are they ready for the Scout challenge?"

"Kent, they're hungry. So yes, they're ready."

At the thought of food, the Scouts focused.

"Excellent. You'll work in groups. The task is simple. Start a fire and bring a small pot of water to a boil."

"That's easy," said Shaine. "We can all do that, except for maybe the newbies."

"Okay. Do it without matches. The groups that are successful will get pieces of this fresh blueberry pie." Kent pointed to one of the tables that had pots of water on it.

Tom found himself partnered with Ack and Borden. Borden said that he'd watched his grandfather use sticks, but it was years ago. Listening to the other groups, Tom learned no one had ever done this before. The boys talked and argued. There was talk of rubbing sticks together, birch bark, pine needles, tinder, kindling and using eyeglasses to focus the sunlight. Jack, Rio, and the campcraft counselors stood back and listened. Some had smiles on their faces.

As if by magic, Earnie appeared. He picked up four pieces of wood, one curved and longer, one straight, about a foot long, one flat, about six inches wide and eight inches long, and a round one, about the size of person's palm.

"Lloyd, Borden, get some pine tree tinder. Tom and Ric, gather dry, thin sticks."

When the materials were in place, Earnie created a bow using a string and the long piece of wood. He placed the straight piece into a notch cut into the flat piece of wood. He used the small, cupped piece of wood to hold the top of the straight piece. He began to pull the bow back and forth, so the straight piece spun quickly. Smoke began to rise from its bottom end. Earnie knelt and blew carefully. A red ember took life. On it, he gently placed several very thin pine twigs. They flamed. Soon, a fire was blazing.

The boys were amazed. Earnie had done the impossible with almost no effort. Everyone was eager to try. When the campcraft instructors handed out sets of fire bows, Tom suspected that they had been set up by Earnie's success.

Tom and the Scouts discovered that what looked easy was challenging.

Ack tried first, without success.

"Can I try?" Tom asked.

"Sure, be my guest."

Tom created smoke but couldn't get an ember. It annoyed him that Rio was taking pictures and repeatedly asking him to smile.

"Borden, it's your turn."

Working carefully, Borden produced a glowing ember. Using the thinnest pieces of pine tree tinder, he generated a flame. Together, they added pencil-sized twigs and built a blazing fire. Borden placed a pot of water on the fire. They added wood around the pot, and the water boiled.

"We win!" Borden shouted.

After another few minutes, Ric and Lloyd were successful.

Shaine and Chet created wisps of smoke.

"This pie is so good," said Borden.

"It's not fair," said Shaine. "Our wood was wet. We should all get pie."

"Very sweet." Ack smiled.

"I think they cheated," Shaine grumbled quietly.

"As emerging leaders, you need to practice outdoor skills," Earnie said. "You need to be ready for any and all catastrophes. You never know what will happen. You'll always need a fire - for cooking or for warmth. Ready for a big challenge?"

"Bring it on," said Shaine.

"On your Dumoine trip, you'll get four matches a day for twelve days. You'll make two fires a day. You'll get 48 for the trip. No Scout trip has ever come back with more than 18."

"We'll beat that," said Shaine. "With Ric and Borden, we're golden."

"Time will tell," said Earnie.

A bell rang.

"Afternoon activities are finished," Jack said. "You've got about half an hour of free time before waiter's bell."

Chet, Ric, Lloyd, and Shaine headed to the tetherball court. Tom invited Ack and Borden to join him at the Canoe Dock.

As they approached, George and Omer were talking.

"How's enrollment?" asked Omer.

"It's good in the younger sections. We're full. However, we only have one cabin of Scouts. We have eleven Voyageurs. Can't figure out what's going on with the older boys and their families," said George.

"Catamount is not alone in that. I've heard the same from the other boys' camps here on the Ottawa and in the Park. The coed camps are packed. Has Catamount considered reopening the girls' camp? Otterslide, wasn't it?"

"There's been talk, but you know how the Director feels. After his sister died, he lost interest in the girls' camp."

"I was at Caribou yesterday. The girls want more interactions with the boys."

Tom spoke up. "Excuse me."

"Can we help you?" asked George.

"Omer said to come down if we had time. We've got a few minutes before dinner."

"Thanks for coming," said Omer. "What can I do for you?"

"Well," Tom said. "I was wondering how we can learn to paddle like you."

Omer and George exchanged looks.

"To paddle like Omer, you need to practice, practice, and practice. Come for classes or whenever you have free time. We have few minutes. I'll work with Ack and Borden. Tom, get into a canoe by yourself. Omer will watch you."

Paddling solo was awkward. As Omer instructed, Tom tilted the canoe and kneeled in the curved side. After snaking left and right, he began to feel comfortable paddling in a straight line.

The waiters' bell rang, and the three headed to the dock. Ack left to do his job, so Borden and Tom racked the two canoes.

"Ack learns quickly," said Borden. "He's nervous, but he'll be good."

Dinner was plentiful. The table conversation swirled around sports and potential fire-lighting prowess. Tom continued to watch Ack, who seemed more confident serving his third meal. At announcements everyone learned Omer was presenting a canoe show for the entire camp.

After dismissal, Jack said, "After Omer finishes his show, head to the canoes. We're paddling this evening."

Demonstrating paddling skills at a canoeing camp earned Omer a standing ovation. Again, Tom was fascinated.

As the younger boys headed to their cabins, the Scouts gathered on the dock.

"Paddle with someone new this evening," Jack said.

After a moment of confusion, Shaine stepped in and set up canoeing partners. Tom would be paddling in Lloyd's bow.

The Scouts turned north onto the Ottawa. After half an hour, Jack halted their evening parade.

"Raft up and rest easy. It's a glorious evening."

"We're living in our canoes during the daytime," Shaine whispered, "Next thing you know, we'll be sleeping in them."

"That may happen." Jack glared at Shaine.

"Remember what I said this afternoon?"

Shaine looked down.

"We have three days before we leave for our service trip in Algonquin Park. Tomorrow morning, we paddle and swim. You are free tomorrow afternoon for general activities."

"What does that mean?" Tom asked.

"You can go anywhere you want, rookie," Shaine blurted.

"Yes," said Jack. "It's an opportunity to pass tests and earn points."

"As a new camper, you can go past all the easy tests," said Lloyd. "Last summer, I earned lots of points finishing the Plebe and Middie tests in archery, pottery, and wildlife. You can do a lot of them in a single session."

"Excellent," said Ack. "I want to sit on the 100-point bench."

While Tom shared Ack's desire, he decided to paddle.

"Tuesday is Canada Day," said Jack. "The morning is open activities, and the afternoon is special. Wednesday morning is available for your choices. Wednesday afternoon is trip prep. We depart after breakfast on Thursday. Any questions?"

There were none.

"Letters home are due tomorrow at the end of rest hour," said Jack.

"Are you kidding?" Shaine whined. "We haven't done anything yet."

"That's stupid," said Chet. "We just got here."

"You're supposed to write every Sunday. We'll be on our trip for the first Sunday. You'll have two rest hours to scribble something. I want to see at least half a page."

Writing was not one of Tom's better skills. He was glad that he'd have time. He needed to send letters to his mother and his grandparents.

"I wish to thank everyone for being good models," Rio

127

said. "I'm getting my film processed while we're in the Park. I'll create a slide show when we are back in the camp."

The idea of seeing himself in pictures made Tom uncomfortable.

"We'll be able to see our ugly faces. How gross!" said Ric.

"You may be ugly, but I'm going to be a star." Shaine smiled. "Rio, thanks so much for launching my career."

"Are you going to be the next Jerk or the next Rocky?" asked Chet.

"Neither," said Shaine. "I'm Luke Skywalker material."

"You wish," said Lloyd.

The Scouts joked about who looked like which actor in what film. The Canadians had seen the same films Tom had over the last few years.

"Well, first, you 'stars' need to get back to the cabin for your beauty rest," said Jack. "However, before you paddle back, you need to change partners."

The boys groaned. The trading of canoe mates begun. Once the rearrangements were complete, Tom was paddling in the bow with Chet in the stern. The canoes turned toward camp. The setting sun mirrored off the water and was blinding.

Keeping the canoe straight was a challenge for Chet. He complained that his paddle was too short, the sun made it hard to see, and the breeze made it difficult to steer.

"What's football going to be like this fall?" Tom asked.

"It's going to be great. Shaine might be the starting quarterback on the varsity. He got screwed last fall and played on the JV. The coach didn't like him, so he didn't play much. We make a good one-two punch."

"How so?"

"I'm his receiver. We're a one-two combination."

Chet loved talking about football. Their canoe continued to weave back and forth, but Tom was pleased that Chet had stopped complaining. If their plan worked, after going to university in the States, Chet and Shaine were going to play in the NFL.

Tom continued to ask questions to keep Chet talking.

Tom's muscles began to tire and eventually began to hurt. Chet was not interested in changing sides. Luckily, just as the discomfort was becoming intense, they arrived at the Scout dock and placed the canoes on the racks.

The darkness deepened, and the mosquitoes buzzed.

"Can we get into the cabin?" Shaine pleaded. "We're getting eaten."

From the bushes, Jack picked up a lifejacket. "Once everything is in its proper place. I need to inspect carefully."

The bug swatting intensified. Jack seemed to move in slow motion. The more the boys slapped and waved, the more the insects swarmed.

"Nice job, Scouts. You can go."

The boys rushed up the path. As flashlights came on, Tom was pleased that several boys agreed it was time to sleep.

"Lights out in ten minutes," Jack said.

Everyone scrambled to the washhouse. Tom was the last to finish. As he walked back to the cabin from the washhouse, Earnie appeared beside him.

"Omer and George are paddling early tomorrow. Do you want to join them?"

"Sure. That would be great."

"They said that you can bring someone else."

"I'll ask Ack. But how will we know when they're here?"

"You'll hear them. Remember the other morning? If you don't hear them, I will. I'll wake you."

"Thanks."

"I'll tell Jack and Rio," said Earnie.

Back in the cabin, Tom asked Ack.

"Sounds like fun," said Ack. "What if I'm asleep?"

"I'll wake both of you," said Earnie. "But my guess is the sun will have one of you wide awake."

Tom's sleeping bag felt comfortable. The day had been both good and frustrating. His paddling was getting better. Several of his cabin mates seemed friendly, especially Ack and Borden. He couldn't figure out why Shaine disliked him so much. It was becoming increasingly difficult not to react to his jibes. So far, on balance, Catamount was okay.

Jack continued reading *To Build a Fire*. The cabin was silent. Tom was glad that he knew the story.

# Chapter 6
# Rescue Big Tray

A hand shook Tom's shoulder.

"Are you meeting George and Omer this morning?"

Tom had expected to be awakened by the sun.

"Are they here?"

"I haven't heard them. They'll be here soon."

"Thanks for waking me."

"No problem. On most days, the sun is my alarm clock," said Earnie. "But you've adjusted and are sleeping later."

Tom awakened Ack. Both boys dressed and tiptoed to the point. Their timing was perfect. Two canoes were sliding out of Boat Bay. He showed Ack where he'd gotten into George's canoe and the two climbed down to the ledge.

"Hello," said George. "Sorry to keep you waiting. We're moving a little slowly this morning."

"No problem," said Ack. "If you'd been earlier, we would have still been asleep."

"Okay. Let's go for a paddle," George said. "Where are your lifejackets and paddles?"

"Under our canoes on the Scout Dock," said Tom.

"We'll meet you there." George pulled on his paddle.

Once the boys were ready, Ack sat in front of George, and Tom got in with Omer.

Tom shuffled his knees onto his lifejacket.

"Early in the season, the knees get sore," observed Omer.

The canoes paddled to the center of the Ottawa. Tom concentrated on his strokes.

The morning stillness was nice. As he heard Ack and George begin to chat, Tom knew he had to say something. He hesitated, afraid to say the wrong thing.

"George tells me that this is your first summer at Catamount," said Omer.

"Yes. My father and grandfather went here."

"That's what George said. I don't think I ever met them."

Tom froze, casting about for another topic of conversation. He was used to people asking about his family.

"You paddle nicely," Omer said. "When did you start canoeing?"

"When I was little. My father and grandfather used to take me out in my grandfather's canoe. My grandparents have a place on a lake north of New York City."

"I thought that you'd paddled before. You seem comfortable in a canoe. Did you ever do any overnight trips?"

"We did some amazing trips."

"Tell me about them."

Tom began to tell Omer about paddling from bay to bay exploring the lake with his dad and grandfather. They explored the islands. On the cooler, rainy days, they would make a small fire, cook hot dogs and warm a can of soup. For Tom's seventh birthday, they had portaged into a more remote lake and camped overnight. They'd paddled to the far end of a narrow lake and erected their tent on a rocky point. He described how his grandfather had made a soft bed of pine boughs and his father had protested.

"Your dad was right. If everyone made bough beds, there wouldn't be any pines around the campsites," said Omer. "Things have changed over the years."

Tom tried to think of another question, but Omer asked first.

"What's your favorite memory of those trips?"

Tom thought for a moment.

"I guess it was after supper one night sitting under a tarp watching the rain sweep across the lake. Dad and my grandfather told stories about their northern canoe trips."

Tom paused, lost in his memories.

"Why did the trips stop?" Omer broke his reverie.

"Dad was injured in a car accident and had trouble walking. His health got worse, and he had to use a wheelchair. That meant that Grandfather had to travel more because Dad couldn't work."

There was an awkward silence.

"After he died, something happened between my mother and grandfather and I saw very little of my grandparents. They moved overseas for grandfather's business. Mom was sad and worried about me. For a while, she wouldn't even let me go to the park without her. She seemed scared to be in New York, but she said that she liked the excitement of the city. She got a job at the United Nations, and after a few years, she met Pierre, her new husband."

Tom took a deep breath.

"My reading problems got worse, and school became a bigger hassle. About a year ago, we created a grand plan. As a French diplomat, Pierre was going to be transferred to another country. I would spend the summer overseas with them and come back to the States for boarding school. My grandparents were retiring and moving back to New York. They would be my guardians and I'd spend the short vacations with them."

"What happened?"

"Everything fell apart. I got screwed. My English and history teachers changed the essays on the exams. I failed both classes, so I didn't get into any schools. Mom and Pierre were moving to India. Mom discovered she was pregnant. My grandparents convinced Mom that they would find a school for me, but I'd have to stay in the US. The day after Mom and Pierre left, my grandfather got hurt in a car accident. To get out of the way, I agreed to come to Catamount. So, I'm here."

The silence in the canoe was profound.

"You have a lot happening in your life." said Omer. "It must be nice to be away from all of that."

"It is."

Omer paused.

"How does your mother feel about your being at Catamount?"

"I don't think that she knows."

Tom paused.

"Mom always said that I should work harder. She never seemed to understand that reading and writing are hard for me. I can do it, but I take much longer than other kids. When my grandparents offered to take over my school search, Mom jumped at the opportunity. To be honest, there's a part of me that's glad that we're not fighting. As soon as Mom was on the plane, my grandparents gave me the option to come to camp. They said that the school situation would get figured out in August and that I needed to have some fun and find myself in the woods."

"The North is a great place. If you let it, it'll guide you to where you're supposed to go."

Omer smiled.

"You paddle well but try to use your back and entire body for each stroke. Turn and watch me."

After watching, Tom said, "You're rotating your core and keeping your arms straighter."

"Exactly," said Omer. "You are a keen observer. Now, you try."

As he concentrated, Tom realized that while the change was subtle, its impact was significant. He was beginning to feel his paddle interact with both the water and movement of the canoe.

"Much better. Now, let's see what George and your friend are doing."

As they approached, George said, "Ack is paddling quite nicely."

Ack grinned.

"I have a good teacher."

"Who had a master teacher?" Omer laughed.

"I did." George smiled. "We've got about 15 minutes before the rising bell. Omer, shall we see if these two can learn anything about tandem paddling?"

"Sounds good," said Omer. "Let's put George in my bow. Tom will move to Ack's stern. Then you can try to copy what we do."

After the switch, Ack asked, "Are we ready for this?"

"We'll do the best we can." said Tom, gripping his paddle tightly. "Watch them and we'll do the best we can."

Omer and George's canoe began to slide sideways, first to the right and then back to the left.

"See how one draws and the other pries," said Tom. "Got it?"

"I think. I'll draw to start."

After a couple of awkward attempts, Tom and Ack maneuvered their canoe from side to side. Tom found it much easier to draw, pulling toward the canoe, rather than prying and pushing water away from the boat.

A second task had the canoe circling around a center point. Again, the boys found it much easier to pull as opposed to push. Being in the stern, Tom was responsible for keeping the spinning canoe stationary. Holding multiple reference points was challenging, but he grasped it quickly.

"That's enough for this morning. You've done nicely," said George. "It's time for some coffee."

"And it's Tom's first time to be the waiter," said Ack.

"Thanks. I'd forgotten about it."

"Let's head for the dock," said George. "Omer, do you think the boys can follow us exactly?"

"Maybe. But I doubt it." Omer grinned. "They've made some progress, but they can't stay with us."

Ack nodded to Tom. "We're ready. Bring it on."

This second round of follow-the-leader started by side-slipping in both directions. The boys did the same. Spinning their canoe, George and Omer began to paddle backwards. Tom and Ack floundered in reverse. Another 180-degree rotation had both boats speeding toward the Canoe Dock.

"They're going to do a landing," said Tom.

"What are you talking about?"

"Remember what Omer did in his demos? It will look like they're going to ram into the dock, but, at the last minute, they'll turn 90 degrees."

"We can't do that. I have no idea of what to do."

"You're right," said Tom. "We'll watch."

George and Omer's canoe accelerated toward the Canoe Dock. At the last minute, George and Omer leaned and pulled hard. As if on a dime, their canoe spun 90 degrees and stopped parallel to the dock.

Tom and Ack maneuvered their canoe to the dock.

"We knew we couldn't do a landing, so we didn't try."

"You'll learn," George said. "It takes practice. You have potential as a team. The Master Tandem Canoe Test is one of the hardest at Catamount."

Before Tom could respond, from the water behind them, a voice came. "Nice try. You can't do a simple landing."

It was Shaine. The Scouts were paddling to breakfast.

"We'd have done one," Shaine taunted. "But it wouldn't be safe around all of these canoes. We don't want to do anything dangerous this early on a beautiful day."

Inside, Tom fumed. Before he said anything, Ack responded, his voice dripping with sarcasm.

"Thank you for being so thoughtful. You're always so kind and caring. In fact, Shaine, I would say that you're being brotherly."

Shaine was speechless. Tom saw that Ack's comment brought smiles to several boys.

The bell rang from the Lodge.

"Waiter's bell," said Jack. "Who's today's waiter?"

"I am," Tom said.

"Get going."

Setting up the table went smoothly: a napkin, a cup, and silverware at each place. Getting the individual boxes of cold cereal, the pitcher of milk, and the syrup from the kitchen was easy. Once the meal started, Tom carried the platter of hot pancakes to the table. After everyone was finished, he carried the leftovers to the kitchen and the stacks of plates, silverware, and cups to the dish room. He was relieved that he hadn't had to use the big trays. After dismissal, wiping down the table finished his morning duties.

As he exited the Lodge, from the Canoe Dock, Jack called, "Tom, come join us. Now!"

Once again, Tom found himself in the bow of Rio's canoe. Jack was their instructor, paddling solo.

"We're starting with canoe rescue."

"We could do this in our sleep," Shaine whispered loudly.

"Who wants to be first?" Jack stared at Shaine. "I'll be the rescuer."

"We'll be the number one," said Rio. "One and two,

here we go." Rio rolled the canoe. When Tom hit the water, he realized he hadn't changed into his bathing suit.

As they floundered in the chilly water, Tom held on to his paddle. Jack grabbed the wood from his hand and tossed it into his canoe.

Jack turned the upside-down canoe onto its side. He slid the bow onto his gunwale, yanked, and flipped the wet canoe so that its gunwales rested on the gunwales of his canoe. He paused for a few seconds to let the water drain out, then turned it gunwales-side up and slid it back into the water. Tom marveled at Jack's speed. Even with Jack steadying, Rio struggled to climb into the empty canoe.

Once Rio was ready, Tom muscled his way back into their canoe with no help. Jack threw Tom's paddle to him.

"Start paddling."

Tom and Rio paddled a couple of strokes.

"Stop!" Jack yelled. "What did you see?"

"A canoe-over-canoe rescue," said Shaine. "We've been doing that for years."

"How quickly did it happen?"

"Pretty fast," said Lloyd.

"Why so fast?" Jack asked.

"Maybe, because, we're doing the Dumoine?" Borden questioned.

"Exactly. Now pair up and practice. Everyone gets wet."

The remaining boats partnered. Some rescues went smoothly. Others took considerable time.

"Raft up!" Jack ordered. "On the river, we need to get boats upright and people paddling as quickly as possible. You have to be ready to maneuver immediately. We need to work on speed. It helps to turn the canoe on its side, so you don't have to break the vacuum of an upside-down canoe. In the rescue boat, the stern man handles the overturned canoe while the bowman keeps their canoe perpendicular to the water-filled boat."

As the bowman, Tom understood his role. He had limited confidence in Rio.

"Everyone flip over with a different partner canoe and complete another rescue," said Jack.

Rio chose to partner with Shaine's canoe. The rescues were slow and awkward. Both Rio and Shaine struggled to lift the overturned canoe. Tom was surprised that neither used Jack's side-lift technique.

"Raft up!" Jack shouted.

Jack described the side-lift technique again. Everyone completed a third rescue. Tom and Rio worked with Lloyd and Ack. This time, both Lloyd and Rio used the side-lift, and the rescues went more smoothly.

"Back to the Canoe Dock," Jack said. "Put the canoes on our rack."

Waiting for all the canoes to be stored, Borden handed Tom his towel.

"This will keep you from freezing."

"Thanks," said Tom.

"No problem. We're all in this together."

As the Scouts warmed in the sun, Jack reappeared with a stack of coiled ropes.

"We're going to be using ropes to line up the Kipawa River to the Dumoine's headwaters and when we lower the canoes down rapids that are too big to paddle. Let's go over some knots."

Out of Jack's hearing, Shaine complained again to Chet. "Jack's just wasting our time. This is for the newbies."

Tom grasped the twists and turns of knot-tying better than several of the Scouts, which made him question their knowledge from previous summers.

While waiting for Bronze class, the sky began to cloud. After their warm-up swim, the Scouts threw rescue ropes. They practiced using lifejackets and poles. Even though they kept moving, the shade and the cool water chilled them. After they finished, Tom was bummed when he realized he had no dry clothes.

"I'm here to save you."'

Jack threw Tom a pair of gym shorts and an old sweatshirt.

"Can't have you freeze to death."

"Thanks," said Tom.

The Scouts played tetherball. To everyone's surprise, Ack had a knack for the string and the ball. With his height and leaping ability, he was often a winner. Tom continued to lose far more than he won. When the waiter's bell rang, he was glad to head into the Dining Hall.

Lunch set-up was exactly like breakfast. After grace, the waiters were called by section to carry the big trays loaded with food-filled serving dishes. The Scout table was one of the last called. As Tom muscled the heavy tray loaded with cheeseburgers, fries, and salad, he was glad that it was one of the shorter walks Now he understood why the staff carried the food to the younger boys' tables.

In the middle of lunch, a clipboard for the two afternoon activity periods went around the table.

"We'll all work on Masters-level basketball and softball tests so we can practice for the Lumberjack Roundup," said Shaine.

"But then we won't get any points," Ric said. "Some of us need to earn points while we're in camp, or we'll never get to 600."

"Ack can explain shinty," said Jack. "I'll set up some shinty tests. I can get the Athletic Director to recognize them. He's done this for other foreign sports in the past."

This idea enthused his fellow Scouts. While Tom wanted to earn points, he was more interested in being better prepared for their trips. He signed up for canoeing and campcraft.

Tom was nervous about carrying the big tray back to the kitchen. He was relieved that the waiters paused for each other at the choke points.

After Tom wiped the table, Jack grabbed him and pulled him next to Ack.

"Ack, you and Tom can't sit on the 100-point bench. You have to earn the privilege."

Tom guessed that Ack had attempted to perch on it while waiting for lunch.

"That's not fair," said Ack. "All the other Scouts can sit there. It will take us all month to get 100 points."

"I agree," said Tom.

"It may not be fair, but it's a part of Catamount. At each activity, the tests start simple and develop into Master and Instructor levels."

Jack paused.

"For example, the lowest level softball test is worth 5 points; the Instructor level is 50 points. You need to work on the basic Plebe tests. You can earn points in the next few days, and then after the Algonquin trip. By the end of the session, you can get to 100. I've seen it happen before."

Tom saw Ack relax as he accepted Jack's reasoning.

"I'm going to work on canoeing," said Tom. "You're welcome to join me."

"Thanks for the offer, but I committed to sports this afternoon. Hopefully, Jack can create shinty tests so I can get some easy points."

"I'll do my best," said Jack. "Let's get down to the canoes. We have rest hour."

When the Plebes stared from the shores of Cabin Cove, Tom realized that paddling to and from the cabin was a real privilege.

In the cabin, Jack reminded the boys about their letters home.

"I've got paper and pens if you need them. Tell your

parents about the Algonquin trip and say that you'll write after we get back in camp."

Tom would have preferred to relax, but he knew he had to begin. Putting words on paper was a challenge. His mind moved faster than his fingers wrote. Because of his dyslexia, his spelling was horrible. While he hated having someone correct his errors, he knew it made a difference, but he didn't know anyone well enough to ask for assistance. Most of the time, his mother had been helpful and not too critical. He realized he did not know his mother's address in India. For a moment, he missed her. However, he was sure that she'd be annoyed that his grandparents had sent him to Catamount. In his grandparents' letter, he would enclose a note to his mother.

Der Gema and Gepa,
Camp is going wel. I am lerning to paddle beter. The boys are frendly and the conselors are nice. Gerge has helpd me with my padlin.
We are going on a trip to Algoqin park for 5 days. The food is good. Ack is in the bunk nex to me. he is form scotlan and has movd to canada premenanly.
I hop that Gepa is geting beter. I mis you
Love
Tom
PS - The leter inside is for Mom. Can you send it? I dont have her adress. I hope that you have told her that i am at catamont. I dont want to upset her

Tom's cabin mates were writing or resting. He guessed that a couple might even be sleeping. He had no idea of how much time was left, but knew he needed to continue writing.

Der Mom,

I hop that thins in Inda are going wel. Camp is fun. The boys are nise and the food is good.

"Stop what you're doing. It's time for us to paddle back to the Main Yard for afternoon activities," Jack announced. "Thanks for being quiet. I'll get envelopes tomorrow for those who need them. Put your letters away. You can finish tomorrow."

His writing had been slow and awkward. Tom was pleased that he had finished one letter. He saw the others had written more than a full page. In fact, Ack had written three full sides. Tom was embarrassed that his two letters, combined, were a single page.

During the paddle back to the Canoe Dock, the boys discussed their prowess on the sports fields. The others expected Ack to be an asset in basketball. Tom was not surprised that his name did not come up.

"I haven't played much basketball and I've never played baseball." Ack looked uneasy.

As the Scouts racked their canoes, the afternoon activity bell rang, and they started running up the hill.

"Scouts - stop!!" yelled Jack. "Come back! You left your paddles and lifejackets everywhere. George would be furious if he saw this mess. Straighten everything, now!"

Pulling everything under the canoes took only a minute.

"That wasn't hard, now, was it?" Jack smiled. "If you leave everything neatly so George can't complain, I'll award each of you an extra point for every day we're in camp."

Earning extra points for simple chores brightened everyone's mood.

Tom was alone as the other Scouts ran toward the fields. A part of him wished that he'd gone to sports so he could be part of the group. Another part, the stronger part, wanted to become a better paddler.

George was standing with a group of younger campers. They looked small standing next to the canoe but seemed eager. If Tom had to guess, he'd say they were the youngest campers.

"Tom, get your paddle."

When he returned, the boys were reviewing the parts of canoe. Tom knew this information and felt as though he was in the wrong place. A stern glance from George kept him attentive.

After fifteen minutes, the group carried two canoes to the edge of the dock. Together, six younger boys carried a single canoe rather than two Scouts. As Tom helped the boys negotiate the sharp edge of the dock, he felt good that neither canoe scraped on the wood.

"Tom, get in the stern with these three." George joined the other three. "Teach them the basics."

The three boys in front of Tom had never been in a canoe. He taught them the forward stroke and how to backpaddle. Then, as George had done with him, Tom went over changing positions in a canoe. The boys giggled as they snaked up and down.

The canoes rafted and exchanged boys between boats. With three new boys, Tom tried to repeat his instruction. But the boys insisted they knew how to paddle and change places. Tom decided to have the boys spin the canoe. Once they figured out that one side paddled forward and the other backpaddled, the boys loved going forward, spinning 180 degrees and paddling again.

At the end of the period, George ordered the canoes back the dock. Tom helped the boys lift the canoes out of the water and carry them to the racks.

George called over to another canoe staff member.

"Mark, go put Tom through the two junior tests and the first Middie test."

Tom sat in the bow of a canoe. Mark asked him about

the parts of the canoe. Tom demonstrated all that he'd taught the younger boys. After a short paddle, they switched bow and stern positions and returned to the dock.

"Congratulations, you passed," Mark said. "I'll turn in the paperwork for 20 points - 5 for the first junior, 10 for the second junior test, and 5 for the first Middie test."

Tom was elated.

"Thanks for your help with the Plebes," George said. "You did a nice job with them."

The activity bell rang.

"Are you staying here for the next period?" asked George.

"No, I signed up for campcraft."

"You better go. If you don't show up, we don't want people running around looking for you."

Tom headed to the campcraft area. As he walked past the Trip Shed, Earnie popped out.

"I earned twenty points," said Tom.

"Good job. When you get to campcraft, tell Kent that I said you should work on the basic fire building test."

"Will do."

At campcraft, Tom gave Kent Earnie's message.

"Tom, you're lucky to know Earnie. As a new boy, you want to earn as many points as possible, eh?"

"Yes."

"Let's start with fire because that's the core to a good kitchen."

As a boy, his father and grandfather had taught Tom how to start a fire. After a short refresher, he remembered what to do. By the end of the period, Tom had started a two-match fire and boiled a pot of water, earning ten points.

"Come back tomorrow." Kent said. "You can pass the basic cooking and axemanship tests. Both are ten points."

"Thanks, I'll see you tomorrow."

Seeing no Scouts in the Main Yard, Tom walked to the Canoe Dock.

"How was campcraft?" asked George.

"I passed the basic fire-starting test and earned ten more points. That's 35 points in one afternoon."

"Outstanding, but don't expect every day to be like this."

"I understand. Do I have time to paddle? I'm the waiter."

George thought for a second.

"Yes. You can stay near the dock and work on your solo paddling. Get your paddle and lifejacket. I'll put a boat in the water."

Tom lowered himself into the center of the canoe and tilted it until the right gunwale was inches from the surface. The boat felt tippy but more stable than his first time.

"Paddle in a figure-eight. Your paddle will be on both the inside and the outside as the canoe turns," George said.

After paddling for a couple of minutes, he felt far more confident.

The waiters' bell rang. Tom paddled to the dock and scrambled out of the canoe.

"How did you feel?" asked George.

"Much better."

"That's what you want. It takes time and practice. I'll put the canoe away. Go wait."

"Thanks. I appreciate your help."

After carrying the food to the table, Tom listened to the others talk about basketball and softball. While he was happy to have earned points, he felt distant. Maybe he should have joined the others.

Shaine dominated the discussion. He had opinions about who should play where and when. Tom learned Ack could hit a softball, seemingly forever. This impressed Shaine and the other Scouts. While Ack could cover ground, his fielding skills were weak. His lack of knowledge about details of game play surprised the boys. As a basketball player, Ack blocked shots better than Lloyd or Ric, but his dribbling, passing, and shooting skills were barely adequate.

The easy give-and-take among Ack and the Scouts made Tom jealous. He was not surprised that no one asked him about his afternoon.

After the Scouts finished eating, Tom loaded the big tray with the empty serving dishes. He headed back to the kitchen mixing with the crowd of waiters.

Behind Tom, he heard a soft but distinct – "*Jerry, come here!*"

The boy in front of him stopped abruptly. To avoid a collision, Tom lurched to a halt, and the platters shifted to one side.

In a micro-second, the tray and serving dishes crashed to the floor. The smashing noise froze the Dining Hall. The clapping began. Tom's face turned red. Swiveling to see who had called to Jerry, Tom saw Shaine hurrying to the bathroom.

The staff hushed the clapping, and people began to help. Once the mess was cleared, Tom finished his duties. After dismissal and wiping down the table, he joined the Scouts at the Canoe Dock.

"Jack told us to get our wet stuff from the Swim Shack." said Borden. "I grabbed your towel, wet shorts, and bathing suit. Here's Ack's stuff as well. The washers always take longer after dinner."

"Thanks," said Tom.

"On the way to Voyageur Island, I'm paddling with Rio," Jack said. "We need one three-man boat."

Shaine commandeered Ric and Chet. Lloyd partnered Borden. That left Tom and Ack as partners. Tom stood alone, waiting for Ack.

As the Scouts sat in the canoes, Jack said, "At some point, everybody drops a tray. Try to forget it. We all make mistakes."

Shaine muttered, "Only a spastic is so clumsy. Tommy the topple. An awkward, avalanching American."

Chet and Ric laughed.

"Go get Ack's lifejacket and paddle," said Jack. "Tom, a stern man looks out for his bowman."

Ack and Tom were the last to pull away from the dock.

"What a bummer. You must have wanted to die," said Ack.

"It's okay. Stuff happens."

"That's BS. You're just being brave."

Tom paused.

"You're right. I've never been so embarrassed in my life."

"Sorry," Ack said.

Tom debated telling him about Shaine but decided not to, so he changed the topic.

"I got thirty points this afternoon."

"Excellent. Me too."

"How'd you do that?"

"I passed the Plebe and Middie softball and basketball tests; 5 for each Plebe test and 10 for each Middie. I think Jack was being understanding."

"That's good. I'm set up to get a bunch of points at campcraft tomorrow. Then, do you want to canoe together? You can earn 20 points, easy."

"Outstanding," said Ack.

Before arriving at the island, Jack had the Scouts raft up.

"This evening is an opportunity for you to appreciate Voyageur life. Hopefully, many of you will live on the Island next summer. We're on our best behavior. Eh?"

Having been on the Island before with Duncan and Cecille, Tom was surprised at how much better it seemed with the Voyageurs living on it. The idea of being off by themselves, yet part of the camp community felt adventurous. Tom hadn't noticed that the Voyageurs rarely attended breakfast. They slept in and cooked their own breakfasts. In the evenings, the Voyageurs played horseshoes or volleyball until dark and sat around their fire pit without an established bedtime. The casual lifestyle was appealing.

Jack and the Voyageur counselors organized a volleyball game with mixed teams of Scouts and Voyageurs. Tom played next to Duncan.

"How's camp?"

"It's good so far," said Tom.

"You are a good man to put up with my sister. She thinks she can paddle."

"She knows more than I do."

"At the moment. I have confidence in you. I've seen you paddle. Pretty impressive for someone just starting."

"Thanks." Tom smiled.

Unlimited s'mores around the campfire were a hit. Ric and one of the Voyageurs began an eating contest. The counselors stopped it after eight. When one of the Voyageurs complained about the Olympic boycott, Shaine grumbled about it being unfair. Everyone seemed disappointed and critical of the country to the south. Tom felt eyes glaring at him and wanted to disappear.

"What are you expecting on the Rupert?" Ack asked.

As the Voyageurs talked about their preparation, Tom dreamed of a similar trip. Preparing for five weeks of travel into the northern wilderness of Quebec was exciting. He realized that the evening had been an effective sales pitch.

"Time to head back to our cabin." said Jack.

None of the Scouts wanted to leave. Voyageur life sounded amazing.

"I'm definitely coming back," said Shaine. "Sleeping

late and no lights out. That's cool."

"I'm with you," said Chet.

"Me too," said Ric.

"We'll see." Lloyd added a note of reality. "It sounds fun, but there aren't any showers on the Island."

Spirits were high as the Scouts paddled back to their cabin chatting among themselves. Shaine had been impressed by Ack's volleyball skills. Having established his athletic credentials, Ack was now fully embraced by the Canadians. Tom hoped something would happen so they would accept him in the same way.

Landing and racking canoes was becoming routine. Trying to escape the mosquitoes, everyone raced.

"Come back!" yelled Jack. "Most of you forgot your wet stuff. Hang it on the line. Now!"

Lloyd's flashlight illuminated the clothesline. However, the light attracted insects. Tom was impatient as Jack inspected each boy's stuff.

"Lights out in five," said Jack. "It's late. If you want me to read, get a move on."

While waiting for a sink, Tom whispered to Ack.

"Thanks for changing the topic at the Voyageurs. Being an American can be awkward."

"No problem. Being Scottish can be tricky. We need to stick together. Now, we need to avoid the bugs. They're insane."

A cloud of insects attacked as they scrambled to the cabin.

With the door opening repeatedly, mosquitoes flew inside. The best way to escape the winged marauders was wiggling deep into sleeping bags.

When Jack started reading *To Build a Fire,* Tom was glad that he knew the ending. He didn't pay attention. As he lay in his bunk, he realized that, despite dropping the tray, the day had been a good one. He'd earned lots of points and had made progress as a paddler. Shaine was becoming a pain. Tom needed to figure out what to do, but he hesitated to make waves.

The loon cries whispered over the water. He relaxed.

# Chapter 7
## Canada Day

**Tuesday July 1**

"Up and at 'em! It's Canada Day!"

Jack's cry awakened Tom. Realizing that he'd slept through the early light of dawn and sunrise, he smiled. He had no idea what Canada Day might be, but he decided to wait and see rather than ask questions. Stretching his muscles, he was glad that he'd rested as long as possible. When he didn't hear any movement from his cabin mates, he dozed off again.

Jack's "If we're late for breakfast, we don't eat!" got the Scouts moving.

Dressing and jostling at the washhouse had become familiar.

"Do we need our bathing suits?" Borden yelled.

"Not this morning," said Jack.

The air was chilly and Tom was thankful.

Borden approached as Tom and Ack prepared to launch the canoe. "Can I join you?" he asked. "I'll sit in the middle."

"Welcome aboard," said Ack. "Where are the mosquitoes?"

"Right now, it's too cool for them," said Borden. "They don't like any kind of a breeze. That's why there's no underbrush near the cabins. That allows the air to move."

"What's the washer do?" Tom asked Ack.

"Dry pots and pans in the kitchen. It's easy, but tedious."

As the Scouts waited for breakfast, Shaine sat on the 100-point bench and explained how easy it was to earn this privilege. Tom appreciated that Borden and Lloyd chose to stand with him and Ack.

As breakfast started, Shaine questioned Jack.

"When is the shinty test going to be ready?"

"I'll get to it."

"You said that yesterday."

"These things take time."

"You said that yesterday. I need to earn some points."

"All in good time."

"Good time is this morning. Right?"

"It will be ready when it's ready," said an annoyed Jack.

Tom had a feeling that Shaine would wait another day or two.

At sign-ups, Shaine wanted everyone to go to sports for softball and basketball during second period.

"Lloyd and I are doing the beginning archery test during first period," said Borden. "Then, second period, we're baking at campcraft. The baking test and the lollipop fire are available for ten points apiece every year."

"Baking sounds good to me," said Ric. "I'll be hungry by then."

Tom convinced Ack to join him at canoeing and campcraft.

At announcements, Tom learned that Canada Day was the Canadian 4th of July. The afternoon would be filled with the Canadian games designed by the Apprentices, followed by a cookout in the Main Yard.

The Director set the stage for Canada Day with a dramatic reading of Robert Service's poem, *The Call of the Wild*.

Chet rolled his eyes.

"The Director reads the same poem every year."

"It's stupid," said Shaine.

The "this-is-stupid" sentiment emanated from all the Scouts. Tom realized that, if he'd been at Catamount for years, he'd probably feel the same way.

When Tom arrived for washer duty, the cooks, Mildred and Gordon, greeted him.

"I remember your dad," said Mildred. "How is he?"

With a stab to his insides, Tom said, "He died a few years ago after a car accident."

"So sorry," said Gordon. "He was a good man. Know that you're always welcome here."

"Thanks. I miss him." He paused for a second. "Now, what do I do as the washer?"

As Tom dried the pots and pans, he watched the hustle and bustle. It surprised him that the kitchen staff was already preparing lunch.

The morning activity bell rang as he finished hanging the towels on the wash line behind the kitchen. At the Canoe Dock, George asked Tom to work with Ack. Together they reviewed what Tom had taught the Plebes the day before. When George evaluated Ack, he passed the two Plebe and the first Middie tests.

"Nicely done. Twenty points."

George handed Ack a yellow piece of paper.

"Be sure to put this in the point box next to the office."

George turned to Tom. "You did a nice job as an instructor yesterday and today. You might want to consider becoming a teacher."

"Thanks," said Tom. "Is there a way we can earn more points this morning?"

"We need to get 100 so we can sit on the stupid bench," said Ack.

The second period bell rang from the Lodge, and Tom and Ack's shoulders sagged.

154

"If you want, we can start the second level Middie test during free time. If you've been paying attention in the last couple of days, you've learned most of it. We won't finish. If you're smooth, though, we can get through a couple things."

"Can we try?" asked Tom.

"Sure, but we stop at the waiter's bell, eh?"

"OK, see you later."

Campcraft was fun. Kent modified the fire test so that Ack could pass it and the basic cooking test at the same time. Boiling water and cooking a pancake earned Ack ten points. Tom earned five for his flapjack. They recited the rules for safe axe usage and sharpened an axe. After chopping a log and splitting it into firewood, both passed the basic axemanship test, earning each of them ten more points.

While Tom worked on his tests, he watched Lloyd, Borden, and Ric. Using a reflector oven, they baked a two-layer chocolate cake, earning points and creating a dessert. Tom saw that control of a fire's flames was the key to success.

"Can Ack and I bake tomorrow?" Tom asked.

"If my weather forecast is accurate, that might be a stretch," Kent said.

"What do you mean?"

"The breeze is from the south. Look at the high clouds. If they fill in and the ceiling begins to drop, a warm front is coming. That could bring rain tomorrow."

Tom had never paid much attention to the wind or the clouds. When it rained in the city, he'd used an umbrella, worn a raincoat, or gotten wet.

"What kinds of clouds bring rain?" Tom asked.

As Kent droned on about cirrus and cumulus, warm and cold fronts, and high- and low-pressure systems. Tom lost interest.

"You're a city boy," Ack said. "Every morning in

Scotland, the clouds and the direction of the wind told me what weather was coming."

Tom was skeptical. Canada was not Scotland.

As Ric whipped frosting, he asked, "How much rain do you need for a lollipop fire?"

"A steady rain."

Tom followed up. "What is a lollipop fire?"

"Using only natural materials while it's raining, you build a two-match fire."

"Sounds tough."

"That's why you can pass the test every year."

"Not me. I'm staying dry." said Lloyd.

"Standing in the rain is not my idea of a good time." said Ric. "I don't need points that badly."

"Me neither," said Borden.

Tom was intrigued.

The end of the second activity bell rang. Lloyd, Ric, and Borden promised to bring their cake to lunch.

Tom and Ack headed to the Canoe Dock.

"Thirty points so far today." said Ack. "Yesterday, I got 30. Only 40 to go. How many more do you think I can get at canoeing?"

"You've completed the simple tasks," said George, who was still at the dock. "From here on, things get more complicated."

"What do we have to do?"

"Four things. The first is to complete a Diamond Drill smoothly and accurately without the canoe stopping or either paddler backpaddling."

"The second?"

"Spin the canoe in a 360-degree circle in both directions without drifting off the center point."

"The third and fourth?"

"For the third, you side-slip the length of the Canoe Dock, moving both left and right, while keeping the bow of the canoe within half a meter of the edge of the dock.

And, for the fourth, you execute a smooth, efficient canoe-over-canoe rescue."

With a sinking feeling, Tom asked, "Is that all?"

"Yes." George smiled. "But there's one additional requirement. Each of you needs to accomplish these four things while sitting in both the bow and in the stern."

As the boys got into their canoe, Tom said, "This is going to be harder than I thought."

"I agree. I think we're done with the easy stuff."

George made them complete the Diamond Drill three times before he agreed that they were both accurate and smooth. "Now, change positions," he directed.

In their new positions, Ack said, "Here goes nothing. I've only been in the stern for a few minutes."

The waiters' bell rang.

"Rack the canoe," George said.

"Sorry, Ack," Tom said. "I thought these were easy points."

"No problem. You didn't know." Ack grinned. "If we're going to pass, I need a lot more time in the stern. But, on a canoe trip, it might be good to know how to paddle in both ends of the canoe."

The lunch bell rang.

At lunch, the Scouts talked about Canada Day and its games.

"Some years, the Apprentices are really creative," Lloyd said.

"Last year, we did the same old field-day events," said Borden. "It was kind of boring."

"Not for me," said Shaine. "I won more events than anyone else in the Cadet section."

"Time for chocolate cake," announced Rio.

"Looks outstanding," said Chet. "Good job!"

"Wait for a minute," said Rio. "I need to get my camera."

"Does he have to take a picture of everything?" Ric

asked.

"The Director is happy to have a photographer on staff," Jack said. "Smile. You'll be in the new Catamount slide show that he shows prospective campers."

"Do we have a choice?" asked Borden.

"No." Jack smiled. "Everyone look hungry and happy."

After the paddle back to the cabin for Rest Hour, Jack handed out envelopes with a printed Catamount return address.

Tom re-read the letter to his mother.

Der Mom,
    I hop that thins in Inda are going wel. Camp is fun. The boys are nise and the food is good.

He needed to say more.

The couselors are frendy. Jac is Canadin and Reo is form Swizerland.
    Today, Ack and I pased tsets at camcraft and canoing. We stared on the next cano test. I am lerning to padle by misef whic is fun. We are going on a trip to Algoquin Park for 5 days on Thusday. It will be fun. I will writ you when I get bak
    I miss yu and look foward to seeng you at Chirsmas. Plese say hello to Peair for me.
    Love
    Tom

After rereading his letter, Tom knew that he should have written more. But giving his mother additional information would just make her worry. Then it came to him.

PS I war my lifjaket in the cano all the time

This untruth would ease his mother's anxiety and, given all that was happening in her life, she'd never know the difference. He folded both letters and stuffed them into an envelope.

"Gentlemen, be sure to put your names on the envelopes above the Catamount return address. That way, the office knows who to check off and who to charge for postage," Jack said. "Any questions?"

Tom didn't want to embarrass himself by asking about postage to the US. He figured that the office would know.

"Do we seal the letters?" asked Lloyd.

"No, do NOT seal your letters!" Jack barked. "I forgot to remind you. The office will put the weekly newsletter in each envelope. They're due to the office tomorrow after breakfast. I'll collect them tonight. Eh?"

Tom put the envelope under his sleeping bag and headed to the washhouse. When he returned, he found everyone packing up for the afternoon.

"Bring your wet shoes, bathing suit, towel, and some good running shoes," Ack said. "In some events, we'll get wet. After dinner, the whole camp plays Capture-the-Flag. Jack said that running in wet shoes is a good way to get blisters."

"Thanks."

Tom was grateful that, at the moment, he had two pair of dry shoes.

After racking their canoes, the Scouts joined the rest of the camp in the Main Yard. The Scouts took their customary position in the back.

Speeches started the Canada Day ceremony. On the platform, campers and staff placed flags from England, France, Holland, Norway, Sweden, Switzerland, Jamaica, Kenya, India, and each of the Canadian provinces. Tom found the talking heads boring and focused on the sky. A high haze of clouds was being pushed by a southerly breeze.

When the Director fired a flare over the bay, Tom's reverie was shattered. From behind the northern point, wearing colorful costumes, the Voyageurs sped toward the crowd. Their canoes twisted and wove in an intricate dance. To rousing applause, the final stage of the boats' ballet was the presentation of the Canadian flag. Tom was impressed.

"Not as good as last year," whispered Shaine.

"It was pretty complicated," countered Lloyd.

"Yeah," said Borden. "That would take a lot of time to learn."

"It's sissy paddling," said Shaine.

"Be quiet," snapped Jack.

Singing of *O Canada* ended the ceremony. Tom guessed that this was the Canadian national anthem.

"We're up at the fields to start," Jack said. "These are fun activities. They're competitive, but don't kill yourselves. But we do want to beat the Voyageurs in the tug-a-war, eh?"

The Cadets, Scouts, and Voyageurs gathered on the playing fields. For group events, the Scouts would compete against the Voyageurs.

"The first event is the double wanigan carry," said Jack.

"What are the wooden boxes?" Tom asked Borden quietly.

"They are wanigans and are containers for kitchen stuff and food. For the games, they're empty. On trips, they start heavy."

"Thanks."

Both the Scouts and the Voyageurs had 20 wanigans to carry from start to finish. Wanigans couldn't be thrown or dropped. Everyone had to carry at least one, and boys could run back for a second carry. If a wanigan fell to the ground, it returned to the start.

Shaine took charge.

"There are seven of us, so we need everyone to triple carry. Let's go."

"I'm not sure I can balance with a triple load," said Ric.

"You can. You have to focus!"

"Just don't drop them. Let's get ready to start."

"I'm clueless," Ack said.

"Me too," said Tom. "Borden, what's going on? Ack and I have never carried a wanigan. How do we manage three?"

"An empty wanigan isn't heavy. You use a tumpline to carry it. The strap goes at the hairline on your forehead. The key to carrying extra ones is to walk slowly and don't rock side-to-side. I'll help load you, and someone will unload you at the other side."

Tom was still baffled.

"Get ready," Shaine yelled. "We're going to start."

The whistle blew. Confusion commenced. Shaine and Borden loaded wanigans. Tom saw that carrying wanigans was an acquired skill.

While an empty wanigan only weighed about five pounds, carrying without shoulder straps using a tumpline put a strain on one's neck muscles. Tom felt okay with the first box. But, when Borden loaded the second above the first, the load felt awkward. The third made things unstable, but he found a balance point.

As Tom walked the course, he stepped carefully and tried not to sway. In front of him, Ack's third and second wanigans slid to the ground. Behind Tom, he heard Ric's wanigans tumble.

At the finish line, Shaine, who had carried two, shouted, "Ric, Ack, you are imbeciles! Get over here. Somebody go back and get those wanigans. We're losing."

Borden unloaded Tom's wanigans.

Tom looked back at the course.

"Lloyd, Borden, follow me."

The three ran back to the start where the dropped wanigans had been placed. Each swung two wooden boxes onto their backs and walked to the finish line.

"We could have beaten them," Shaine snapped. "Ric, it's your fault. Ack, I thought you were coordinated."

The three-legged race was next. Shaine ordered Chet to join him. He commanded Ack and Lloyd and Ric and Borden to partner. Tom was alone, waiting to pair with one of the first finishers. One of the Voyageurs was in the same situation.

Shaine and Chet started strong, but Chet tripped. They collapsed in a heap.

"My ankle!" screamed Shaine.

The other pairs walked carefully. After finishing, Borden ran back and paired with Tom. Together they finished behind Shaine and Chet but well behind the similar Voyageur pair.

"Slow and steady beats fast and fumbling," said Borden.

"We could have won," said Shaine, "if Chet had kept pace."

"Jack told us to be calm," said Lloyd.

"I'm calm when I win," Shaine snapped.

The third event was an obstacle course. The participants used paper cups to carry water over and under a series of benches and tables to fill a bucket.

"We need a plan," said Tom.

"We just need to run as fast as possible," said Shaine.

"Maybe we need to be careful and concentrate on not spilling water."

"I think Tom's right," said Borden. "My guess is that the Voyageurs will try for speed."

"I agree," said Lloyd. "Let's be precise."

Ack and Ric nodded.

A whistle sounded. The Voyageurs sprinted, and the Scouts shuffled carefully. Everyone got soaked. The race took forever.

As Shaine filled the bucket to overflowing, he screamed, "We won!"

"I hope we don't do that again," said Chet.

"But we won. We beat the Voyageurs!"

"They stopped competing three or four minutes ago," said Ack. "They let us win."

"But we won. That's what counts."

"If you say so."

The Scouts dried in the sun as they waited for the next event.

The fourth event was a single-person challenge. The two competitors each stood on a foot-high section of telephone pole. Each person held one end of a long rope. The task was simple: to pull your opponent off his perch.

"We will compete among ourselves for the Scout champion. The Voyageurs will do the same," Jack said. "Then, the two winners will pull for the camp championship."

*So much for informal, fun-time competition*, Tom thought.

Once again, Shaine took command and set the practice pairings. Tom saw that being too tall or very large were liabilities. During the practice time, he pulled against all the Scouts except Ric and Shaine. Tom understood this event and won many of the practice pull-offs. When he saw Shaine watching, he intentionally lost a few.

In his first competitive match, Tom bested Ack, whose height made his balance uneven.

Next came Ric. Tom had watched him practice. For his size, Ric was quick, but he lunged. At the start, Tom pulled, but let Ric get more rope. Then they pulled gently, testing each other's strength and strategy. Tom waited. Ric yanked too hard. Tom released tension on his rope. Ric lost his balance and fell backwards.

Shaine and Tom stood to determine the Scout champion. Shaine had easily beaten his three opponents. The intensity around them increased.

"3, 2, 1, PULL!"

Back and forth, the two pulled smoothly or yanked aggressively. Both stood solid, feet planted, knees bent. A crowd gathered. Shaine poised, preparing. He jerked, and Tom relaxed his rope. Shaine's arms flailed as he recoiled backwards. He balanced on one foot. Tom yanked. Shaine tumbled to the ground.

"You cheated!" yelled Shaine.

"No, he didn't," said the judge.

Several of the watchers murmured, "Nicely done."

The Voyageur champion was waiting. As the two stepped onto their poles, the crowd swelled.

Tom heard cheering. This was no longer casual competition.

"3, 2, 1, PULL!"

Each boy pulled as much rope as he could. Tom sensed that each had about half of the total length, plenty to work with. He pulled, released rope, yanked, and tugged. His opponent did the same. As each maneuvered for an opening, time stood still.

The longer the two remained entwined, the louder the crowd shouted. Behind Tom's challenger, one of the crowd staggered into view. Ever so slightly, his challenger turned. With power, Tom yanked. The boy began to lose his balance. Tom pulled harder. The boy stepped to the ground.

The Scouts erupted into celebration.

Tom extended his hand. "Congratulations. That was a hell of a match."

"Yes, it was. I'm Peter. Nice to meet you."

Tom and Peter shook hands.

"Did you ever do karate?" Peter asked. "You're the only person other than myself I've seen use that stance on the pole. I practiced karate for the last three years."

"In fact, I did, when I was younger."

In second grade after his third temper-induced fight, the adults had forced Tom to take two years of karate and judo. He thought that he'd forgotten all of what he'd learned. He wondered briefly what else was hiding in his mind.

"You learned to balance. Hopefully, we'll meet again."

"Yes. It would be a good match."

"Indeed." Peter grinned. "I believe that it's time for the real tug-o-war. We'll win that one."

The crowd gathered around the long, thick rope and watched as the Cadet cabins paired off. Then the Cadet champion pulled against the Scouts. It was no contest, as the Scouts were clearly bigger and stronger.

The Scouts gathered before their match against seven of the Voyageurs.

"I've got a plan," said Shaine. "We start with a quick yank. Then, we pause for a micro-second when they respond. They'll lose their balance, so we pull as hard as we can."

"I'm not so sure about taking a pause," said Borden.

Tom agreed with Borden but stayed quiet.

Shaine lined up the Scouts with Ric, the biggest, as the anchor.

"Get ready," Shaine shouted. "We've got this! Go, Scouts!"

"On your mark."

The crowd quieted.

"Get set."

"PULL!"

At first, Shaine's plan worked, and several Voyageurs stumbled when the Scouts relaxed. However, so did Lloyd and Ric. For a few seconds, the two teams strained evenly. Then, slowly but surely, the Voyageurs pulled the

Scouts across the centerline.

"Nice try," said Jack. "It was a noble effort. They were bigger and stronger."

"If we'd followed my plan, we would have won," Shaine grumbled. "The front people didn't pull as hard as those in the back."

"It's no big deal," said Ack. "The Voyageurs are older and stronger."

"I don't remember the Voyageurs ever losing," said Borden.

"But we have to try," said Shaine. "We'd win if we did it again."

"In your dreams," said Lloyd.

"Time to head to Boat Bay for the water activities," said Jack.

As they walked down the road, Shaine slid next to Tom.

"You're welcome," whispered Shaine.

"What?"

"The boy who stumbled out of the crowd and distracted Peter, I helped him."

"You what?"

"Yeah, I pushed. He staggered. You won. Congratulations."

Shaine moved away, grinning.

Tom was shocked. Who should he tell? If Tom said anything, Shaine would deny it and Tom didn't want to piss off Shaine. Getting the congratulations and claps on the back had felt good. He decided to do what he did when confused: nothing. Tom didn't feel good about it, but he wasn't sure who he could trust.

As the Scouts changed into their bathing suits, Jack said, "Wear your wet shoes. We don't want any broken toes."

While waiting on the dock, Tom realized that his shadow had become hazy. The clouds were thickening.

The breeze continued from the south. Maybe Kent's forecast was going to be correct.

"The Apprentices were creative for these two events. One is historic and the other is literature-based," Jack said. "Have fun. This is silly stuff."

Large floating logs filled a small area inside the swim dock. The competitors wore thick keyhole lifejackets and helmets.

"I don't get this," said Tom.

"Stupid southerner," said Shaine. "It's a log jam."

Turning to Tom and Ack, Lloyd said, "We did this a couple of years ago. In the old days, the lumberjacks cut the trees in the winter and dragged them onto the frozen lakes. In the spring flood, the log drivers would keep things moving down the river to the sawmills."

Two staff held thick poles with metal points at the tips and with what looked like giant steel fishhooks swinging below.

Pointing, Tom asked, "What are those?"

"They're peaveys," snarled Shaine. "Everyone knows that."

"They're used to maneuver the big logs. In the forest, they're used to roll the logs. We'll use them at the Lumberjack Roundup for one of the competitions," said Ric. "It takes some practice, but it's not hard if you're strong."

"During the spring runoff, the drivers used them to guide the logs. Sometimes drivers had to dance across the logs and push them back into the current. And sometimes the logs would jam together and create an obstruction. Then, they would have to set dynamite to break up the jams," said Borden.

"Balance and quick feet are the keys," said Lloyd. "The logs look stable, but when you step on them, they roll and rock up and down. You don't want to get caught under them."

The floating logs no longer looked harmless.

"If you get over without falling in the water, we get a point," said Jack. "Then, if you make it back, we get five points. The Voyageurs have challenged us. The most points win. Be careful."

"3, 2, 1, GO!"

Tom made three steps on the heaving logs and was almost halfway before he slipped. As he crashed onto the wet logs, he was glad to have padding. Chet and Borden made it across without falling into the water. Only Borden danced back to the start.

"None of the Voyageurs made it," Jack said.

"We win," shouted Shaine. "Scouts rock!"

Standing in the breeze, Tom had the feeling that most of the Scouts didn't care.

Robin Hood and Little John's battle was the next event. Carrying a foam-filled sack, each boy faced off against a cabin mate, both balanced on a 4 x 4 above the water. Given the chill in the air, Tom was glad that the contestants were still wearing lifejackets and helmets.

"This is just for the Scout champion," said Jack. "No larger camp-wide championship."

Rio had been snapping photos all day.

"Smile for the camera lens," he said.

Relieved from the pressure of competition, the boys posed for what they hoped would be funny pictures.

In Tom's first match-up, he fell to Borden, who went on to win three in a row. Ric knocked off Borden and reigned supreme, besting all who challenged him. Doubting that he had a chance because of Ric's size and strength, Tom opted to watch.

After drying off, the Scouts moved to the Canoe Dock.

"Now, we have something we can really win," said Shaine. "The war canoes!"

"What's a war canoe?" Tom asked.

"Silly American. He's got lots to learn, if he survives."

"It's a 36-foot canoe," Lloyd said. "They were used in the fur trade and were called Montreal canoes."

Tom and his fellow Scouts clambered into the largest canoes he'd ever seen.

"There are nine Voyageurs and only seven of us. This isn't right," Shaine complained.

"Don't worry," said Jack. "Help is on the way."

Jack and Rio stepped into the big canoe.

"We're even now. I'll take the stern."

Reluctantly, Shaine moved away from the stern. Tom felt better and saw that his fellow Scouts were more comfortable with Jack in control.

"Ack, take the bow left. Lloyd, bow right. You have the longest arms. The rest of you pair up by size."

Tom sat on the right side in the third seat. Shaine sat beside him paddling on the left.

Holding the longest paddle that Tom had ever seen, Jack stood in the stern,

"Gentlemen, we're in the big time. This is not a sprint. We go out and around the canoe sitting in the middle of the river. My guess is that it's five or six minutes out. Then, it's back to the finish line. The key to victory is to keep a steady pace paddling together. Ready?"

The Scouts shouted, "Yes, Captain Jack."

"Ack, draw. Lloyd, pry. Right side, forward. Left side, hold steady."

Slowly, the Scout canoe turned. The two big canoes maneuvered awkwardly to the starting line.

"3, 2, 1, GO!"

The two boats paralleled on the way out. About twenty meters from the turn-about canoe, the Voyageur canoe sprinted and pulled ahead by a few meters.

"Damn!" said Jack. "They have the inside position."

The Voyageurs executed a tight spin. To avoid hitting the Voyageur canoe, Jack had to turn outside both the stationary boat and the other war canoe.

As the Scout canoe pointed to the finish line, Jack quietly called for a faster pace. Paddling more rapidly, they gained on the Voyageurs.

"Faster. Paddle. Paddle harder!" Shaine yelled. "Paddle! Paddle! Faster! Faster!"

The boys in front and behind Shaine tried to paddle faster. In doing so, they lost timing with their fellow paddlers. Paddles hit paddles. Confusion reigned.

"Stroke! Stroke! Stroke!" Jack yelled.

With the disruption, the Voyageurs sped up and won.

"Shaine, the stern has command of the boat," Jack snapped. "Never do that again. Do you understand?"

Shaine nodded and looked away.

"Now for the final event," said Jack. "The crazy coracles."

"They're lame," muttered Shaine.

"We're against the Voyageurs," Jack said. "You'll be in two teams, three in one boat, four in the other. The Voyageurs will have four and five."

Quietly, so as to avoid Shaine hearing, Tom asked, "What's a coracle?"

"It's a round kids' swimming pool. One of the backyard inflatables," said Lloyd. "It has something to do with some kind of English boat."

"They're impossible to keep straight," said Borden.

"What happens?" Tom asked.

"We race around the first buoy of the Diamond Drill and back to shore. It's about thirty meters in each direction, but it can take forever. It's fun to watch."

"But not so fun to paddle," said Ric.

"I've got a plan," Shaine piped up. "My crew is Ric, Chet, Lloyd, and me."

While Shaine huddled with his crew, Tom looked at Borden and Ack.

"Any ideas?"

His coracle mates were silent.

Tom spoke up. "With three, we are light. We'll float higher in the water. We'll go faster. We'll paddle together at an easy pace. At the buoy, we'll spin. Any questions?"

"Sounds good to me," said Borden.

"I have no idea." Ack grinned. "But I doubt that any of the other groups has a better plan."

The three loaded into their swimming pool, which rocked and squirmed.

"This is insane," said Ack.

"It's just as awkward for everyone else," said Borden.

As they splashed to the starting line, Tom watched the other coracles.

"We're definitely more buoyant than the others."

"Maybe some will sink," said Ack.

"We can hope," said Borden.

Lining up took several minutes.

"On your mark. Ready, set. GO!"

"Paddle calmly, paddle easily," Tom said quietly.

Their coracle inched ahead of the other three. Shaine's boat and one of the Voyageur's coracles began to fill with water. They slowed dramatically. At the buoy, the three spun their pool and maintained their deliberate pace. They won to loud cheers.

The Voyageur crew of four finished second. After bailing as they paddled, Shaine's pool finished a distant third. The floundering Voyageur coracle sank.

Jack shook the winners' hands as Rio took photos.

"Nice job! You three redeemed the Scouts. Many thanks."

"They only had three," said Shaine. "That's not fair."

"You picked the teams," said Borden.

"And you captained our boat," said Lloyd. "You said you wanted the best paddlers."

"Boys, calm down," said Rio. "It's time for more pictures."

Posing while damp was chilling. Quickly, the Scouts

stood next to the multi-colored coracles. Rio took time to arrange a second grouping with the Lodge in the background and George and the Director surrounded by the Scouts.

"It's so good to have a qualified photographer around here," said the Director. "Keep up the good work."

Rio beamed. Tom shivered and sensed the Scouts were tired of posing.

As they changed into dry clothes, Borden and Ack extolled Tom's brilliant strategy.

"I didn't do it," Tom said. "We were a team."

After the Scouts dressed, Jack led them up to the Lodge.

"Congratulations, you are officially big and strong. It's time to move tables outside."

"What a pain!" Shaine mumbled under his breath. "We pay to come here and now they want us to work."

"Shaine, we help whenever it's asked," responded Jack sharply. "That's the Catamount way."

With the previous summer of practice, the Voyageurs had perfected table-carrying. The Scouts welcomed their suggestions for managing the doors and the stairs. After the first few tables, the newcomers turned and twisted with efficiency. Tom was pleased that carrying the tables warmed his hands and feet.

The dinner bell rang. The entire camp formed a line beginning with the youngest campers and ending with the Director. Overhead, the sky had clouded over. Kent's weather forecast appeared to be right on track.

"We should get to go first," said Shaine. "We won the most events. To the winners go the spoils."

"A good leader always makes sure he takes care of his followers," said Jack. "That's why the Director always gets his food last."

The Scouts and the Voyageurs ate together. Their competition had made for a degree of camaraderie.

The Voyageurs continued to talk about the preparation for their trip. The Rupert sounded exciting, strenuous, and dangerous. Tom realized that completing a northern river trip would deepen his connection with his grandfather and, sadly, with his father.

"Last year, what was the Dumoine like?" Ack asked.

As the Voyageurs answered, Tom couldn't tell if they were being completely honest. Sometimes, they seemed to heighten the challenges, and at other times, Tom sensed they downplayed the risks.

"Ack, what do the Scots think about the Olympic boycott?"

Tom looked down, wishing to be invisible.

"Not sure," Ack said.

"I think it's a good thing," one of the Voyageurs said.

"I disagree," said another.

"Well, at least we won't be missing anything while we're in the wilds of Quebec," commented a third.

"Without the dumb boycott, I'd be in Moscow right now watching my brother paddle," Shaine said loudly.

Shaine's outburst steered the conversation to the world of paddling. Tom learned that the Olympians paddled on flat water using special racing canoes. All the boys hoped that white-water racing would be part of the Olympics in the future.

When the talk moved to the Blue Jays and baseball, Chet leaned over to Tom.

"Don't mind Shaine. He's had this bee in his bonnet for months. I think the reality was that his brother wasn't going to make the team. The boycott is a good excuse. He loves to complain."

"Thanks," said Tom.

As supper ended, the Director announced an all-camp Capture-the-Flag, and a cheer rang out.

Moving the tables back into the Dining Hall went more smoothly. After the clean-up was finished, everyone walked to the sports fields.

"Tom, I've never played before. What are the rules?" Ack asked.

Tom had played Capture-the-Flag during his school's outdoor education trips. He hesitated, wondering about specific Catamount rules. Before he could speak, Ric explained.

"They divide the entire camp into shirts and skins with an equal number on both sides. The younger sections are divided with half of the cabins wearing shirts and the other half without. The sprint track at the end of the sports fields and the camp road that runs along the ridge define the play area. The midline starts with the 50-yard line on the fields and continues up the hill to the cut brush under the hydro line."

"The what?" asked Tom.

"The big electric line," said Lloyd. "We call electricity 'hydro.' Most of our power comes from hydroelectric dams on the Ottawa, at Niagara Falls, and up North."

"We'll be on one side and the Voyageurs on the other," Ric continued. "We're skins. Any questions?"

During the game, Tom saw his fellow Scouts in motion. Everyone could run. Shaine was both fast and agile. Chet was quick. Ric and Borden were straight-line sprinters. Lloyd and Ack had stamina. Tom was happy to learn that his speed and endurance were among the best.

Shaine led numerous mass attacks of Plebes and Middies. The younger boys seemed to respond to his commanding shouts. Chet ran as his blocker. The charges resulted in many being tagged and sent to jail. The other Scouts sprinted to the jail to free their teammates. The game swung back and forth without a score.

When the center judge shouted, "Five-minute warning," Tom had an idea.

"Ack, Borden, Lloyd. The four of us will circle around in the woods to behind their flag. Ric, can you try to get

Shaine and Chet to the far end and have them lead another attack? The Voyageurs will focus on them. Then from the trees, Lloyd can sprint and grab the flag. He can throw it to Ack. Ack will pass it to me. Before I get caught, I'll give it to Borden. He's the fastest sprinter."

"Sounds good," said Ric.

"Works for me," said Lloyd.

"Let's go," said Ack.

The plan worked perfectly. Borden crossed the centerline with the flag, and the Scout-led side won.

On the walk down to the Main Yard, Shaine boasted that his feint was the reason for their victory.

At the Canoe Dock, Borden asked, "Jack, is there time for a dip?"

Tom was afraid to ask about the specifics of a dip.

"Sure," said Jack. "But you need to get your bathing suits and towels from the Swim Dock. We have to get to the cabin before it's dark."

The Scouts rushed to the clothesline and hurriedly paddled to their dock. Tom learned that a dip meant swimming without a bathing suit. At first, the idea of being naked in front of his cabin mates was awkward. He sensed they shared his unease, but everyone stripped down and slipped into the lake.

The water cooled his body and relaxed the tension in his tired muscles. Standing on the sandy bottom with the water lapping at his shoulders was delightful. Skinny dipping wasn't so bad.

"I love this," said Borden. "We don't have to worry about wet bathing suits."

"This is delightful," said Ric. "No worries."

"Only at camp can you do this," said Lloyd. "No one else would understand."

"They don't know what they're missing," said Chet.

After a few minutes, Jack said, "While this is joyful, bedtime calls. Tomorrow is trip prep. It's a big day."

As Tom climbed out of the water, he did not join the debate about drip drying vs. using a towel. A damp towel was the same as a wet bathing suit; something to deal with. The breeze was gentle, so it didn't cool him too quickly. For a change, there were only a few mosquitoes. As he air-dried on the dock, he noticed that the cloud ceiling had dropped. Tom wondered what a rainy day at camp would be like.

When he walked into the cabin, Shaine was reading Tom's letter aloud, emphasizing the misspelling and awkwardness of his words. He froze, paralyzed by embarrassment. Some of his cabin mates were snickering.

Tom's temper boiled and his face burned. Without thinking, he lunged forward and grabbed the letter. His hands curled, and an anticipatory hush fell. Shaine stepped back with a sly smile on his face, waiting.

"Gentlemen! Is there a problem?" Jack's voice boomed as he entered the cabin.

Tom stepped back and took a deep breath.

"No!" After an awkward couple of seconds he continued, "Shaine was helping me with my letter. You see, I'm dyslexic, and spelling is a problem. Shaine was correcting my misspellings."

Shaine relaxed.

"Is that so?" Jack asked, using his "I don't believe you" voice.

Tom walked toward his bunk. He spun and, almost shouting, said, "Yes. I know Shaine would never make fun of anyone with a disability. That's not the Catamount or the Canadian way."

"Of course not. Is it, gentlemen?" said Jack.

A chorus of "no's" echoed.

"Lights out in two minutes."

Quickly, the boys moved to their bunks.

With a quiet voice, Jack asked, "Shall I finish *To Build a Fire*?"

This received a hushed "yes."

Earnie strode into the cabin. "This is one of my favorites. Give me a minute and I'll be in my bunk."

The boys climbed into their sleeping bags. Flashlights went dark. The cabin was quiet. Jack started reading.

Tom cooled. He'd almost lost his temper, which he knew would be bad. After being suspended twice, he had learned to count to ten. He knew that he was not a verbal match for Shaine and he hated being at such a disadvantage. Shaine was a bully and Tom was his target.

Shaine's quick tongue made him the leader, even though his judgement was sometimes flawed. His skills were good, but from what Tom had seen, others were just as good or better. Shaine was a problem, and one without an easy solution. Tom wasn't sure how long he could take it. Luckily, he had the escape option.

On the positive, he'd earned twenty points at campcraft. Canada Day had been good. The Scout-led team had won Capture-the-Flag. Winning the individual rope-pull and the coracle race had put him on equal footing with the old timers. He felt like he was part of the group, no longer an outsider.

The calls of the loons echoed peacefully over the river. Tom's sleeping bag felt cozy. As Jack's voice droned, he was glad that he knew the ending, so he relaxed.

# Chapter 8
# Lollipop Packing

"Get up and get dressed. Quickly!" Earnie yelled. "We overslept."

Raindrops drummed steadily on the roof.

"We need to hustle," Jack shouted. "We don't want to miss breakfast."

"If we're late for breakfast, we'll be the laughingstock of the entire camp," said Borden.

"Wear your wet shoes," Jack said. "Your feet will get soaked today, without question."

Tom's sweatshirt got damp while running to and from the washhouse, and his toes squished after he stepped into a puddle. He was bummed that he'd forgotten to wear his wet shoes. However, his original wet shoes had dried. He was glad that his two pair were interchangeable. Managing the wet and dry would take getting used to.

With a steady rain, he needed a raincoat and dove into his duffels. He wished that he'd paid more attention to what his grandmother had packed. He wondered why he had two button-down school shirts. At the bottom sat his London Fog raincoat. He pulled it on over his sweatshirt.

"Here's a baseball cap to keep the rain off your face," Borden said.

"Thanks," Tom said. "I hadn't thought about that."

"You'll adjust. We have to learn and relearn the little tricks every year."

178

Tom wondered what other things were waiting for him to discover. What would trip prep be like in the rain?

As they put the canoes in the water, Shaine said, "You look so stylish."

"So sophisticated," said Ric.

"So New York City," said Chet.

"Very professional," said Lloyd.

"He's off to business in the woods." Shaine snickered.

Tom was embarrassed.

"My jacket is the new GoreTex stuff," said Shaine.

"Mine too," said Chet. "It's supposed to breathe so you don't sweat."

Stretching their arms, the two displayed their brightly colored jackets. The others had on rubberized jackets in green or tan that were designed for hunters or construction workers.

"Ack, what are you wearing?" asked Shaine. "It looks like a dress."

"It's a cagoule. It's standard issue in Scotland. It keeps your legs drier. People have worn these for centuries. Mine works well."

"Well, at least you're prepared. Tom is on his way to the office. I hope his papers don't get wet."

Tom bristled but couldn't think of anything to say.

The paddle to the Canoe Dock was dreary. Each boy concentrated on staying as dry as possible.

As the Scouts racked their canoes, the breakfast bell rang. The younger boys ran from the shelter of the Boat House.

"We Scouts planned this perfectly," Shaine said as they joined the crowd. "We're too smart to wait like drowning rats."

The warm oatmeal and hot chocolate brightened the boys' spirits in the dining room. When he realized that his job for the day was 'Main Yard grounds,' some of Tom's glow slipped away.

Midway through the meal and with great ceremony, Jack announced, "River Mail. Here's a letter for Tom, from Camp Caribou."

The table was hushed as Tom opened the bright pink envelope. The letter was from Cecille.

"Tommy's got a girlfriend," Shaine said with a wicked grin.

Tom's face turned red.

"Is she pretty?" asked Ric.

"I'll bet she's a plain-Jane," said Chet.

"Quick work," said Lloyd. "We haven't even seen the girls. Tom's a magician."

"It's Duncan's sister," said Tom. "I met her on Opening Day. George had me help his family take his stuff to the Island."

"Nice work." Chet winked. "I remember her from last summer. She's a hottie with a body."

While his cabin mates ribbed him, Tom opened the letter. He pretended to read and then stuffed the paper into his pocket. He'd read it during rest hour when he had time to work through Cecille's flowery handwriting. Deciphering the words would take time.

"It's a thank-you note for helping Duncan's family paddle to and from the Island. I bet she felt like she had to do this," Tom said. "My mother makes me write thank-you notes for everything."

"Mine too," said Lloyd.

"Me too," said Chet. "It's such a drag."

"Yeah, and my mom checks my spelling," said Ric.

Tom turned the conversation to other parental stupid expectations and was pleased to hear that there were many.

As everyone finished eating. Jack said, "I like expectations. This morning, you're free for morning activities. During rest hour, you'll finish your letters home and organize your trip clothes. We'll spend our afternoon packing in the Trip Shed. We leave tomorrow morning."

Rainy day announcements had a different tone, focused on covered spaces. However, in the Sports announcement, Jack seemed to welcome the wet weather.

"During second period, we're playing flag football. I'm not saying that this will be the annual mud bowl, but who knows?"

Most of the Scouts greeted the concept of a slippery game enthusiastically. Tom wanted to try a lollipop fire but couldn't convince anyone to join him.

After dismissal, the Scouts and much of the camp waited on the porch of the Lodge. The wind-driven rain swept over the grass in the Main Yard like a series of waves across a lake. Tom was delighted to learn that there would be no grounds job.

Earnie touched Tom's shoulder. "I understand that you're going to try a lollipop fire. There's a small grove of birch trees near the Middie end of Cabin Cove. It's hidden by a thicket of cedars."

Tom was unsure of what to do with this information, but he said, "Thanks."

"Birch bark has oils in it. It will flame even if it's damp. Don't take much from any single tree. Tear it into thin strips."

Tom's 'thank you' was grateful.

"And get your kindling and tinder from close to the trunk of the pines. You'll need to go further into the woods to get what you need. Use the twigs without moss that are the size between pencil leads and full-size pencils. They'll be dry inside."

Tom's smile was bright, and he hoped his words showed his enthusiasm.

"Thank you. I'll do my best."

"I'd say good luck, but what's needed is skill and patience."

The morning activity bell rang.

Pulling down his baseball cap to keep the rain out of his eyes, Tom decided he would not melt as he trotted up to campcraft.

Someone had rigged a big green tarp over a picnic table. Tom was one of a handful of campers.

"A lollipop fire is simple," Kent explained. "Using only natural materials, you build a fire with two matches. The fire must boil two inches of water in a Billy-can."

"Can we use birch bark?" asked one of the younger campers.

"Yes, but only for a lollipop fire. Never for regular fires. You can use a strip the size of your palm. We don't want to damage the birch trees. When you travel in the park or use established campsites, you'll see dead trees stripped of their bark."

"I don't see any birch trees," said another camper.

"There are a few around. You need to find them. Any questions?"

There were none.

"Off you go," said Kent.

Tom waited until the other campers had scattered before he walked into the forest. A ten-minute walk took him to the birch trees. On his return, he gathered kindling and tinder from beneath the overhanging limbs of pine trees. After the intensity of the early morning's rain, he was surprised to find dry, pencil-sized branches. Back at campcraft, he piled his materials on the sheltered table.

"To boil water, you'll need some larger wood," said Kent. "Go find some branches the size of your thumb that have been leaning against something. Anything on the ground will be wet."

Tom collected several long sticks and broke them into firewood lengths. Waiting for a pause in the rain, Tom watched several younger campers make ineffective attempts. Sequencing was critical.

At the next lapse, Tom grabbed his supplies. After he'd constructed his teepee, a deluge unloaded. He pulled off his raincoat and covered his wood. As his sweatshirt became soaked, he shivered and wondered if this was worth it. When the rain stopped again, he leaped into action. He struck his first match. Thankfully, it lit.

Tom stuck the flame into its proper place. The birch bark flared. The tinder ignited. However, after a minute, his teepee was a smoldering mess. Tom was shattered. He was sure that he'd followed each step carefully.

"Nice try," said Kent. "You've got another match."

"What did I do wrong?"

"In situations like this, a good fire-maker builds as he goes. Watch."

From the campcraft supplies, Kent grabbed a large handful of tinder, a couple of birch bark slices, and some pencil-length pieces of kindling.

"Watch closely."

Kent stuck a match and held it under the big bundle in his other hand. At first, the bark lit. Then the little sticks flamed. Carefully, without burning his hand, he placed the blazing bundle in the firepit. Quickly, with care, he placed a dozen individual sticks and gently blew into the developing fire. As the flames grew, he added more and larger lengths of wood. Soon a roaring blaze warmed the hands of the campers standing around it.

Tom repeated what he'd just seen. The flame leaped from the match to the birch bark and to the tinder. Just before the fire scorched his hand, he set the bundle down. Then, rapidly, one at a time, he placed pencil-sized pieces of wood on the flaming mass.

As he blew into the fire, a memory popped into his head - "*Blow strong, but remember that you are whispering to the spirits of trees.*" He slacked his blowing. The flames took flight.

Soon, Tom's fire was solid. It was time to boil the Billy-can of water. He'd forgotten about building a spit to hang the pot. As he despaired, Kent came over with a Billy-can. Using a red bandana to shield his hand, he placed the can directly on top of the fire, twisting it back and forth to create a solid base.

"Build the fire around the sides of the can."

Once the water boiled, everyone enjoyed hot chocolate.

While sipping the warm drink, Kent asked, "What made you weaken your blowing? I was sure that you'd blow out the flames. That's what most people do on their first attempt."

"It just came to me."

Tom paused, unsure how to continue.

"I heard a saying in my mind - *Blow strong but remember that you are whispering to the spirits of trees.* I don't know where it came from."

"It came from Catamount. We used to say that when I was a young camper. Thanks for reminding me. I'll use it in the future."

Tom wondered if he had heard it from his grandfather or his father. Probably both.

The lunch bell rang, and everyone scurried to the Lodge. Fire-starting had taken more time than Tom had realized.

While eating seconds and thirds of warm, gooey macs and cheese, the Scouts talked about their exploits of the mud bowl. The players had enjoyed slipping and sliding. Borden's full-frontal face-plant sounded impressive.

"Sounds like it was fun," Tom said.

"It was," Ric said. "How was your lollipop fire?"

"I was successful."

"Good job. I couldn't do one."

"Me neither," said Lloyd. "I don't have the patience."

"And you don't like to get wet," Ric said.

During table clearing, Earnie called Jack and Rio away

from the table. When they returned, they did not look happy.

"Gentlemen, the cabin failed inspection today. That's unacceptable. Part of rest hour will be a special cabin cleaning," Jack barked.

The conversation became subdued as the boys wondered about the implications of 'special.'

The rain stopped. The paddle to the cabin was quiet. Upon arrival, Jack insisted that all belongings and clothing be placed inside a trunk, a duffel, or a laundry bag. The sweepers aimed for vacuum-like cleanliness.

After the cabin was spotless, Jack called the boys together.

"For our packing session, bring your sleeping bag, your ground cloth, your clothes, and anything else that you want to bring. Keep your stuff to a minimum. In a minute or two, I'm coming around to check. After I've OK'd you, finish your letters home."

Jack seemed to take delight in removing anything that was more than a change of clothes. After Jack moved on, Tom added a couple of things he had removed.

Tom pulled out Cecille's letter.

*Dear Tom,*

*Thank you for being so kind and helpful to me and my family when we were at Catamount. I do hope that you've had a good start to camp. I know that being a new camper can sometimes be hard, but be yourself, and your cabin mates will get to know you. You were so friendly, and I enjoyed getting to know you. I am eager to hear about life in New York City. It must be so exciting. Arnprior is so dull most of the time.*

*Camp has started well for me. I'm working on my master style paddle skills and hope to be ready to take the final test before the month ends. Our trip this session will be in Algonquin Park. We are taking 10 days to go from the northwest corner to Whitney in the southeast. Mary Rose, our counselor, says that we'll have the wind at our backs for much of it, so we'll be able to do some sailing. But the Park means lots of portages, so we'll be traveling slowly. I wish that Caribou would let us do rivers. We paddle and portage just as well as boys, but you get to do more exciting trips - it's not fair!*

*All the girls are looking forward to meeting you and your fellow Scouts at the Circus next week. Please write back. Getting River Mail is special.*
*Your friend,*
*Cecille*

Getting the letter felt good. Cecille was a nice girl, and he was looking forward to seeing her at the Circus even though he knew he'd get grief from his cabin mates. Cecille wasn't a girlfriend, just a friendly girl that he'd met while paddling her brother to the Island. She'd asked him to write back, so he'd send a brief note. He was sure that getting River Mail in front of her cabin mates would be special. Girls liked that kind of thing. Tom was unsure of what to say. He was scared about her reaction to his poor spelling and simple words. Slowly, he wrote.

Dear Cecille,
Thank you for yor letter. You are kind to writ to me. Tomorow we are going on a 4 nite trip to Algonqun Park. We ar packin in a fu minites. I hope to see you at the sircus.
Your freind
Tom
PS - I am dyslecsit so my spellin is bad - sorry

Tom folded the letter into an envelope and sealed it and then realized he didn't know how to address it. As he walked to Jack, he hid Cecille's letter behind the one for his grandparents. Jack was scribbling a letter of his own.

"Here's my letter home. And I have a letter to go back to Caribou. How do I address it?"

Jack's head popped up. Far more loudly than he needed to, he said, "Writing back so quickly? She must be special."

Tom's face warmed.

"Put Cecille's name on the front and Camp Caribou under it for the address. I'll make sure it gets there." Jack winked at Tom and whispered, "It'll go with the one I'm sending."

"Thanks," Tom mumbled.

The cabin erupted into a flurry of questions - Does she have any good-looking friends? What cabin is she in? How's her body?

Tom's face reddened, and he looked for a way to hide. Looking at Ric's belongings, he noticed a sheath knife.

Loudly, Tom asked, "Do I need to bring a knife on the trip?"

What had been an unspoken question was in the open. A hush fell over the cabin.

Jack looked at Rio and nodded.

"That is a great question," said Rio. "It is the one that I should have asked before the staff trip. Probably, but not always, the answer is no. Unless you plan a lot of fishing and will need a knife to clean up the fish. In the wanigans are kitchen knives, and we will have an axe. Carrying a maybe-needed knife is extra weight that you have to carry when you portage."

Rio sensed the disappointment and disbelief.

"I didn't believe it. I feared bears, so I took a big Swiss mountain knife that my grandfather gave me. It is beautiful."

Reaching into his locker trunk, Rio pulled out a polished leather sheath. He slid out a silvery blade and eased it back into its sheath.

"My knife, it sat in my bedroll for the entire trip. Then, one morning, I thought I had lost the knife. I panicked, but Jack discovered it. Then, during the portage coming up Heartbreak Hill, I was sorry I brought it."

There was a pause.

"Does that mean we can or can't bring a knife?"

Shaine asked.

"It's your choice," Jack said. "If you bring one, it gets rolled in your bedroll. If you lose it, too bad. If you get cut using it, don't expect me to be gentle when I clean your wound."

Confusion appeared on the faces of several Scouts. Tom didn't care because he didn't have a knife. His grandmother had told him that he wouldn't need one.

In the distance, the afternoon activity bell rang.

"Let me have your letters," Jack said. "Get your stuff together and try to get all of your gear into your daypack. I doubt the rain is finished."

As the Scouts assembled on the cabin's porch, Tom thought they looked like the homeless men living under the bridges in the city. Most carried both a small pack bulging with clothing and a sleeping bag crammed into a stuff sack. Only Borden and Lloyd were carrying what looked like rolled-up ponchos.

Jack glanced at the clouds.

"Let's get going. If we get caught in the rain, it will be a mess."

The boys paddled quickly and reached the Trip Shed just before another rain shower erupted. Earnie stepped out from the supply room.

"I hope that some of you remember how this works. For those who don't and the newcomers, I'll go over it. Look at the lines on the floor."

Tom hadn't noticed the painted lines and felt stupid. What else was he not seeing?

"Each of you will have a yellow rectangle. The red squares in the center are in columns of threes and rows of seven. They are for food, days and weeks."

"Put your clothing and sleeping bag on top of your ground cloth," said Earnie.

Having no idea of what a ground cloth was, Tom tensed. He didn't have one. When he looked around, realizing that he was not alone, he relaxed a little.

"Jack, go into the supply room and get new ground cloths for those who need them. Be sure to record who gets them so their families can be billed."

Tom unfurled a 3 x 7 rubberized cloth sheet. He had no clue as to its purpose.

"Who remembers how to roll?" Earnie asked.

Borden raised his hand.

"Step into the center," said Jack. "Do your thing."

Borden spread out his ground cloth. Lengthwise, he folded his sleeping bag in half. He put his extra clothes and his flashlight on top of the sleeping bag. Borden pulled the edges of the ground cloth so they met in the middle. As tightly as possible, he rolled the ground cloth so that the sleeping bag and clothes were fully enclosed. To finish, Borden wrapped two short lengths of webbing around the roll and tightened them. He finished by tying the ends of the webbing to form a handle.

"Catch!"

With a flourish, Borden threw his bedroll to Earnie.

"Well done!" Smiling, Earnie hefted the bedroll. "There's no doubt that this would float. Good job."

Borden beamed proudly.

"Suck up," Shaine whispered.

"Will we have to do float tests?" Ric asked.

Others looked concerned. Tom was glad that he wasn't the only one who was apprehensive.

"Given the weather, we won't be doing any tests. I'm sure that everyone will roll effectively," said Jack. "You need dry sleeping bags tonight and for our trip."

Tom wasn't overly confident in his ability to create a waterproof bedroll and he noticed that a few others relaxed. Maybe they shared his hesitancy.

"Practice rolling your bedrolls," Earnie said. "We have extra webbing for those who need it. While you're rolling, we'll be double-checking your spare clothing and any extra stuff."

As Tom finished, Earnie came over. "That looks pretty big. What do you have in it? Unroll it and let's look."

Tom had packed two extra t-shirts, two pairs of underwear, two pairs of jeans, a heavy sweatshirt, a pair of dock shoes, extra socks, and his flashlight.

"What are you taking in your daypack?"

"My raincoat and a sweatshirt."

"No wool, no sun protection. That raincoat is questionable."

Ernie continued, "Replace the sweatshirt with a long-sleeved shirt. It will keep your arms and neck from getting burned or eaten."

Tom understood sunburn prevention. But being eaten seemed radical.

"Lose the second sweatshirt and the extra jeans. You only need one of everything that you're not wearing."

"Okay." This sounded extreme, but Tom would follow Earnie's advice.

"Cotton kills when it gets wet. I'll get you a wool shirt, then you can dump the sweatshirt. It won't be stylish, but it'll keep you warm. I doubt that any wool pants remain in the used clothing locker. I'm sure that the Voyageurs have already rifled through it."

Earnie looked Tom straight in the eyes.

"Promise me you won't wear the jeans in the rain. Wet jeans make you cold quicker than being naked. Do you have any wool socks? Probably not. I'll find you a pair or two. Do you have another pair of runners? If the dock shoes get wet, they'll never dry. With a second pair of runners, you have backup shoes in case you need them."

Tom nodded.

Earnie stepped closer.

"What are you planning to wear when paddling?"

"Shorts and a T-shirt."

"What underneath?"

"Underwear." Tom squirmed.

"Cotton?"

"Yes."

"Do you have anything quick drying – a racing swimsuit or running shorts?"

"Yes, I've got both. I think."

"Choose one. When it's swim time, take off your shorts. They'll stay dry so you won't have to wear wet clothing. Eh?"

"Yes."

This made sense to Tom. Managing his damp bathing suit had been problematic. On the Saturday canoe/cookout trip, he'd seen Borden and Lloyd take off their shorts and swim in running shorts.

"By the way, have you showered since you've been here?" Earnie asked quietly.

The question shocked Tom. In the city, he showered and wore clean clothes every day. He'd never thought about showering at camp. He'd changed his t-shirts and underwear only twice.

"No," Tom whispered. He was mortified. Luckily, as far as he could tell, no one seemed to have noticed.

"That's what I guessed."

Tom disliked the 'I know what's going on' look on Earnie's face.

"You've been in and out of the water every day, so there's no need right now. Before you leave, put on a clean shirt. It will get filthy. However, shower as soon as you get back to camp. You'll smell horrible because of the campfire smoke."

"Earnie, which pair of pants should I take?" Lloyd asked.

Tom was glad to have the attention move away from him. He knew Earnie was trying to be helpful, but everything he said felt like criticism. He wished this trip could be like the fun times he'd had with his grandfather and his father. They had taken care of everything.

"Catch," yelled Shaine.

Before a tennis ball hit Tom's face, he grabbed it. He tossed it back over the line of bedrolls.

Those who had been 'OK'd' were playing volleyball. The ball arched back to him and Tom bobbled it to Borden, who smacked it back to the other side.

Once everyone finished with their bedrolls, Jack ended the game.

"We'll be out for five days and four nights, so we'll need four breakfasts, five lunches, and four dinners. Breakfast on the first day and dinner on the last day will be here at camp. We need food for twelve people. Who wants to help create the menu?"

Lloyd and Borden volunteered and huddled with Earnie. Tom had been concerned that Shaine would try to dominate.

"We need to get our equipment together," said Jack. "Shaine, get four green canvas packs for our bedrolls and tents. Ric and Chet, get a kitchen and a baking wanigan. Then, get two empty food wanigans. Tom and Ack, come with me to get tents."

Once they piled the equipment in the center, Lloyd said, "Time for the menu."

"Trip food sucks," said Shaine. "Do we have steaks?"

"No!" grinned Borden. "But we have Spam."

"Gross!" said Ric.

"Fry it and cover it with brown sugar," said Borden. "It becomes one of the foods of the gods."

"Not in my religion," said Chet.

"We'll bring a can of pineapple and add some cinnamon," Borden said. "It's delicious that way."

"Let's hear the full menu," said Jack.

"Breakfasts will be two granolas and two oatmeals, each with an addition - bacon, pancakes, cinnamon rolls, and Spam."

"No comments," snapped Jack. "Continue."

"Lunches will be PB and J on bread, bannock or hard crackers with sardines and cheese. We'll have a bag of gorp every day, either for lunch or afternoon snack. The four dinners will be macs and cheese, rice and chicken, beef stroganoff, and spaghetti."

"Comments?" asked Lloyd.

"Desserts?" Chet asked.

"Two puddings, a banana bread, and brownies."

"Any vegetables to eat?" queried Rio.

"Salads - the first two days. Then, dried peas and carrots for one and green beans for the other."

With emphasis, Earnie asked, "Any meaningful observations?"

No one said anything, which did not surprise Tom.

"Well, let's start bagging," said Jack.

All the bulk dried food had to be packaged into gallon-sized plastic bags. Everything was double-bagged, one inside the other, both tied off. The operation of scooping, measuring, bagging, and tying was labor-intense, but the process went smoothly. Each completed meal was placed into one of the red squares so that things could be double-checked.

Once bagging was complete, Earnie loaded the wanigans. "We'll put the lunch stuff with the baking materials; hopefully, that will help balance the loads."

"Thank God," said Chet. "The one that I had to carry last summer weighed a ton. It never got lighter."

"Keeping them balanced," said Jack, "is the responsibility of the GFDs."

This term was new to Tom. From the others' reaction, no one else had heard it before, so he asked, "What's a GFD?"

"The GFDs, Guides for the Day, will lead from sunup to lights out. They'll cook breakfast and dinner. They read the maps and tell us where to go. They'll pick the lunch spot, the campsite, and organize the kitchen area."

"Sounds cool," said Shaine.

Tom suspected that Shaine saw himself permanently in this role.

"As a team, two or three of you will be Guides for a Day," continued Jack.

"What's everyone else do?" asked Borden.

"Another team gathers firewood, and the third group does dishes."

"How are these groups made up?" questioned Shaine.

"We'll choose names out of a hat," said Earnie.

Shaine wasn't pleased, but Tom sensed that Shaine knew that challenging Earnie would not be a good idea.

Rio brought out a small box, pieces of paper, and pencils.

"Please, everyone write your name upon the paper, and please, then place the paper in the box."

Tom tried not to smile at Rio's English.

"These will be your GFD and tent groups for the trip," said Jack.

Rio drew the first two, Shaine and Chet.

"Outstanding!" said Shaine. "A two-man tent. Luxury."

Jack scowled.

"Next."

Rio picked out the next two, Ric and Lloyd.

This meant a three-man tent of Ack, Borden, and Tom. While this might mean some crowding, Tom was pleased to be with them. Having Borden's experience would be a comfort when it was their day to lead.

"These are the groups." Earnie looked directly at each boy. "There will be no discussion. If you are unhappy, I don't want to know. The GFD program will continue on the Dumoine. You'll have three sets of different partners on the river."

Noticeably, but briefly, he stared at Shaine.

"As Scouts, you're taking responsibility for day-to-day decisions. One of your key tasks is cooperating. With everyone!"

"The GFDs will start on the second day," said Jack. "That will give each tent group a night to sort things out. Tomorrow, the counselors will be the guides."

"We'll volunteer to be the first group," Shaine said. "That way, we can show everyone how it's done."

Tom doubted that the smiles on everyone's faces were sincere. Shaine as an authority figure was not appealing. He hoped the counselors would watch carefully.

"We'll do second," Borden said.

"That's fine with us," Ric said. "That leaves the best for last."

"Who is our tenth person? Is Jack our guide or do we have an assistant counselor?" asked Lloyd.

"We're special. We get a senior guide," said Jack. "After dinner, our guide will join us to review the route and explain our service task."

A bell rang. Somehow, the bell rang at the necessary time, every time, every day. It mystified Tom.

"We're done for the afternoon. You're free until dinner," said Jack. "We'll be back here for our final briefing after supper."

The Scouts headed to the Main Yard. Tom would have liked to paddle, but given the dreary weather, he stayed with the group. Despite intermittent drizzle, tetherball began. Having played only once, he scrutinized the game for a few minutes. Then he joined the challengers' line.

When it was his turn to enter the court, Tom faced Chet. Both were agile. The ball went round and round. Ultimately, experience won. Tom returned to the challengers' line.

The more that Tom watched, the better he grasped the interactions of the rope, the ball and the player's hand.

When Tom next stepped into the court, Shaine had

reigned supreme over a series of opponents. With each victory, Shaine's taunts became more intense.

"An American abomination," Shaine snapped as he served.

Tom leaped and hit.

Shaine jumped and blocked.

"The numbskull can't spell."

Tom vaulted and batted.

Eventually, Shaine prevailed.

"Silly city slicker."

Tom tried not to let the comments bother him. As he waited with the other challengers, Tom detected a pattern in Shaine's hits and blocks.

"Back again, awkward American," Shaine jeered as Tom's turn came again. "You're going down, dumb ass."

The watchers quieted. At one point, Tom was close to defeat. Knowing Shaine's pattern, Tom blasted the ball in a high spiral. Shaine leaped, blocking. Back and forth swung the ball, sometimes predictably and, other times whirling out of control.

The dinner bell rang, and the clouds opened. The crowd ran for the Lodge.

As the rain beat down, both boys concentrated. Each leaped high to hit. Shaine's arm met Tom's. At the same time, his knee smashed into Tom's groin. He crumpled. Shaine smashed the ball, and it snaked around the center pole for the win.

"Nice game, loser."

Shaine stamped in a puddle as he walked by.

The mud dripped down Tom's face. As he stumbled to his feet, he clenched his fists. From the top of the dry porch, Shaine glared triumphantly. Before walking into the Dining Room, he paused and took several deep breaths.

After grace, Jack said, "No mud at the table. Go wash up. Both hands and face."

After pulling off his dirty, wet sweatshirt, Tom walked to the washroom. His anger began to subside as he splashed hot water on his hands and face.

The intense drumming of rain on the Dining Hall's roof subdued dinner conversation. The Scouts sat by tent groups. Away from Shaine, Tom squeezed between Ack and Borden.

"I hear Shaine pummeled you," said Ack. "From what I saw, you almost had him."

"I did, but.... I'll tell you later."

Steamy beef stew and hot biscuits warmed Tom's insides and calmed his mind.

"I love being outside," said Borden. "Cooking over an open fire is fun. Paddling in the Park means lots of portaging. Nobody likes that. Ack, you'll see that Algonquin is so beautiful."

"I'm sure it is," Ack said. "But there's nothing like the wind and rain of the Highlands. It makes this stuff look tame. My grandfather loved bad weather. He thrived in high winds and downpours. He always worried about snow, but we never had much."

"Nothing is like an October storm at a hunting camp. We always felt warm and safe in our cabin. My grandfather always worried about getting frozen in, but we never did."

"Sounds like my grandfather," said Tom. "He and my dad always talked about the storms that they survived in the North when we sat around the fire on our canoe trips."

"I thought you lived in New York City," said Borden. "Where did you go on canoe trips?"

"My grandparents own a cottage about an hour north of the city. It's on a long lake connected to two others. There are a few cabins on our lake and none on the other two."

"When I used to hike with my grandfather, we might

not see a manmade structure for days. The heather is wild," said Ack.

"There are parts of the North that have never been explored," said Borden. "That's true wilderness."

After the meal, the Scouts trooped back to the Trip Shed for their briefing.

"Thank God the rain has stopped," said Shaine.

"Who do you think our guide will be?" Chet asked.

"Probably one of the senior staff," said Ric. "They do the early trips before the problems arise."

"They only do short trips," said Lloyd.

"Maybe it'll be Kent," said Borden. "He's a great cook."

"Maybe Erl," said Lloyd. "He told some great stories on one of my Middie trips."

When Jack, Rio, and Earnie walked in, a hush fell. By the way Earnie was walking, Tom knew he was their guide.

"Scouts, please welcome our guide, Earnie," said Jack. Tom smiled.

"Lloyd and Borden, go into the equipment room and carry out the big map of Algonquin Park."

Once the map was leaning against the wall, Earnie pointed.

"We start and end at the Rock Lake landing. We'll be paddling in a big circle. Our trip has two goals. The first is service to the Park. Our route contains a couple of less used portages. We'll clear them as necessary. This means that we'll be carrying extra forest tools."

Tom heard a low groan he thought came from Shaine.

"By doing this route, we avoid the Devil Staircase portages, one up, one down."

The Scouts smiled.

"The second goal is to get you ready for the Dumoine. Every day, you'll paddle with new people and in different places in the canoes."

"What's the point of doing this?" asked Shaine. "We already know where everyone should paddle."

"You may feel that you do, but people change. The Dumoine is rugged. For everyone's safety, we want the right people doing the right things. Don't we?"

"I guess so."

Tom was beginning to realize that, when confronted, Shaine backed down.

"Rio, our resident scientist, will keep track of who paddles with who," Jack said.

From Rio's reaction, Tom guessed that this was a surprise to him.

"I will tell you, each one, the canoe rotations when we start the paddling for each day," said Rio. "A morning surprise."

"Well said. Now, it's time to double-check your bedroll with your tent mates. Unroll, inspect, re-roll," said Earnie. "Then, without a tent, pack a bedroll pack with your tentmates. Take it with you when you paddle to the cabin tonight. Bring it back in the morning."

Even with Borden helping, the rolling process was time-consuming for Ack and Tom.

"Borden, what are you going to wear under your shorts on the trip?" Tom asked quietly.

"Yeah," Ack said. "I don't want to give Shaine an opportunity to make fun of me."

"A racing swimsuit. It dries the fastest. I know it looks weird, but running shorts stay damp longer."

"What about a towel?" Tom asked.

"No. A few people bring them, but they become a hassle. They never dry and are a pain on the portages."

Once the bedroll packs were ready, Jack had the boys double-checked the four wanigans. Tom had thought the double-checking process was overblown, but they discovered they were missing a second bag of powdered milk.

"Who was bagging the powdered milk?" Jack questioned.

No one responded, but Tom saw Chet glance at Shaine.

Shaking his head, Jack said, "Let's get back to the cabin. Your excess clothing goes in your daypacks. I don't want to see anything on the floor. Put the wanigans and tools next to the door. Let's sweep up the floor. Earnie will inspect his Trip Shed when he returns."

Tom hadn't noticed that Earnie had disappeared. As they put away the brooms and dustpans, Earnie reappeared carrying a plastic trash bag.

"Looks good. Let's head down to the Canoe Dock. Be sure to bring all of your stuff."

As they put the canoe in the water, Borden said, "I'll take the bow."

"I'll take the middle." said Ack. "I want to try out the new seat. The bedroll pack looks comfortable."

Tom was happy to be in the stern. With two paddlers pulling in front of him, Tom focused intently on his paddling and the canoe tracked straighter with fewer adjustments.

As they paddled, the undersides of the clouds turned bright red. In the west, a line of blue sky was moving in.

"Do those colors mean anything?" Tom asked.

"Red sky at night, sailors' delight. It's clearing," said Borden. "It'll be a cold night. Tomorrow should be a good day to paddle."

After the Scouts carried their packs up to the cabin, they stood around wondering what to do.

"Put away everything that you're not taking," said Earnie. "We don't want any confusion in the morning. No one wants to leave anything important behind. If you forget anything, we're not coming back."

"It's going to be dark in less than half an hour," said Jack.

200

Tom pulled out a duffel and put away his excess clothes.

"I found this wool jacket in the used clothing cabinet. It'll keep you warmer than your cotton sweatshirt."

Earnie handed Tom a frayed brown shirt with a green patch on the left elbow. He also gave him a pair of misshapen gray socks.

"Wear these with your wet shoes. The wool will keep your feet warm."

"Thanks."

Staying warm was one of Tom's concerns. He was overjoyed that Earnie had followed through. He was sure that at some point the well-worn gifts would be targets for Shaine, so he was glad when Earnie gave Ack a similar shirt.

"I'm building a fire," said Earnie. "When you're completely ready for our adventure, you're welcome to join me."

As Tom stuffed his cotton clothing into his duffel, he felt his plastic emergency box. Out of it, he surreptitiously pulled a $20 bill. He smiled, knowing his grandfather would be proud of his preparedness. Then the guilt hit. He hadn't thought about his grandfather in days.

"Come on," Ack said. "We're as ready as we can be."

The Scouts drifted outside. Darkness had fallen. As the boys sat, they gazed into the flames, each one lost in his own thoughts. The sky had cleared, and the stars were twinkling. The temperature was dropping.

Once everyone was ready, Earnie did what Tom expected.

"Gentlemen, as most of you know, I don't get out on many trips these days. I consider it an honor to join you as we help the Park. As you know, the Algonquin is the oldest wilderness park in the world. As paddlers, we share in an ancient tradition of canoe travel that goes back thousands of years. Each of us is on our own journey of discovery as we grow up and as we age. As Catamount men, we must always remember our ABC's - *Adventure, Brotherhood, and Courage.* We don't know what awaits us, but we go together, prepared and eager for the challenges ahead."

Tom had heard this talk before but sitting on a rocky point overlooking a wide expanse of still water, Earnie's words meant more. The fire crackled as the wood burned to glowing embers. The stars sparkled. A loon's cry echoed over the water.

"Time for lights out, gentlemen," Jack said.

"And we mean quiet. Go to sleep," said Earnie.

In his sleeping bag, Tom tossed and turned. The creaking of the other bunks showed he was not alone. Tom's mind whirled. He wasn't sure that he could handle Shaine's spitefulness much longer and was afraid he'd lose his temper. He'd worked hard with a counselor over the past few years but if he lost it, he knew the blow-up would be bad. With Earnie as their guide, he hoped things would be under control. Shaine was subtle, but not stupid. Part of Tom was looking forward to the trip, but he'd done nothing like this in his life. Was he ready? What would happen in the wilds? If it was a disaster, he did have an escape option. But what would his grandfather say? The last thing Tom wanted to do was disappoint him.

Gradually, the scraping and scratching stopped. Tom embraced the darkness and slept.

# Chapter 9
## First Portage

The sounds of Earnie whispering with two men brought Tom to full consciousness. Sitting up quickly, he bonked his head on the slant of the roof.

Tom muffled his "Shit!"

"Tom, are you okay?"

"Yeah." Tom nodded into the blinding flashlight.

"It's 3:00 am. There's a problem over at the Lodge. It's no big deal. It's doesn't concern any of the campers. Go back to sleep. I'll see you in the morning."

Tom heard the concern in Earnie's voice. He'd heard it's-no-big-deal too many times in his life to believe it. After the men left, he tiptoed to the rocky point. No sounds or lights came from any of the campers' cabins around the Cove. Tom listened intently. Everything seemed peaceful. The rocks beneath his bare feet were cold. He stepped into the grass to pee into the bushes and quietly walked back to his bunk.

Waiting for sleep to return, he thought about the past few days. There had been some good and some not so good. Overall, camp was okay. Some of his cabin mates were promising as friends. A couple were questionable. One didn't like him. He felt he could depend on the adults. As he drifted off, he ruminated on Catamount's ABCs and wondered about how adventure, brotherhood, and courage would play out on the trip.

"Rise and shine!" Jack yelled. "It's trip time."

Outside the cabin, the sky was a deep blue without a hint of white. A sharp exhale created a cloud of condensation.

"A cold front went through," said Jack. "We're in for some great northern days."

Outside Tom's sleeping bag, the air was crisp. His 'new' wool shirt felt warm. As he spread his groundsheet on the cabin floor, he decided to say nothing about Earnie being summoned in the middle of the night. He began to lay out his clothing.

"You won't need that wool shirt. Roll it," Borden said. "The day will warm up quickly."

Reluctantly, Tom placed the shirt on top of his sleeping bag.

"Borden, this is a stupid question. What do we sleep on if it's cold like last night?"

"The ground and your groundsheet. Picking a tent site is important. You try to get one that's flat with no roots or rocks. The best ones have a mat of pine needles."

"Thanks."

"No problem. This is new to you. I'm here to help. Ask away. I have answers."

"Thanks. Again!"

The cabin was quieter than normal while the Scouts rolled their belongings. Tom sensed purpose in everyone's actions. When he needed help squeezing his bedroll, Borden added a pair of hands. Tom did the same for Ack.

As the three stuffed their bedrolls into their canvas pack, Ack said, "I hope there's room for the tent."

"It'll be tight," said Borden. "After a few days, it's easy."

"Hopefully with more room than in our daypack," Ack said. "Tom, your city-slicker raincoat is massive."

Tom's face reddened.

When all the Scouts had rolled, Jack said, "We want to

get on the water as soon as possible, so we're going to load the trailer before breakfast. First step: packs, lifejackets, daypacks, and canoes get carried to the Trip Shed. We'll stuff the tents into our packs and tie the axes and saws onto the top of the wanigans. Then, we'll load our bedroll packs, wanigans, paddles, and lifejackets into the trailer's bottom. Finally, we'll tie the canoes onto the racks. We want to leave immediately after we eat. Any questions?"

Tom couldn't decide whether Jack's insistence in continually restating the day's plan was reassuring or annoying.

"Do we need to get extra paddles?" Borden asked.

"Yes," said Jack. "Thanks for remembering. Each tent group should grab one from the Boat House. Don't forget to wear a hat and have your cup available. Let's load up."

Once the pack and daypack were in the canoe, Borden said, "I'll try the middle."

"I'll take the bow," Ack said.

Tom was surprised, but happy to be in the stern. He'd assumed that, with Borden's experience, he would want to be in charge.

At the Canoe Dock, Tom said, "Since I'm in the stern, I'll carry the canoe."

"Sounds good to me," Borden said. "I'll do the bedroll pack and two paddles."

"How do I manage all of our other stuff?" Ack asked.

"Wear the daypack. Loop our lifejackets on the extra paddle," Borden said. "You'll get the hang of it."

As the boys passed the Lodge, Earnie walked out. "Jack, Rio. Come into the office."

Outside the Trip Shed, another counselor, new to Tom, awaited them.

"Go inside. Have a seat. Earnie will be over in a minute."

The boys wondered what was happening. In

whispered tones, Tom told them about Earnie's being summoned in the middle of the night. Before imaginations could race out of control, Earnie, Jack, and Rio walked in. Silence fell.

"Gentlemen, last night, the Director was hurt in a car accident and is in hospital." Earnie paused. "This means that I won't be able to come on the trip with you. Let me introduce Doug Jacques as your guide."

The Scout's new leader was an inch or two shorter than Jack. He looked strong but didn't have the muscles of a trained athlete. His light, wispy mustache seemed to be a continuation of his mottled brown hair. Doug's tan was dark, and his eyes showed lines from spending hours in the sun.

"He's a good guy," said Jack. "We were campers together. We did our Scout and Voyageur trips together."

"To me, he was great on the staff trip," Rio said. "He is a serious portager who can carry like a fur trader of the old days."

Tom had no idea what a fur trader should look like. Doug reminded him of a pirate or an outlaw; someone who shouldn't be crossed.

"I remember you," said Ric. "You were on my Temagami trip last year. You slept in a hammock."

"Yes, I did," said Doug. "Now, let's get the trailer loaded. We don't want to miss breakfast."

Except for Ack and Tom, everyone seemed to know exactly what to do. Borden guided Ack and Tom's last-minute decisions about where packs and equipment were best secured in the trailer. Ric and Chet carefully stowed their fishing rods inside the van with tales of previous successes and jokes about the size and numbers of future catches.

After everything was loaded, Earnie gathered the boys.

"At announcements this morning, we will not say

anything about the car accident. Until we know more about the Director's condition, we feel that it's best for camp life to continue normally. So, please don't talk about this in the Lodge or the washrooms. Okay? Thank you."

He paused.

"Gentlemen, have a great trip. I was looking forward to getting out, but duty calls. Remember *Adventure, Brotherhood,* and *Courage.*"

Just as Earnie finished, the breakfast bell rang. Again, Tom marveled at the timing of the bells and how they seemed to ring at exactly the right time, every time.

The conversation over breakfast centered on who would paddle with whom in which canoe. While Shaine disagreed, Tom thought that the consensus was that Borden and Lloyd were the strongest paddlers. No one disagreed that Borden and Ric were the best portagers.

After breakfast, Jack said, "Everyone go to the washroom. We have a long ride in the van."

As Tom walked through the dining hall toward the parking lot, he heard Earnie talking to Jack and Doug. Hoping to hear something important, Tom paused.

"Remember, if there's a difficult decision to make, it's the guide's responsibility. Now, what are the three C's for adults on trips?"

In unison, Jack and Doug said, "Care, Caution, and Cooperation."

"The three Cs and the ABCs have worked at Catamount for decades. Everyone knows them and lives by them. Understood?" said Earnie.

Several other boys walked out of the washroom. Tom joined them before he was discovered listening.

Loading the van was a process. The inside was crammed with the ten paddlers, their daypacks, and the big lunch cooler. The driver, Henry, was a favorite among the boys. They jokingly pestered him to turn up the radio. They pleaded with him to stop in Pembroke so they could enjoy "civilized" food at the McDonald's.

While they drove, Tom watched the road. Last night's car accident had brought up memories of his father's accident and reawakened his unease about his grandfather's recovery. He kept his eye on Henry, but he seemed to be a competent driver.

The forest on both sides of the road seemed endless. His mother's voice about the perils of the outdoors rattled in his head. She had been uncomfortable in the woods, fearful of bugs, snakes, bears, and wolves. A sly grin crept to his face as he realized that she'd be freaking out if she knew what he was doing. She was halfway around the world. He was on his own and he smiled.

Pembroke was smaller than Tom had expected. The boys howled for a stop, but Henry drove past the McDonald's. On the far side of town, a shopping area appeared. Henry pulled into a gas station next to a Tim Hortons donut store.

"Pee break," Jack announced. "In and out. Behave. Be polite. Use the gas station and Tim Hortons."

Most of the boys ran into the Tim Hortons. As they waited in line for the bathroom, they gazed at the donuts.

"Anybody got any money?" Ric asked.

When no one said "yes," Tom had an idea. He was the last to exit the bathroom and pulled out his $20 bill.

When he walked out with three dozen donuts, Jack barked, "How did you get those?"

"I had a twenty in my shorts. My grandfather told me to always carry some cash, especially when I don't know where I'm going or what I'm doing."

"Always prepared. I like that." Doug smiled.

"Me too." Jack smacked his lips. "Let's start with two per person. Gentlemen, line up."

The boys crowded.

"Stop!" Doug bellowed. "Everyone will get their donuts. Create a straight line by the date of your birthday.

The first of the month is at the head of the line. Anyone 30 or 31 at the back."

The Scouts organized themselves, and each boy selected his donuts. After paying for petrol, Henry selected his two.

"We will distribute the last of the donuts for meritorious conduct at the launch point," said Doug.

"I could eat a dozen donuts in three minutes," said Ric.

"No way," said Chet. "I bet that it would take you six."

"That's 30 seconds a donut," said Shaine. "Even I could do that."

"Load up. We have to get moving," Jack said.

For the next half hour, a conversation swirled about how many donuts each could eat at one sitting. After arduous give and take, they decided that a fair competition would be eating a dozen donuts while being timed, and not puking within the next hour. Once the donut eating contest was settled, the coming Canadian football and NHL seasons became the topics of discussion.

The donuts had been successful, and Tom felt that he'd earned some street cred. The longer they drove, the fewer little towns they passed through.

At the entrance to Algonquin Park, the attendant waved the van and trailer through the gate. The forest didn't seem different inside the park; it continued uninterrupted. After another hour, the van turned onto a dirt road. Tom and the boys enjoyed seeing how high each pothole would bounce a person. After a dusty 15 minutes, the van stopped at a small brick building.

A uniformed ranger came out as the boys disembarked. After chatting with Doug and Jack, he said. "Boys, thank you for coming to Algonquin Park. We appreciate your help in maintaining it. Camps like

Catamount have a long history of traveling through the Park. We want to keep it positive. The washroom is that brown brick building over there."

The boys scrambled to use the facility. As Tom exited, the van and trailer and an official-looking green truck drove past. The Scouts walked down a well-used gravel road to a half-empty dirt parking lot with a boat landing on a small river. Jack and Doug examined a map with the ranger while the boys unloaded the trailer. Tom was annoyed to see the ranger eating a donut and the box resting on the hood of his truck.

At the boat launch, Rio began unpacking the lunch cooler.

"Chet, Ric, Lloyd, can you organize the ham, cheese, and bread to make the sandwiches for each of us? Shaine, hand out apples to those who wish one to eat."

As the boys munched on their lunch, the ranger addressed the group.

"Boys, thank you for helping keep the portages clear. I have a favor to ask of you. On the big lakes, please be quiet after dark. I know that boys will be boys. We want you to have fun. But remember that sound carries long distances over water. On the big lakes, other people will be camping. Please keep your voices down, eh?"

A chorus of "Yes, sir!" sounded.

The ranger got into his truck and drove away.

"Now, what everyone has been waiting for – the boat pairings for today." Rio pulled out a piece of paper.

"Lloyd with Jack. Tom with Doug. Chet, Ric, and Shaine. And Ack, Borden and me."

Shaine looked happy. Tom wasn't sure that Chet and Ric shared his enthusiasm.

"My boat will have the kitchen wanigan," said Doug. "Jack will take the baking and lunch wanigan. The other two are equal in weight, so it doesn't make a difference."

After putting the canoes in the river along the dock,

the Scouts loaded them. Henry waved goodbye and drove away.

"I'll start in the stern," Doug said. "You can take the stern after the portage."

This surprised and pleased Tom.

As the four canoes pushed away from the dock, Doug turned to Jack.

"Do you want lead or tail?"

"I'll take tail. I haven't been here," Jack said. "You know where you're going, so you can lead the parade."

"Tom, please paddle on the left."

As their canoe moved to take the lead, Tom saw Jack arrange his map so it was visible as he paddled. Behind him, Tom heard Doug do the same. The narrow river curved to the left, to the right, and back to the left. After a ten-minute paddle, the four canoes entered a big lake.

A massive red cliff on its left shoreline dominated Tom's first wild lake. A row of colored tents and trailers sat along its base. From behind, a breeze created wavelets. Several canoes and small motorboats danced on the lake's surface. Far down the right shore, a distant opening seemed to call to Tom.

"I love starting a trip with a tailwind," Doug said. "But it won't last. It'll turn into a headwind before we get to portage."

The blue of the sky, the white of the clouds, and the sharp green of the shoreline excited Tom. Unexpectedly, he felt at peace and pulled steadily on his paddle. Tom sensed everyone appreciated the wind at their backs. He felt energized by the Park's beauty.

After about ten minutes, Tom's muscles began to ache.

"Three-minute break," called Doug. "Tom, paddle on the right. We'll alternate sides. Let me know when. I'm an ambidextrous paddler."

As the four boats rafted together, Tom noticed that the breeze had died. His back and arms were tight. Everyone stretched their shoulders and twisted their backs.

Lloyd asked, "Can we drink the water?"

"Considering the motorboats on Rock Lake, not the best idea," Doug said. "Wait until we get closer to the portage. The boats can't get up the channel; too shallow, too many rocks."

"Shall we paddle, gentlemen?" Jack's voice rose. "We have a bit of a headwind. See that dock jutting out from the far point? First boat past it gets choice of campsites tonight. GO!"

The breeze was now blowing in their faces. To compensate, Tom dug his paddle deeper into the water.

"No need to pull any harder at the moment. The wind's not too bad," Doug said. "What happened to the wind? We went from a tailwind to a headwind."

"I don't know." Tom was mystified.

"What's happening in the woods to our right?"

"The land is getting steeper. It's a big hill."

"What's the hill doing to the wind?"

"Blocking it." Tom said.

"Where is our headwind coming from?"

"Around the hill?"

"Yes," Doug said. "The wind gets bent around obstacles. It pushed us as we started. Now, it's in our faces. In a few minutes, when we get into open water, the wind will be on our right side. The hill acts like an eddy in a river."

"Makes sense."

Tom remembered hearing something about eddies in rivers from his father. As Tom thought about air and water, he realized that both could bend and be focused by their environment.

Doug's wind analysis was right on target. When their canoe entered a large bay, the wind hit their canoe from the side and intensified. Just as Tom's arms and back were giving out, Doug called, "Switch sides."

Using a new set of muscles was invigorating.

"We win!" shouted Tom as they passed the dilapidated dock.

"Rest easy," Doug said. "We're in a wind shadow created by the trees."

Tom rubbed his hands.

"Hot spots?" asked Doug.

"Yes."

"You don't want to get blisters," said Doug. "Don't grip the paddle so tightly. Relax your hands. Move your fingers so that you're not pulling in the same way every time."

"I'll try."

Lloyd and Jack joined them, and they watched both Rio's and Shaine's canoes struggle with the wind.

"That was a bear," Shaine said.

"Yeah," said Chet. "The wind kept blowing us off course."

"Take five," said Jack, rolling his eyes.

Several boys rubbed their hands and dipped them in the cool water.

"All of you are moving your fingers so you won't get blisters as you paddle, eh?" Doug said. "You can drink here. This area is too shallow for the motorboats."

Doug dipped his cup and drank. Tom panicked; he'd forgotten a cup. From the canoe beside him, Borden handed him his cup. The water was clear and cool.

After everyone had a drink, Doug said, "We need to keep moving. I assume you would prefer a campsite with a good beach."

"Let's go," Chet said.

"Onward to glory," Ric said.

"Do we have more headwinds?" asked Shaine.

"Depends on where we're going," said Doug. "Does anyone other than Jack and Rio know where we're headed?"

No one knew. The boys looked at each other. Tom saw that some cared, and some didn't.

"Can anyone read a map?" asked Doug.

Borden and Lloyd responded positively.

"Excellent. Tell us where we are."

Doug handed his map to Tom, who shared it with Borden in the canoe next to him. Both studied it. Jack gave his map to Lloyd.

"Shaine, do you want to look at mine?" Rio passed his to Shaine. All seven of the boys examined the maps.

"Is this the big hill?" Borden pointed at a series of circles on the map.

A steep cliff sat behind them across the bay.

"Is that the cliff?"

Tom's finger pointed at the map where the lines were close to each other.

"Yes."

Borden placed his finger on the map.

Tom nodded.

"We know where we are," said Borden.

"Are you sure? 100%?" asked Doug.

"About 95%."

"Then, where do we go?"

"We go down this bay." Tom pointed in the direction they had been heading. "When it ends, I think we have a 375-meter portage into Pen Lake."

"Shaine, Lloyd, do you agree?"

"I guess so," said Lloyd.

Shaine paused and looked around.

"Probably."

"Borden and Tom are correct," Doug said. "Good job, gentlemen. Let's go for a paddle. We have a portage waiting. Remember to move your fingers. Keep a relaxed grip on your paddle, no blisters. I'll take the lead."

As the Scouts paddled down the bay, the lake narrowed with low gray granite outcroppings on the left and an expanse of green marsh on the right. The conversation quieted as the canoes began to maneuver around rocks. A few sat above the surface and others lurked just below the waterline. After a couple of near misses, Tom's vision sharpened and he began to see them more clearly.

Behind them, a dull scrape squeaked.

"Keep your eyes open," Jack yelled. "We don't want any cuts in the canvas."

The bay narrowed into a shallow stream. About 50 meters ahead was a flat rock face with a bright yellow sign on a tree.

"Is that sign the start of the portage?" asked Tom.

"Yes. They make this one easy to see. Some hide under branches. Yellow signs are portages. Orange signs indicate campsites."

About five meters from the unloading area, Doug said, "Raft up. Our wood and canvas canoes are not the unbreakable aluminum boats from your past summers. Unload and load the canoes while they float. Loaded boats are not to touch dry ground, a rock, or the bottom of the lake."

Tom saw Shaine glance at his feet and the dry rocks.

"Your feet will get wet. Be careful. The rocks are slippery. Work together and move your stuff away from the unloading area."

"We want to be as efficient as possible." said Jack. "No wasted energy. With two two-man boats, this will take planning. By the end of the trip, we may be able to do one-carry portages."

"We need to be good organizationals." Rio said. "Each canoe needs to plan itself carefully."

All the boys grinned. Tom felt badly. He hoped Rio wasn't upset when the Scouts gawked at his words.

"We'll share the extra carrying. This one's not long. I'll come back after dropping off our canoe." said Doug.

"Jack will be the last to start his carry. That way, he'll know exactly how many people need to carry a second load."

"That means everyone drops their first load and starts back," said Jack. "Any questions?"

There were none. While Tom had several, he kept quiet. He hoped he could do what was needed without looking foolish.

"We'll take the lead," Doug said. "Tom, what's our plan?"

"As the bowman, I'll hold the canoe. You'll unload the pack and the wanigan. I assume you are going to carry the canoe?"

"Yes," replied Doug. "And my daypack."

"I'll carry the wanigan."

"That will leave me the bedroll pack and the paddles. Sounds good."

"Lifejackets?" asked Tom.

"Each wears his own," said Doug. "It provides a bit of padding when you carry the wanigan. Let's get started."

Doug stepped into the water and signaled for Tom to stand next to him. Intentionally getting his feet wet still felt strange. He held the canoe. Doug swung the wanigan onto the wide dry rock. Next came the bedroll pack, the paddles, and lifejackets. Doug pulled on his lifejacket and his personal pack. While standing in the water, he flipped the canoe onto his shoulders.

"I'll see you on the other side," Doug said. "Move our stuff away from the landing area."

Tom carried the wanigan up to a grassy area at the edge of the trail. When he returned for the pack and their paddles, chaos reigned at the landing site. Both Rio's and Shaine's canoes jockeyed to unload. Paddles and lifejackets were thrown. Some boys splashed in the shallow water; others tried to keep their feet dry.

"Thanks for getting your stuff out of the way," said

Borden. "This is crazy."

"What do I need to do?"

"Get started."

Tom moved to his wanigan. He'd never lifted one by himself.

"Let me help," said Borden. "Getting the tumpline in the right place is an art."

Together they lifted the wanigan. Tom twisted so the load rested high on his back. Borden placed the wide part of the tump at Tom's hairline. The weight was awkward, but it was not as heavy as Tom had thought it would be. He was grateful that his lifejacket padded his back.

"Walk smoothly so the wanigan doesn't bounce. I find a slow jog or fast trot to be the best," said Borden.

Tom welcomed the advice and walked into the woods on a wide, well-defined path. He wondered how long 375 meters would take.

At first, the going was smooth. Then the path dipped to a low area, oozing with black mud and rocks. Soggy footprints faced in both directions. Tom tried to dance from dry rock to dry rock, but the weight of the wanigan pulled him into the muck. So much for clean shoes.

The trail rose and fell. The low points sucked at his shoes. The steps up required careful balance. 375 meters was far longer than Tom had imagined. The leather strap pulled deeply on his forehead, and his neck ached. Sweat began to drip into his eyes.

Finally, at the top of a rise, a sparkly lake stretched into the distance. A cooling breeze floated through the trees. A narrow wooden dock stuck out from a small beach strewn with driftwood. High-stepping over the last roots on the path, Tom trudged onto the sand and stumbled on a rock. The wanigan slipped and pounded onto the dock.

"Not so hard, Tom." Doug smiled. "You never know what's in there. You did well for your first portage.

Carrying a full wanigan is not for the faint of heart."

"Thanks." Tom smiled. Given the shooting pains in his neck muscles, he didn't care if anything had been damaged. He was overjoyed to be finished.

"It's amazing how every portage seems to have more uphills and mud puddles." Doug grinned. "But I love them. They build character."

As Tom rotated his neck, the muscles screamed.

"Thanks for carrying the wanigan. Few rookies accept the challenge on their first portage."

Doug pulled his cup out of his pack, dipped it into the lake, and drank. Tom knew he was supposed to use his own cup. Doug handed him a cup of water.

"We're not supposed to share cups, but you don't have yours with you. I assume it's in the daypack."

The liquid tasted like pure gold.

"That was wonderful." Tom hung his head. "I forgot a cup."

"No problem. We always have an extra or two. I'll give it to you at the campsite, quietly."

"Thanks."

"I'm headed back for the second load."

"I'm right behind you," said Tom.

"Sure. We always appreciate extra hands."

As Tom and Doug walked back down the trail, they passed the other Scouts, each fully loaded. As the stern paddler, Tom had assumed that Shaine would shoulder the canoe, but he was surprised to see him carrying his canoe's bedroll pack and paddles. Well behind, Ric bore their canoe, sweating profusely.

"How much further?"

"About 100 meters," Doug said.

"Thanks."

About ten meters later, Doug said, "Time to pick up some birchbark."

He stepped a few meters off the trail and reached

down to a fallen birch tree.

"I always grab some birchbark and put it in my shorts pocket. This way, you have some good fire starter close at hand when you need it."

This made sense to Tom, and he picked at a thicker piece.

"I suggest that you find something that's a little thinner so it folds nicely and you can't feel it."

Again, this was self-evident, and Tom felt stupid.

As if Doug was reading Tom's mind, he said, "Don't worry. There are hundreds of little tricks. It takes years, and even then, you forget."

Tom smiled and stuffed a thin palm-sized fold into his left rear pocket.

Back on the trail, after another minute, a second upside-down canoe appeared. Rio was struggling with his canoe.

"How much further?" asked Rio.

"About 200 meters," said Doug.

"Okay." Rio staggered.

"Take a break," said Doug. "I'll teepee the canoe."

Stepping out from under the canoe, Rio looked frustrated and embarrassed.

"Tom, come hold the canoe. Rio and I are going to carry it together."

"No. I will do it by myself."

"Not if it's going to kill you. With two, it's much lighter."

"I guess so," said Rio. "Only this one time. Okay?"

While Tom held the canoe, the two hoisted it onto their shoulders.

"Tom, go get our stuff. The others will come back and help. You be the last. Double check to see that nothing has been left behind."

Shortly, the fourth canoe appeared. Tom stepped off the trail. Jack seemed to glide over the roots and stones.

As he passed, he said, "I do love a short portage. It gets the blood running, eh?"

Back at the start, Tom found two bedrolls and three personal packs. Off to the side sat the fishing rods, three paddles, a lifejacket, and a cup. He pulled everything into the open.

In a couple of minutes, Borden, Lloyd, Ack, and Chet arrived. Lloyd and Borden shouldered the bedroll packs. The remaining three pulled on the daypacks and divided the other items.

"Do we have everything? Doug told me to double-check."

"Looks good to me," said Ack.

"Me too," said Chet. "Let's boogie."

With the others around, the portage didn't seem as long. After they finished, everyone brought out their cups and drank from the lake.

"Here, use mine," Doug handed his cup to Tom. "As far as I know, I'm healthy."

The cool water tasted pure. Water was water, but dipping a cup and drinking from a wilderness lake was special. A second cupful quenched his thirst.

Tom returned the cup, trying to be inconspicuous.

With volume, Doug yelled, "Who wants to go for a swim?"

A chorus of "I do's" rang out.

"Well, gentlemen. Put your cups away. Let's load up and paddle. If it's available, there's a great swimming campsite down the lake."

After Doug put his cup into his daypack, Tom stood in the water holding the canoe. Doug put the wanigan behind the bow seat and the bedroll pack behind the center thwart. Then, he stepped into the canoe and settled his daypack into the bow. Once Doug had his paddle in hand, Tom pushed off and settled into the stern seat.

"Where are we headed?"

"Between the islands. There's a narrow channel between the big rocks."

Paddling down the lake was fun. The air was crystal clear. The greens of the trees seemed sharper on Pen Lake. Tom felt he was leading a flotilla. The breeze strengthened, but it didn't impact his steering. From behind, the waves pushed the canoes. While he had to concentrate to keep on course, he felt alive. The wildness enthralled him.

As they approached the first campsite, two overturned canoes showed it was occupied. Far in front of them, a beach beckoned. As they got closer, Tom saw an orange sign. No canoes sat on the sand, and no tents were lurking amongst the tree trunks.

"Looks available," said Doug. "Raft up."

Once the four canoes were together, Doug said, "We start by carrying the packs and wanigans to the fire pit area. We need to build a temporary canoe rack on the beach using the driftwood. We don't want the canoes to touch the sand. Paddles go under the canoes. Lifejackets can be pillows or go under the canoes. Questions?"

Doug paused and, with emphasis, stated, "Once the canoes, the packs, and all of our gear are secure, we'll select tent sites. No cheating."

Tom saw several of the experienced boys roll their eyes and guessed that competition for sites was intense.

The arrival process went smoothly. Lloyd and Borden dragged small logs and created a canoe rack. The others carried packs and wanigans to the fire pit. Everyone helped carry the canoes.

When the Scouts gathered around the fire pit, the eager anticipation of his fellow campers surprised Tom.

"My canoe won the race." Doug said. "Since we're not sleeping by canoe, that means we have two winners - the staff and Tom, Borden, and Ack's tent. Both have first pick. Each will have a one-minute head start."

Tom saw Jack and Borden tense.

"GO!" Doug said.

Jack ran toward the point. Borden headed behind the fire pit. Tom and Ack followed.

At the first tent site, Borden said, "Too many roots."

He moved to a second and a third. Tom and Ack followed, surprised at Borden's pickiness.

"This one is the best. It's off the trail and has a nice layer of pine needles. We can string up a rope between these trees and set up the tent without a center pole. And we're not too close to the thunder box."

"What's the thunder box?" asked Tom.

"It's the open-air outhouse. Follow the main path up the hill. My guess is that once you get to the top of the rise, you'll see a wooden box. You pull up the lid and do your business. After you're finished, you put the wad back in the center of the campsite."

"What's the wad?" asked Ack.

"It's the toilet paper. One of the counselors carries a roll in their daypack. At a campsite, it sits near the kitchen. In the morning, sometimes there's a waiting line. Go early, eh?"

"Thanks for the tip."

Tom was thankful to have learned this information privately. If he'd waited until the call of nature had become intense, it could have been embarrassing.

"You guys get the pack and my daypack," said Borden. "I'll guard the tent site, eh?"

When Tom and Ack walked by, the other two groups were arguing about who had been first to which tent site.

Back at their site, Borden and Ack suspended the top of the tent while Tom staked its corners with stout sticks. He was looking forward to not having to maneuver around a center pole.

"Who wants which side?" asked Borden.

"Your choice," responded Tom.

"Okay. Let's see how the ground feels." Borden rolled around. "I'll take the left side."

"Ack, your choice," Tom said.

Ack lay in the center and rolled to the right.

"I'll take center."

As the boys unfurled their bedrolls, Borden said, "Spread your ground cloth so that it overlaps the flaps on the tent's inside edges. That way, we keep out bugs and rain. If you need to pad something, use your extra clothing under your sleeping bag. This is a good site. For some tent sites, it makes a difference."

"What do you do for a pillow?" asked Ack.

"I roll my pants inside my shirt."

"What about your lifejacket?" asked Tom.

"It's too big and bulky. I leave mine under the canoe with my paddle."

"Makes sense."

Tom fashioned a pillow-like tube using his extra t-shirt and pants.

Ack used his lifejacket. "This may not be the best, but I'll try it."

A few minutes later, Jack called the Scouts to the kitchen area. Once everyone assembled, he said, "Time for firewood."

"Don't we have woodies for that?" said Shaine.

"We do, but given that we can't go swimming until we have enough wood, I thought it might be nice if everyone helped. What do you think?"

"Makes sense to me," Ric said as he grabbed an ax.

"No axes," said Doug.

"How come?"

"This is a well-used campsite. We don't want to leave any scars on the area. Do we?"

"I guess not."

"There's driftwood along the shore," Doug said. "I'm sure there's dry wood in the forest. Sooner you finish, the sooner we swim."

"Follow me."

Borden headed off into the woods. Tom wondered where he was leading when he went past branches lying on the ground.

After going over a rise, Borden said, "Here's what we want, a stand of maple trees with dead, standing saplings beneath them."

Borden pointed to little trees one to three inches in diameter.

"You can pull them over."

With a sharp crack, Borden broke off a dead sapling at ground level.

"Get a bunch of these. My granddad showed me how to do this. Pile them together and drag the load back to the campsite. By pulling entire trees, you get more wood and don't have to make lots of trips."

Joyous tree crashing ensued, and in a few minutes, each boy had loaded his arms. While pulling entire trees across the forest floor was awkward, the others welcomed their arrival back at the fire pit. Stomping the dead trees into useable lengths was as much fun as crashing the trees.

Doug insisted they sort the pile by diameter.

"Great work," said Jack. "Well-organized stacks make it easier to manage the fire. Ready to swim?"

"Yes!" was the loud response.

After throwing off their t-shirts, Shaine and Ric ran into the water. Tom felt awkward stepping out of his shorts while wearing his racing suit, but when the others did the same, he relaxed. The sun had warmed the water. The sandy bottom felt delightful on his feet.

Rio got out his camera and snapped photos.

After a few minutes, most of the boys exited the water and sat on logs to air dry.

"Canoes coming," Jack said. "Be friendly. I bet they

wanted this place."

Everyone waved as the two canoes paddled past.

"Looks like they're headed to the portage rather than down the lake to a campsite," Doug said. "I hope they make Welcome before it gets dark."

"What do you mean?" asked Tom.

"The next campsites are on Welcome Lake. The portages are long, so they take more time than many think. The Rock Lake loop is popular for visitors to the Park, especially Europeans in their twenties."

"That seems pretty adventurous." Tom was fascinated. "How do they get their equipment?"

"The outfitters rent them everything for three or four nights. Most of them have hiked and camped. Very few have canoed and portaged, so they overestimate their abilities."

"Sounds like they're set up for problems."

"Sometimes. Most of them are fine. When they get home, they have a Canadian adventure story."

"I see."

"Just like the tales you'll tell your friends in the city, eh?"

"Yeah, I guess so."

Unexpectedly, the weight of not knowing where he was going in the fall crashed into Tom. He wondered if he would have any school friends with whom to share his stories.

After everyone was dry, Jack yelled, "Organization time. All hands to the fire pit."

When everyone had gathered, Jack said, "Starting tomorrow morning, Shaine and Chet are in charge. They'll cook breakfast. Everyone else stay away from the kitchen until it's time to eat. After the meal, the washers do dishes. Once they're finished, the GFDs pack up while the others roll their gear. Any questions?"

There were none.

"The GFDs read the day's maps and set the pace of travel. They pick the lunch spot and manage the food. They decide on the campsite for the night and cook dinner. When we bake, we'll ask for volunteers. Then the GFDs pack up for the night. On Saturday morning, the next group of GFDs — Borden, Ack, and Tom — will wake everyone up and cook breakfast. They lead us through the day. Anything need clarification?"

Again, no one asked any questions.

"The GFDs become the washers, the washers become woodies, and the woodies turn into GFDs. Today, the counselors are the GFDs. Ric and Lloyd are washers. Borden, Ack, and Tom are woodies. Tomorrow, Shaine and Chet are the guides. Borden's group are the washers, and Lloyd's group are our wood gatherers. Okay?"

It was clear to Tom. His fellow paddlers nodded.

"For most of you, this is review, but listen carefully," said Doug. "The campsite rules are simple. Number 1 – Except to use the thunder box, never leave the campsite area alone; always have a partner. Exploring is a good, but tell one of the staff where you're going. Number 2 - No one is ever barefoot; always have shoes on your feet unless you're swimming. Number 3 - No swimming without a staff person as a lifeguard. Number 4 - No wrestling, no pranks, no tree climbing. No stupid stuff. We don't want Jack to become our doctor. Any questions?"

Again, there was silence.

"Clear the kitchen," said Jack. "Once the fire is burning, dinner will be about half an hour."

The Scouts headed to the beach. Most began skipping stones. Tom and Ack sat on one of the logs.

"This is so different from the heather. There are so many trees and no mountains."

"Yeah. In New York, you see buildings and concrete. This is so peaceful."

The two boys shared more about their backgrounds.

Ack's parents had divorced after his father had an affair with his secretary. Ack's grandfather had welcomed him and his mother into the family estate where they'd lived in a small cottage. After his grandfather died, his mother received a letter saying that they were to leave the property at the end of the school year. They flew to Canada where Ack's grandparents lived in a two-bedroom apartment outside of Toronto. Until his mother found a job and a place to live, the four of them would be living in a very small space. Ack's grandfather had attended Catamount and arranged for Ack to go to camp for the summer.

"That's a lot to handle." After a pause, Tom smiled. "Canada seems like an okay place. But so far, I've only been in the Toronto airport and at Catamount."

"I was here a couple times as a little boy. Most of the time, my grandparents came to visit us in Scotland. They got along with my dad's father." Ack smiled. "What's your story?"

Tom's trauma spilled out. After his father's accident, he hadn't understood the tensions between his mother and his grandparents. After the funeral, his grandparents had moved overseas and he'd missed them tremendously. Several times he'd had to change schools because of poor grades and temper outbursts. When his mother started dating Pierre, Tom was glad for the distraction. Once they were married, Pierre was not sympathetic to Tom's academic struggles, which created hostility between the two of them. After he failed his exams and wasn't accepted into boarding school, life at home had become intolerable. In many ways, he was glad that his mother and Pierre were overseas. He hoped his grandmother would be able to solve his school problem. His grandfather's car accident had brought back memories of losing his father. While Tom was happy to

227

be away from the strain of his grandfather's health concerns, he missed not knowing what was happening.

"I thought my life was complicated," Ack said. "Yours seems more chaotic than mine."

Borden joined them.

"What've you been talking about?"

"Our grandfathers, our mothers, and how things change," responded Ack.

"My grandfather's a good guy," Borden said. "He's a great fisherman and avid hunter. He gets a moose every fall."

"Dinner time" rang out and everyone rushed to the fire area. The wanigans had been organized into a long serving station.

"Line up by the first letter of your last name," Rio commanded.

Tom was at the end. Without any fanfare, Doug handed Tom a faded yellow cup with a loop of string through its handle.

"I'll explain the string later."

With precision, Jack piled two huge serving spoons full of spaghetti onto each plastic plate. Doug added a pile of green salad, and Rio a brownie.

"One cup of bug juice to start," said Jack.

Everyone ate quickly.

"Seconds!" Doug called.

This time, each person received one large spoonful.

As the last serving emptied the big pot, Doug said, "Perfect. No thirds."

"Don't wander away," said Jack. "We need to review the dish process."

"We know it," Shaine said.

"Then, explain it," Jack barked.

"Let's wait until everyone has finished eating."

After the Scouts finished eating, Shaine stood and grabbed the wad. "Nature calls. Where's the thunder box?"

Borden pointed to the path. "It's up the hill."

After Shaine left, Jack stood. "Since Shaine knows this, I'll go over how we wash everything. Mean green is the washing bin. Start with the least dirty and finish by scrubbing the pots. Mellow yellow is the bin with the hot clean rinse water. If you want to rinse out your cup, do it at the beginning. Each person is responsible for his own cup. Any questions?"

There were no questions.

"We've got a while until it gets dark," Doug said. "Darkness means quiet. Sleep is important. In the morning, be quiet. For a day or two, some of you will wake up with the sun. It comes up about 5:30 am."

"We're the GFDs tomorrow," asked Chet. "What if we're sound sleepers?"

"I always get up early," said Doug. "I'll be sure you're up to cook breakfast. Anything else?"

Except for the washers, everyone else went down on the beach, and a rock skipping competition ensued. The rays of the setting sun warmed the beach. The glare off the water was intense.

As the sun sank behind the trees across the lake, the evening began to cool.

"Where does one pee?" Tom asked.

"Walk behind the tents," Borden said.

On his way back to the beach, Tom grabbed his wool shirt and his flashlight.

When he arrived, the other boys were headed toward their tents. Tom found himself the only camper.

"They're going to get shirts or stay in their tents. The bugs will be coming out, and the temperature is going to drop."

Doug was holding a steaming cup. "Do you want a cup of herbal tea?"

Tom thought for a moment.

"No, thank you."

"Probably a wise choice if you don't want to pee in the middle of the night. I've always had to pee at night. I love chamomile in the evening."

Doug put his cup to his lips.

"What about the string on my cup?"

"It's for looping over a branch near the kitchen. And you can use it to tie your cup to the canoe or your daypack. If it's visible on a tree limb or tied to something, it's harder to lose, eh?"

"Okay." Tom wondered if anyone would lose his cup on this trip. He guessed yes.

"Thanks for the donuts. I imagine you were a little pissed when we gave the extras to the ranger."

"No big deal." Tom wondered how Doug had read his mind.

"We should have asked, but the timing didn't work. The donuts will keep Catamount in his good graces. We want the Park people to look at us positively. Sometimes people complain about the camp groups."

"How come?" asked Tom.

"The noise. Some people see us breaking the rules and think it's unfair."

"What do you mean, unfair?"

"For the general public, the maximum number at a campsite is nine. We have ten on this trip. Most camps have cabins of eight or ten so that means trips are ten to fourteen with staff. That would mean using two campsites, which would be a problem on some lakes."

Doug sipped his tea.

"Camps have been in the Park since in early 1900s. We help the Park with service trips and seasonal clean-ups, and we want to keep our special status." Doug stood. "I'll be back in a minute."

As Tom sat alone, the sun's glow faded. In the distance, a loon called. A second answered down the lake.

Their echoing cries amplified the quiet. The silence felt welcoming. As Tom looked straight up, stars began to appear. He slipped on his wool shirt.

"Fire's out." Doug sat on a log and glanced upwards. "Ever seen the Milky Way?"

"Don't think so."

"If we're lucky, we'll see it before we get eaten by the mosquitoes."

As the blackness deepened, more stars filled the sky. Tom began to slap mosquitoes. A dull hum intensified from the woods. Tom had never seen so many stars, nor felt so many mosquitoes.

"I'm going to my tent." Doug said. "Feel free to stay. See you in the morning."

"Good night."

The ever-increasing points of light fascinated Tom. But after a few minutes, the bugs won. When he stood, he was surprised that he cast a faint star-shadow.

The darkness under the trees was not as intense as he had expected, and he didn't need his flashlight to find his way back to the tent.

"Can I come in?"

"Angle towards your sleeping bag," Ack said.

Tom dove into the tent.

"Killing time," Borden said. "I hope we can get all of them. There's nothing worse than that one mosquito that you can't get."

While the three boys attacked the intruders, they heard talking from the other Scout tents.

In the distance, Jack's voice rang out. "Tomorrow's a long day. It's quiet time. Go to sleep."

The bug hunt seemed endless. Every time they thought they had eliminated the blood-sucking pests, one or two would buzz when flashlights were turned off. Finally, they heard no buzzing in the darkness.

"I'm tired," Borden said. "I'm going to sleep."

"Me too," said Ack.

"Likewise."

Tom crawled into his sleeping bag, wiggling into the pine needles. The ground felt as soft as his bunk. Today had been good. His donuts had been a hit with his fellow Scouts and with Doug. The Park was beautiful. He had accurately read the map. He'd survived his first portage with no serious repercussions. His neck and arms were sore. The spaghetti had been tasty. There didn't seem to be any more mosquitoes in the tent.

What would tomorrow bring? The idea of a longer portage made him uneasy. New challenges would emerge. The whispers from the other tents died to silence. The loon calls echoed.

# Chapter 10
# Learning to Leapfrog

The crackling fire awakened Tom. His nylon cocoon was warm, but the ground beneath him felt harder than it had last night. The longer he was awake, the more uncomfortable he became. Ack and Borden were still asleep, so Tom wiggled into his clothes and crawled outside. The air was crisp. He pulled on his wool shirt and thought about going back into the tent for his long pants. Standing in a ray of sunshine, his legs warmed. Hopefully, the air would follow.

Carrying his damp shoes and almost-dry socks, he walked to the fire pit. Doug watched flames surround a small coffee pot.

"Good morning," said Doug quietly. "Put your shoes on. Remember the campsite rules and the fruit basket."

"Good morning." Tom stretched his hands to warm them from the small fire.

"It's a little early to wake up everyone."

Doug stood, fixated on the coffee pot.

"Can I have a cup of coffee?" Tom asked, knowing that the answer was probably negative.

"No. Campers aren't allowed to have coffee."

"But I drink it in the city."

"You're not in the city. You're on a Catamount canoe trip. Rules say no coffee, so no coffee."

Using a folded bandana to protect his fingers, Doug grabbed the coffeepot and filled his cup. "Do you want something hot? Herbal tea or hot chocolate?"

"Hot chocolate would be nice."

"I'll get some water. Put on your shoes. I know damp socks and wet shoes are no fun, but you don't want to hurt your feet. Remember the fruit basket."

This was the second time Doug referenced a fruit basket. Tom was perplexed, but he didn't want to look ignorant.

Carrying a small pot, Doug walked down to the lake. Balanced on a couple of large rocks, he filled the pot. Tom shivered as he pulled on his moist socks. His damp shoes reinforced the chill.

When he returned, Doug said, "Wet socks and shoes are uncomfortable. With repetition, you get used to them."

Doug placed a few sticks beneath the water pot.

"Hot water in a few minutes. I'll get out the hot chocolate. Get your cup."

Looped over a branch, the faded-yellow cup was hanging where Tom had left it. Doug handed Tom a spoon and opened a bag of brown powder.

"Two spoonsful. No more. It needs to last."

Doug sipped his coffee. Silently, they watched the pot of water. It was taking forever to boil. Doug added a couple of sticks. Flames shot up. In a minute, bubbles appeared. Doug ladled hot water into Tom's cup.

"Thanks."

After stirring his hot chocolate, Tom looked for a place to put the spoon.

"It's yours for breakfast. Lick it clean and put it in your pocket, or somewhere you won't lose it. We don't carry many extra utensils." said Doug.

After another sip of coffee, Doug glanced at the watch hanging from his belt.

"In ten minutes, I'll wake up the GFDs. I'm going down to the beach. Feel free to join me. The day's starting to warm."

Tom followed. The lake was a mirror. Wisps of low clouds hung on its surface. A single line of ducks swam and cut a widening V.

"A family of Mergansers," said Doug. "They're the most common duck in the Park."

Tom didn't know how to respond. He felt compelled to say something, so after an awkward silence, he asked, "What's the fruit basket? I didn't see that we packed one?"

"Sorry about that," Doug smiled. "I forget that there're new campers that don't understand the things I take for granted."

After a long sip of coffee, he said, "If I asked you to pack a fruit basket for a trip, what would you bring?"

"Apples, oranges," Tom paused. "Pears, bananas, peaches, pineapples, grapes, but they might get smashed."

"What if we wanted to make lemonade?"

"I'd bring lemons. They're pretty sturdy. Didn't they take them on long time sailing ships?"

"You're right. They did, to prevent scurvy. But they didn't bring sugar."

"Yuck."

"That's the idea."

Tom was puzzled.

"A canoe trip is like a fruit basket. We plan, we pack, we prepare, so everything will be good. Somewhere on the trip, something will happen. An accident, a fall, or something gets lost or broken. Stuff happens, the lemon. Instead of grabbing a sweet fruit, you get something sour. Understand?"

"I think so."

"Shoes and feet are a good example. Bare feet would be fine at most of the campsites. But what would happen if someone stepped on a piece of old glass or a rusted can?

Out here, we can't take them to the hospital, eh?"

"I see."

Tom vowed to wear his shoes.

"That's why you have dry shoes to wear around the campsite. Your feet need to dry out. I see that you've got wool socks. That's good. Wool keeps you warm when it's wet. But it takes forever to dry. Eventually, you get used to pulling on damp socks every morning."

Doug sipped his coffee and looked at his watch.

"Time to get the GFDs. You and your tent mates are washers today. You may want to roll before breakfast."

The sun had burned off the fog and the sky was a deep blue without clouds. Tom sipped his hot chocolate. There was so much to learn, but this was better than school. No books. No tests. No essays. No research reports. Everything was real.

Another line of Mergansers sliced across the lake. Suddenly, at the same instant, the entire parade of ducks dove under water. As they popped up one by one, Tom wondered how they coordinated. Maybe, someday, he'd study wildlife at school.

As soon as Doug awakened Shaine and Chet, their loud "wakey, wakey" stirred everyone. Tom walked off the beach. At the fire pit, the GFDs were opening the wanigans.

"Good morning," said Chet. "What are you doing?"

"You're not supposed to be here," Shaine said. "Get moving. You're in the way."

"I'm going to our tent. We're the washers, so I'm rolling before breakfast."

Tom hoped Shaine would become more pleasant as the morning progressed.

Back at their tent, Borden was outside rolling his sleeping bag.

"Tom, pull your stuff out of the tent. There's more space, so it's easier to roll."

"Thanks, Borden. How'd you sleep?"

"Like a log. How about you?"

"Okay. The ground was hard when I woke up."

"It was, but you get used to it pretty quick. My grandfather says that after a night or two in the bush, he could sleep on concrete."

Tom started rolling.

"Aren't you going to roll your wool shirt? It's going to be hot today."

"How do you know?"

"Yesterday was sunny with a strong northern breeze. Last night, it was clear and cool. It's sunny and clear now. That means today will be warm with less of a breeze."

"Okay. I believe you."

"You may want to stick your long sleeve shirt into the daypack."

"How come?"

"Sun and bug protection, if we need it."

"Thanks for the heads-up."

Ack stuck his head out of the tent.

"Thanks for the shirt info. I'm rolling inside."

After rolling their belongings, the three collapsed their tent. Tom carried their fully loaded pack to the beach. "Breakfast-is-ready" rang out from the fire pit. The meal was simple - oatmeal with raisins and brown sugar, Tang, and hot chocolate. Jack pontificated about oatmeal being the food of the gods.

After eating, Tom filled an empty pot with water and put it on the fire. Ack and Borden organized for clean-up. Once the water was hot, three inches went into the bottom of mean green with a few drops of liquid soap. They rinsed the bowls and spoons in the steamy water of mellow yellow. Everything air-dried on wanigan lids.

Rio moved like a bumblebee with his camera, snapping photos. He asked them to smile and look at the camera. Tom didn't think anyone would be interested in pictures of boys doing dishes.

"The dirty dishwater needs to be buried back in the woods," Borden said.

"I'll do it," Tom said.

"Go 200 feet or more into the forest and bury the soapy water six to eight inches below the surface," Doug said. "Afterwards, camouflage the area so no one knows you've been there. That's Leave-No-Trace camping."

Finding an appropriate spot was no problem. After brushing aside the mat of leaves, Tom dug into the black dirt. After burying the waste, he spread debris and small sticks to disguise the area. He hoped in a day or two no one would know that the area had been disturbed.

After Tom returned with the empty tub, he watched Shaine tell Chet how to load the kitchen wanigan. Everything had a specific place. They organized the second wanigan for lunch.

As others packed their tents and bedrolls, Tom took the bum-wad and walked to the thunder box. Sitting on a wooden box surrounded by trees was a different experience. He wondered if Rio had taken pictures of the thunder box. As he returned, Ack asked for the wad. Tom threw it to him with a comment about the nice view.

After everything was packed, the Scouts gathered on the beach. Jack asked, "Where are Shaine and Chet? They are the GFDs."

There was a chorus of "don't know."

"I'll go prod them," said Jack.

"I'll start the briefing."

Doug spread a Park map on top of a canoe.

"We begin by paddling across Pen Lake. Three portages take us into Welcome Lake. The first is short, about the same as Pen Lake. The next two are much longer. Assuming it's okay with the GFDs, we'll probably eat lunch at Welcome Lake. We'll finish the day at a campsite on Frank Lake."

"Do we have to stay there? What if we're slower?" Lloyd pointed at the map. "There are a bunch of campsites on Welcome."

"We have a reservation on Frank. But this time of year, the Park isn't crowded, so we have flexibility."

"That's good," said Lloyd. "The portages sound tough."

"They're fine. You'll be surprised at how quickly we move. Later in the summer, when the interior is crowded, we would be bound by our reservation. That's how the Park assures that each group has a campsite every evening. Let's get the canoes in the water."

Tom was pleased that they had flexibility. Like some of the others, he was apprehensive about the long carries.

As the canoes were being floated, Jack walked out from the woods.

"They're coming. Finally."

Chet carried their pack onto the beach and threw the wad to Doug.

"Nature called."

"Took your time," said Ric sarcastically.

"Great view. These things can't be rushed." Chet smiled.

"No, they can't." Ric nodded.

Doug handed the map to Shaine. "You and Chet are in charge. Anything you want to know? I did an overview of the route."

The two examined the map.

"Do we need to know specifics about the day?" Doug asked.

"We paddle. We portage. We paddle. Let's load the boats," Shaine said. "Rio, do we have new paddling groups?"

"No. We, the counselors, talked last night and decided it is better to polish your portaging technique by using the same people again today. Okay?"

This made sense to Tom.

"I'm going to take pictures of us loading the canoes," said Rio.

Tom was beginning to feel that the photo process was becoming a drag. He sensed he was not alone.

After loading their canoe, Doug said, "After the portages, I'll take the bow."

"Okay."

After a ten-minute paddle, Doug gathered the canoes.

"Shaine, Chet, do you want to say anything about the portage?"

Shaine looked at Chet.

"No. Let's get started."

"In that case, I have some ideas. Should we rotate the order of landing so that a different staff member is the last to leave the portage? If so, my canoe will be the last to unload."

"Sounds good to me," said Chet.

"Any questions about anything?" Doug asked.

A silence answered.

"Jack, take the lead," said Doug. "This portage is 430 meters."

The portage began at the end of a narrow stream. As they waited their turn, Tom saw that some still tried to keep their feet dry while others stepped freely into the water.

"Do dry feet make any difference as you carry?" Tom asked.

"Some say 'yes' and some say 'no'." Doug smiled. "Even if I tried to stay dry, my feet would get wet."

Knowing his luck, Tom decided not to worry about keeping his feet dry. He knew they'd get wet.

Before they landed, Doug asked, "Do you want any bug dope?"

"How bad will the bugs be?"

Doug handed Tom a small bottle.

"I imagine they'll be bad. It's warming up. There won't be any breeze in the trees. The path yesterday was pretty wide and carried a nice draft."

Tom squeezed a few drops into his palm.

"Use it sparingly. We don't have an unlimited supply. Don't get any in your eyes and try to keep it away from plastics. It may melt them."

Tom rubbed the liquid on his face, neck, and arms.

"Don't forget your ears and your legs."

Tom took a few more drops before he returned the bottle.

Wanting to demonstrate his willingness, Tom said, "I'll start with the wanigan."

"Thanks. Take it halfway and then come back for the bedroll pack and the paddles. This way, we both do an extra half and neither of us has to do two complete walks. Understand?"

The idea made sense. Tom wondered how the other boats were organizing. As he watched, he suspected that only Jack and Lloyd had a plan.

When they finally landed, they found a wanigan, several paddles, a couple of lifejackets, and the fishing rods sitting randomly.

"Exactly what I expected. It's a mess," said Doug. "Hold the canoe. I'll put our extra stuff off the side of the trail."

After unloading, Doug helped Tom get the box on his back and the tump on his forehead.

"Off you go. I'll be right behind you."

The leather strap at Tom's hairline felt better than it had yesterday. However, after a hundred meters, Tom's neck began to scream. The leather ground into his forehead, and he was sweating heavily. He was thankful that he had accepted Doug's offer of insect repellent when he noticed that the swarming mosquitoes didn't land on his skin, although he did gag when he swallowed a few of the flying beasts.

"We're about halfway," said Doug. "Drop the wanigan and go get the rest of our stuff."

Tom carefully swung the wanigan to the ground. Without weight, the walk back to the beginning was delightful. The sunlight danced through the leaves. The birds chirped in the canopy. Several chipmunks scurried across the path. The forest was alive. He walked quickly and the bugs didn't have time to concentrate on him.

As Tom finished organizing the stuff at the landing area, Borden, Ack, and Lloyd appeared.

"We saw your wanigan. Good thinking," said Lloyd. "We're the cleanup crew."

"Jack was right," said Borden. "We left gear behind. We didn't plan."

"Thanks for sorting out this stuff," said Ack. "Let's get started."

The four picked up everything and began the walk. With others around, time passed more quickly, and the bugs didn't seem so bad. Before too long, the sparkle of a lake appeared.

"Got everything?" questioned Jack.

"Yes," said Lloyd.

The canoes were floating. Tom stepped through the mud and lowered his pack into their canoe. The black ooze wanted to suck off his shoes.

"Let's get started. The bugs are attacking. We start the next portage over there." Shaine pointed to the far side of a small lake.

"Don't forget your fishing rods." Borden almost threw them at Chet and Ric. "I hope you catch something."

The canoes rafted together in the middle of the lake. Everyone drank. The sun was bright and a gentle breeze cooled them. After their morning workout the Scouts were feeling justified in relaxing.

"Do you want the good news or the bad news?" Doug

asked.

The boys' attention riveted on Doug.

"The good news," Ric said, sounding suspicious.

"The map is wrong, so we don't have to trudge through a long swampy section of the portages."

With a sense of unease, Shaine asked, "So what's the bad news?"

"Instead of two more portages, there's only one. It's a long one."

A collective groan floated over the calm of the little lake.

"How far?" asked Chet.

"2200 meters."

"No way," said Shaine.

"If you'd asked for a briefing as you studied the map, you would have known. The GFDs are responsible for planning the day," said Doug.

"You set us up," Chet said.

Doug smiled.

"Consider this a learning opportunity. The ranger told us the Park rerouted the portage. The new one bypasses a little pond and two sections of knee-deep muck. Those sections were known for eating shoes."

"This means that we need to plan carefully," said Jack. "GFDs, what's your plan?"

Shaine and Chet looked at each other and shrugged their shoulders.

"Suck it up and carry," Chet said, hesitantly. "Jack says long portages build character. Right, Jack?"

"You're reading my mind. But I think that there might be a better plan." Jack turned to Tom. "2200 meters is about a mile and a third."

"That's a killer," Ric said. "That's a long way to carry."

Ric said what most of the boys were thinking. Tom felt the beginnings of apprehension.

"Can I make a suggestion?" asked Rio.

"I guess so." Shaine's voice showed that he questioned what a new, foreign counselor could add. Tom wondered as well.

"We could do like what we did on the staff canoe trip," Rio said. "We had a very long carry. A 3500-meter portage up and down a big hill. We frog leaped. We divided the portage into four stages and we stopped every 875 meters. Many carried a different something for each stage."

Rio let everyone think about his idea.

"I think we could frog leap to break this portage into three stages of 733 meters."

The two GFDs looked at each other. Shaine nodded to Chet.

"Sounds good to us," Chet said. "Each canoe can come up with its own plan."

"We have an extra pack in Jack's boat and mine," said Doug. "Is it fair for us to always have an extra walk while carrying group equipment?"

After the Scouts argued for several minutes, Doug stepped in. "Shall I offer a suggestion? Let's do two legs. It's easier to organize."

The boys accepted Doug's guidance. Tom understood the group's rotations because he and Doug had done this on the last portage. Again, he volunteered to carry the wanigan for the first half. When Doug asked him if he wanted to carry the canoe for the second, he accepted the challenge.

"My boat will start last," Doug said. "I'll be the sweep person."

"We'll go first because we have the lunch wanigan." Jack grinned.

"There's a swimming beach at the end of the portage," Doug said. "Shall we get started?"

The portage went smoothly. This time, Tom's muscles didn't hurt as much with the wanigan. At his turn for the canoe, Doug showed him how to use a lifejacket to pad his shoulders and neck. As he walked with the boat, he found that a slow trot kept it from rocking too much.

The canoe seemed to get heavier the longer Tom walked. As with his first wanigan carry, just as he thought he had reached the end of his endurance, Welcome Lake glistened through the trees. On the gravel beach, Jack teepeed the canoe, and Tom walked out from under it. He felt a swell of success. With sweat dripping, he marched straight into the water to join the others cooling themselves.

"Lunch is ready!" called Jack. "Line up by last letter of your last name."

F meant Tom was in the middle. His W had meant that he was usually at the end of lines. He appreciated the change.

While the sun and the breeze dried their clothing, the boys devoured PB & J sandwiches and crunched on apples. They moaned about the roots and rocks and complained about the weight of their loads, but Tom sensed that everyone was proud of their accomplishments. Listening to the back and forth, he suspected that not everyone had carried a canoe. Successfully carrying a canoe meant he was no longer a newbie.

As they prepared for the afternoon's paddle, Doug said, "Your turn for the stern."

Tom's stomach knotted. On a trip, being a camper stern man was an honor. In the protected bays at camp, he could keep a canoe in a straight line. But, could he steer a loaded canoe on an open lake in a breeze this strong? The last thing he wanted to do was look incompetent.

As they loaded the packs, Doug yelled. "We'll be on the water for an hour or more. Hats and sunscreen, eh?"

Doug threw Tom an orange bottle. He squeezed goo on his arms and legs.

"Don't forget your nose and ears. You don't want them to fry."

Tom rubbed on more lotion.

When everyone was sun protected, Doug said, "GFDs, lead off. We'll take the tail. Tom, wait a minute or two."

After the other three canoes were moving, Tom said, "Let's paddle. Please start on the left."

After a dozen strokes, the canoe reached cruising speed. A breeze pushed the canoe to the left. Tom's steering correction took a little longer, and he struggled to stay in time with Doug. To his chagrin, Tom accidentally splashed him with his paddle on his forward motion.

"Thanks for cooling me down," Doug said.

After about five minutes, Tom said, "Switch sides."

Paddling on the left was not Tom's natural strength. After only two minutes, Tom called to switch sides and struggled to stay on course. Although their canoe was last, he sensed that everyone could see how poorly he was paddling. He concentrated on keeping the canoe moving in a straight line. His back hurt, and his arms were sore. Switching sides often eased Tom's muscles, but he knew too much alternating was poor form.

Way past time, Shaine called, "Time for a break. It's a hot one."

The four canoes drifted together. Because Tom had fixated on his paddling, he hadn't realized that they had crossed the entire lake. In front of them, the mouth of a small river opened.

"You did a nice job, Tom," said Doug.

"Thanks," said Tom, not believing him.

"Can I make a suggestion?" Doug said.

"Sure." *Here it comes*, thought Tom. *He's going to tell me I'm horrible.*

"Watch my paddle."

Doug did a short stroke and keeping the blade in the

246

water, sliced it forward with no apparent correction. It looked effortless. Doug did it again, and then a third time.

"I'm sure that you've seen this before with George. It's the Canadian stroke. The correction is a natural part of the paddle's return for the next stroke. It's all in the blade's angle. It takes practice."

From a neighboring boat, Borden said, "And an insane amount of attention. That's why I don't like paddling in the stern. It takes too much mental effort."

Shrugging his shoulders, Tom smiled.

"You'll get it," said Doug. "GFDs, is it time to move?"

"I guess so." Shaine nodded to his canoe mates.

"Let's go for a paddle!" Ric shouted.

"Onward to glory!" Chet yelled.

Tom adjusted his paddling and found it easier to keep the canoe headed where he intended. Having more control, he relaxed a little. Going upstream required concentration to keep the current from grabbing and turning the canoe.

While the blue above was awe-inspiring, the greens and browns of marsh grasses focused the eye on the immediate. In front of them, a family of ducks fled up the creek, fluttering, stopping, and flurrying. A beaver lodge sitting among the lily pads sparked talk about the endurance of the old-time fur traders. Tom was amazed that they paddled from sunrise to sundown, and each man portaged 180 pounds at a time.

The river narrowed and began to twist at times, almost reversing its direction. Seeing what was around the next bend was exciting. Tom worked hard to stay out of both the downstream current and the dense lily pads.

At the next wide area, Shaine called for a break.

"GFDs, what's coming up?" Doug asked.

The three examined the map.

"We continue paddling upstream through a long marsh," Shaine said.

"What does that mean?" asked Doug.

"No wind and, maybe, lots of bugs," said Chet.

Under his breath but loud enough to be heard, Shaine mumbled, "What a drag."

"You're spot on," said Doug. "I'm glad you are in control. Take the lead. We'll be the tail."

The stream continued to wind like a snake's back. After Doug did a cross draw to prevent the bow from ramming into the steep mud bank, the two communicated constantly. Tom appreciated Doug's skill and saw that Rio had been right. Precise maneuvering required strong teamwork.

Because of the tall grass and the creek's twists, the lead canoe was often out of sight. When they came around the next bend, the canoes were rafted below a sizeable beaver dam.

"What's the plan?" Doug asked.

"A short portage," Chet said.

"Is there a path?"

"Don't see one," said Shaine. "This sucks."

"Let's organize two lines so we can lift the canoes over the dam," Doug said.

"Sounds good," said Chet. "Who's first?"

"My boat," said Jack.

"Can my boat be the last?" Rio stepped into the grass with his camera. "Photograph time. Everyone please always smile."

While Shaine held the canoe, Jack and Lloyd stepped onto the dam. Chet and Ric followed, forming two parallel lines. Shaine pushed the bow of one canoe to them and they lifted the canoe up and over.

"Shaine, push the next canoe over and take a place in the line," said Jack.

The second canoe went up and over.

"We're next," said Doug. "Step carefully. You don't want to slide into one of the holes in the dam. The water gets deep in a hurry."

While Rio scrambled around taking pictures, everyone smiled awkwardly. Balancing on the slippery sticks was a challenge. Both the third and fourth canoes moved quickly, but reloading the floating canoes was crowded and confusing. As the boys scrambled from branch to branch, the disturbed water turned a muddy brown. Ric lost his footing and slid into the chest-deep soup. When he climbed into his canoe, the top part of his t-shirt was white and the bottom was the color of chocolate milk. Shaine and Chet laughed.

"It's the Mud Man, the monster from the muck."

"Is that being brotherly?" Doug snapped.

After an awkward silence, he continued, "GFDs take the lead."

The canoes crossed the little lake and reentered the winding stream. After a dozen turns, the water ended at a portage.

"It's only 320 meters," Shaine said. "A short one."

As the canoes in front of them unloaded, Tom said, "I'm in the stern. I'll take the canoe."

"No argument from me," Doug said.

This portage felt better. The boat didn't seem as wobbly or as heavy as it had on the previous carry.

After loading the canoes, they paddled through two oval lakes connected by a narrow gap. Halfway across the second, they paused while Shaine and Chet studied the map.

"This is Frank Lake. We need to find the campsite," said Shaine. "We're done for the day."

Finding the campsite was a challenge because it was tucked up a narrow, marshy bay. After tromping through knee-deep mud and climbing a shoulder-high ledge, Tom was not impressed. The tent sites were small, and there was no swimming area.

"GFDs, what do you think?" asked Doug.

"It's not great, but it'll do," said Chet.

"Yeah," said Shaine. "It'll work. It'll be tight, but that's okay."

"Are there any other options?" asked Jack.

"This is the only campsite on the lake," said Shaine.

"May I make a suggestion?" said Doug. "It's only mid-afternoon. While this is our reserved site, if we do the next portage, we'll have better choices on Lake Louisa. We moved faster than we'd planned. Louisa is a big lake with well over twenty campsites. This time of year, I doubt that it'll be crowded. Moving also puts us ahead of schedule, which is always a good thing."

"Sounds good to me," said Lloyd. "This one will be really buggy."

"How long is the portage?" asked Ric.

Looking at the map, Chet said, "It's almost 2000 meters. That's long."

"That's long." Shaine stared at his fellow Scouts. "I say we stay."

"This campsite sucks," said Borden.

The breeze died, and mosquitoes began to swarm.

"Too many bugs," said Ack. "I say we move and soon."

"Shall we take a vote?" asked Jack. "The counselors won't vote. It's up to you."

The vote was five to two in favor of traveling. Tom was glad to be moving on.

After a ten-minute paddle, the group decided to split the long portage into two sections. Tom would start with the canoe and return for a bedroll pack. His balance carrying the boat was getting better. Handling the big pack and two paddles seemed easy compared to either the wanigan or the canoe. As he twisted over roots down the steep steps to the lake, he realized he wasn't hurting as much as before. Completing two long portages in one day gave Tom a sense of real accomplishment.

When Doug placed the canoe into the waters of Lake Louisa, he said, "This has been a good day. We've learned to portage efficiently."

Many of the Scouts smiled.

"Can we pose for pictures?" Rio began to unpack his camera.

"Let's not," said Shaine. "I'm hot. I want to swim."

"Me too," said Chet.

"I'm hot as hell," said Ric.

"Maybe there would be better pictures at the campsite," said Borden.

"Okay, but the light is perfect," said a disappointed Rio.

"Let's paddle and find a campsite," Shaine said. "This has been a killer day. And, I have to manage cooking dinner."

Tom saw Doug and Jack exchange a glance.

"The closest campsite is on the point at the mouth of this bay," said Shaine.

On a mirror-like surface, the canoes cut shallow wakes that curled to the gray-green mosses and sharp, narrow pines along the edge. As they rounded the point, Lake Louisa opened. To the east, it stretched beyond the horizon and was dotted with islands of all sizes. To the west, a small mountain ended its expanse. Another bay beckoned across its width. The campsite sat above a rocky ledge with a diving platform.

While unloading, the Scouts were excited to see multiple tent sites and a well-defined kitchen area surrounded by sitting logs. Because of a thick layer of pine needles, good sleeping areas were plentiful. Ack, Borden, and Tom selected a site back in the forest. Using a center pole leaning against a tree, the three erected their tent quickly and were the first to leap into the cool, clear water.

"Cannonball contest!" Ack yelled.

His splash sprayed Rio and Jack.

"No big problems," Rio wiped the water drops off his camera.

Shaine did a flip.

"I can spin around more than anyone."

"No way," said Borden.

The contest began.

Rio photographed the turns, the splashes, and the boys' grins. Like many of the Scouts, Tom flopped on his butt. The final two were Shaine and Ack. The group declared Shaine the winner after he completed a one and half, going in headfirst.

"Anybody hungry?" called Doug.

The Scouts encouraged the GFDs to speed dinner.

After dinner prep was underway, Doug asked, "Who wants to help bake a couple of apple pies?"

Tom, Ric, and Ack volunteered. They peeled, cored, cut, and mixed apples with sugar and cinnamon. Then they blended margarine and flour to create the pie crust.

"How do we roll the dough?" asked Tom.

"We use what we have," Doug said. "What do we have that's long, and also flat?"

"A canoe paddle," said Ack.

Using the paddle's shaft, Ric rolled the dough into flat circles on top of a wanigan lid. Using the paddle blade, he slid the crusts into pie pans. Tom spooned in the apple mixture. Ack placed the top crust and cut openings for the steam to escape. Afterwards, the uncooked pies were placed safely away from the kitchen so they wouldn't be underfoot during dinner.

By the time the pots of chicken stew and rice were taken off the fire, Tom was starving and wolfed down his first serving. Everyone had seconds, two spoons of rice and one of stew. When thirds were called, Tom was one of the six still eager to eat. After looking at the pots, he doubted that there was enough for all six.

"Circle up," said Jack. "We'll raffle."

The boys formed a circle, shot fingers, and counted around.

"Ric, you win. We'll start with half a serving spoon of rice and the same of stew."

Tom was fourth and received half a spoon of rice and a dab of sauce.

As he mopped up the last of his meal, Tom remembered that he and his tent mates were washers. Carefully, so no waste polluted the lake, he filled the cooking pots with water and put them on the fire. Because the bowls had been cleaned completely by the hungry campers, the process of mean green and mellow yellow went quickly.

When washing was completed, Doug called the bakers back to the fire.

"Ric, place a reflector oven in front of the fire's flames. Tom, off to the side, build a bed of coals. Ack, get the pies."

"Why do we have only one reflector oven?" Ric asked.

"I brought a Fry-Bake. It rests on the coals, and you build a small fire on its top. I want to see which is better."

Once everything was ready, Doug placed the pies in baking position.

"Who's managing which pie?"

"I'll watch the reflector," said Ack.

"You need steady flames, not a roaring blaze but more than low coals."

"I'll do the Fry-Bake," said Tom.

"Put the lid on the pan and start a small fire on its top. It can't get too big, and you don't want it to go out."

Tom nodded.

"How long until the pies are ready?" Lloyd asked.

"About 40 minutes. Chet, Ric, this is perfect place to try your luck. Louisa has lake trout."

With an eager audience, the two started casting into

the lake.

Doug oversaw the bakers. Ack managed the flames for the reflector oven. Tom added a stick or two to the twiggy fire. He stared intently at the Fry-Bake, not wanting to be blamed for undercooking or overcooking.

Borden wandered up from the lakeside. "Where did the Fry-Bake come from?"

"From my time at NOLS," said Doug.

"What's NOLS?" asked Ack.

"It's the National Outdoor Leadership School. It's in the Rockies. I did a semester last fall."

"That sounds exciting."

"It was great. We backpacked in the high mountains, spent six weeks in the southwestern deserts in Utah, and came back to Wyoming for a month on skis and snowshoes."

As Doug recounted the skills he learned and the different environments, Tom was intrigued. NOLS sounded like a school that he'd actually enjoy.

"Check the pies."

The crust was browned and the insides were boiling.

After the pies cooled, Doug cut them into sixths. They conducted another raffle for the choice of first piece. Tom was glad to see that the pieces of pie were placed into hands so no bowls or spoons would need cleaning. As the boys wolfed down their pie, Rio took pictures.

"This is fantastic," Ric said.

"It's mighty tasty," said Lloyd. "I'm impressed."

While the crust wasn't flakey, Tom loved the sugary apples.

"I think we've found our bakers." said Borden.

"I agree," said Shaine. "We don't want to mess with success."

As the compliments continued, Tom felt a sense of well-being.

As dusk darkened to night, Doug announced, "Shaine

and Chet, it's time to pack for the night. Tom, Ack, and Borden, you're the GFDs tomorrow."

"What's the menu?" Borden asked.

"Granola and pancakes for breakfast. Lunch is PB & J on rye crisp with oranges. Beef stroganoff for dinner. After dinner, we'll need to bake bannock."

"I'm so glad that the bakers are the GFDs." With an edge to his voice, Shaine said, "I'd be afraid to mess up our first bannock."

All eyes focused on Tom, and he felt an unwelcome sense of expectation fall on his shoulders.

"What's bannock?" asked Ack.

"It's bread that's easy to cook and hearty to eat," said Jack. "You'll do fine."

"Time for bed," Doug said. "We've got portages tomorrow, so we need our beauty rest."

"Getting up early for your coffee?" Tom asked.

"Of course. It's the best time of the day."

"Can you wake me?"

"Sure."

"Be quiet if it's early." Borden grinned. "I like my sleep."

"Me too," said Ack. "My sleeping bag is calling. Good night."

The Scouts sat staring into the fire. A loon called. A second loon answered. Their echoing continued.

"Their sound is hypnotic," Tom said.

"It is," Lloyd said. "You hear nothing like this in the city."

After a few minutes, the mosquitoes began to buzz more intently.

"I'm out of here. Too many bugs. They can feast on the Yankee." With a flourish, Shaine led Chet, Lloyd, and Ric to their tents, leaving Tom the only camper.

The darkness was intense, but it felt peaceful, almost protective. Without the others, Tom felt he could relax.

The water lapped at the rocks, and branches whispered softly. After a few minutes, the flames died to glowing coals.

"Time for shuteye. Head to your tent," Doug said. "I'll douse the fire. You did well today. Have a restful night."

Tom tumbled into the tent. With limited conversation but intense focus, the three killed the flying nuisances and slid into their sleeping bags.

The day had been long and Tom's neck muscles were sore. The pine needles cushioned him. He felt that his success at carrying the canoe and baking pies had earned his place as an equal member of the Scouts. He wondered why Shaine had been quiet for most of the day; he'd expected him to be a dominating GFD. He appreciated Doug's last comment, but he worried about what new demands being a leader would bring.

From far down the lake, the cries of the loons whispered.

# Chapter 11
## Accidents

Bird calls stirred Tom at the first light of dawn. Again, the ground that had felt so welcoming the night before did not feel so soft this morning. He twisted and turned, wondering what time it was. When he heard sticks breaking, he dressed and exited the tent.

"You're up early," Doug said. "I was going to wake you once I'd made coffee."

"The birds," said Tom.

"In another day or two, you'll get used to them."

"Maybe. It's so quiet out here, I hear every little sound. It's so different from the city."

"Yes." Doug handed Tom the coffee pot and a small two-liter pot. "Please go fill these."

Tom returned and placed them on the grill above the fire.

"What color was the sky?" asked Doug.

"Not sure. Why do you ask?"

"Go check. Then I'll tell you why."

In a few minutes, Tom returned. "I've never seen the sun rise over the trees. The sky was reddish in the east. After the sun rose above the treetops, the clouds turned white."

"Red sky in morning, sailors take warning. Ever hear this?"

"Don't think so. What's it mean?"

"It's an old weather saying. 'Red sky in morning,

sailors take warning. Red sky at night, sailors delight.' It's accurate most of the time."

When the water boiled, Doug scooped six spoonsful of coffee into the hot water and placed the pot on the edge of the grill.

"It takes a few minutes for the coffee to brew. Go get your cup. I'll get the hot chocolate powder."

Tom made a cup of hot chocolate. Doug stirred the coffee pot, waited a minute, banged the spoon on the side of the pot, waited another minute, and poured himself a cup of coffee. Tom hadn't realized that making coffee was such a process.

"I love a cup of coffee in the morning." Doug glanced at his watch. "Let's go see what the wind's doing. In ten minutes, you can wake up your fellow GFDs."

The sun was warming the rocks. A gentle breeze was stirring.

"From what direction is the breeze?" asked Doug.

The sun had risen to Tom's right, the east. That meant they were facing north. The breeze was moving up the bay behind him.

"From the south?"

"You're right. What does that mean?"

Tom guessed, "We don't have a headwind?"

"You are correct in part. Does it mean anything else about the weather?"

"I don't know. Kent told me about clouds and fronts at campcraft, but I don't remember much."

"There's more to this weather forecasting ditty. 'Wind from the south, rain in your mouth. Wind from the east, weather's a beast. Wind from the north, sun sallies forth. Wind from the west, weather's the best.'"

"That's neat. Does it work all the time?"

"Most of the time. It's not as accurate when it's hot in the middle of the summer."

Doug launched into an explanation of moisture in the

atmosphere, cloud types, and warm and cold fronts. Tom realized that there was a lot to learn about the weather and listened intently.

"Does this mean that we'll have rain tomorrow?"

"Probably. It may start tonight. We'll see. It's time for you to get Borden and Ack. I'll meet you at the wanigans, eh?"

Tom's fellow GFDs were stirring. He told them he'd make hot chocolate.

"Where are your cups?"

"Next to the wanigans."

"Your hot drinks await."

A few minutes later, Ack and Borden joined Doug and Tom in the kitchen area.

After everyone had a hot drink, Borden yelled, "Wakey, wakey. We're wasting daylight. Up and at 'em."

The first part of breakfast prep was easy, adding water to the powdered milk and dividing the granola into ten bowls. Tom built up the fire while Ack mixed the pancake batter and Borden created syrup using brown sugar and maple flavoring.

The Scouts munched on their granola as they arrived. Borden started making pancakes on the griddle.

"Two to start," said Jack.

Not everyone wanted a third, but Ric, Lloyd, and Borden were happy to finish their sixth. Rio continued to be annoyingly in the wrong place at the wrong time as he photographed their breakfast.

Once they finished cooking, the three retreated to roll their belongings and pack their tent. Borden carried the pack to the canoes, while Tom and Ack organized the lunch wanigan. They began to redistribute food to balance the wanigans.

"Could we combine the food into one wanigan and repack to organize a one-trip portage?" asked Tom.

"We could put two bedrolls and a tent inside the

empty wanigan and eliminate one pack," said Borden.

"After that, we'd have to stuff the other bedrolls and tent into the two canvas packs," Ack said. "Is that possible?"

"Don't know until we try."

Doug yelled, "Scouts gather at the fire pit. The GFDs have an idea."

Borden explained their reorganization plan. Everyone seemed to support the idea.

"Sounds good," said Jack. "Bring your stuff to the open area by the canoes."

Half of the plan worked. Ric helped Jack reorganize the kitchen and lunch wanigans by packing more food into them. That created an empty wanigan into which Lloyd crammed two bedrolls. Ack refolded one of the tents so it fit under the flap of their pack. They had eliminated one bedroll pack. Tom had forgotten about the empty bedroll pack, and it got jammed into one of the remaining big canvas packs. They still had eleven loads for ten people. An air of disappointment hung over the Scouts.

Shaine predictably articulated what some were feeling. "This was a stupid idea. I bet it was something crazy from south of the border. All we did was waste time."

"This was a nice try," said Doug. "Maybe it will work later in the trip."

"We did take off one of the big loads," said Rio. "We are trying to strive for maximum efficiency in all that we undertake. Are we not?"

"It would be nice to be able to do a one-carry portage," said Jack. He turned to Shaine. "While I don't mind strolling through the woods, I am sure there are others who are not as appreciative of nature's glory."

Shaine stared at Jack. "And we didn't consider the daypacks, the life jackets, and the paddles."

"Yeah," said Chet. "That's what bogs us down."

Doug spoke sharply, "It was good thinking. Not all ideas work out the first try. As we portage, think about efficiency. Now, I suggest we rearrange so the eleven loads are equally balanced."

With only minor repacking, everything was ready.

Doug opened the day's maps.

"Since we're all here, I'll do the daily briefing, eh?"

Doug looked at the three GFDs. Tom nodded, as did Borden and Ack.

"After a short paddle, we have a 1460-meter portage into North Grace Lake. After this delightful stroll in the woods, we paddle two-and-a-half miles to two more portages. The first is only 170 meters and the second, 810, gets us into McGarvey Lake."

Borden pointed at McGarvey. "Would that be a good time for lunch?"

"Probably. Depends on how people feel."

Tom would have liked more precision, but he was beginning to appreciate the need to be flexible.

Doug continued, "After lunch, we paddle about a mile and a half to the start of our two service portages."

"What do we do there?" asked Tom. "Are the GFDs in charge?"

"If you don't mind, Jack and I will take control at that point."

The three nodded to Doug.

"These are longer, less-traveled portages. Our job is to make sure they're clear. This may involve cutting up a downed tree or fixing a path through a swampy area. That's why we brought the equipment."

"Do you mean the axes?" Ric asked. "I won the chopping contest last summer at the Lumberjack Roundup. I'm ready."

"No problem," said Doug. "If there's ax work to do, you're our man."

Ric smiled.

"Do we have new canoe groups today?" Tom asked.

"Yes." Jack motioned to Rio, who read from a small notebook.

"Tom and Chet will paddle with me. In Jack's canoe will be Shaine. Borden will paddle with Doug. And, finally, Ack and Ric will be with Lloyd, who will begin the day in the stern."

Tom sighed, but he'd make the best of it.

Once their canoe was packed and in the water, Tom said, "I'll start in the middle."

"Thanks," said Chet. "We'll switch after lunch."

Rio nodded and began arranging his waterproof camera box and the map.

"I have to be ready to know where we are going and also be ready to take photographs for the Director."

"As GFD, shouldn't I have the map?" Tom asked.

"Yes, that is correct. But I must see it. You can turn around."

The canoe rocked repeatedly as Rio moved his camera box and the map from place to place in his search for optimum positioning. Tom was annoyed by the time their canoe started paddling.

At the first portage, the three agreed to leapfrog. Tom was to carry the wanigan and the canoe.

"Yesterday, we learned my camera box fits perfectly on top of the wanigan, so we do not have an extra load to worry about carrying an extra time."

When Rio placed his box behind his head, Tom tried not to roll his eyes.

The portage went smoothly, including the midway load exchange. The mosquitoes were manageable, individually biting but not swarming. The forest was alive with dappled sunlight. Birds called. Chipmunks scrambled among the rocks and roots. Both the wanigan and the canoe felt more secure on his back. Tom sensed

262

that the portage had gone more quickly than the last one, but with loads being switched midway, it was hard to tell.

On the lake in front of them, a strong crosswind created wicked white caps.

"Lifejackets," said Doug. "Be careful."

Rio signaled to Doug, and the two stepped away to talk.

When Rio returned, quietly, he asked, "Tom, Chet, do either of each of you wish to paddle in the stern? I am not comfortable with the windiness."

"Not me," said Chet.

"I'll try," said Tom.

After a tippy and splashy slog across the windswept lake, they made it to the calm behind a point. The crossing had been stressful. Each of the three was wet, but Tom felt he'd handled it well.

"We'll stay close to shore. The trees will block the wind so there will be a narrow strip of calm water along the shore. We'll have easier paddling," said Doug. "Stay close together."

As they started, Jack asked, "How about 20 questions?"

"Excellent," said Ric. "What are the categories?"

"How about people, animals, books, and movies?" asked Chet.

"Sounds good to me," said Jack. "I'll start."

"Is it a person?" shouted Lloyd.

"Yes."

"Is the person alive?" asked Shaine.

"No."

"Is this person a character in a book?" asked Ack.

"No. That's your third question."

Not wanting to look foolish, Tom listened. The boys determined it was a historical figure, and, on the 15th question, Lloyd guessed Alexander MacKenzie and was correct.

"Who's he?" Tom asked.

"He was one of the first to go across North America to both the Pacific and Arctic Oceans. Everybody knows that," said Shaine.

Choosing not to react, Tom focused on paddling. His muscles seemed stronger. His Canadian stroke felt more natural. Going in a straight line was easier.

At the next portage, the short one, Tom carried the canoe and a daypack. Chet managed the wanigan with Rio's camera box. Rio carried the bedroll pack and their paddles.

Once the canoes were reloaded, Doug said, "Congratulations. With Borden carrying both a wanigan and a big pack, we did a one-carry portage. Thanks to Tom's suggestion."

"And Doug gets credit for helping Ric and me tie our fishing rods to the canoes," said Chet.

"That's what really helped," said Shaine loudly. "Good Canadian ingenuity."

After a short paddle, they faced the longer portage.

"How do we want to do this one?" Tom asked. "We did a one-carry on the last one, but that was short."

"Let's switch halfway," said Chet. "I'll do the wanigan and the bedroll. I'd rather not do the canoe. My shoulders are bony."

"Okay with me," said Tom. "I'll start with the canoe, go halfway, and then finish with the wanigan."

"That is okay with me for this time," said Rio.

Tom gathered Rio wasn't happy carrying the canoe.

As they hoisted loads, Ack yelled, "Lunch is at the other end. Doug says there's a great place to relax."

The Scouts smiled.

The portage went smoothly until the end. Rio tripped on a tree root and dropped the canoe. Physically, he was fine, but the canoe had a three-inch canvas tear near the bow.

"It'll be fine," said Doug. "It's above the waterline. We'll duct tape it now and do a full repair tonight."

"How do we do that?" Tom asked.

"With Ambroid. You'll see. It's not hard, but it takes skill. Get lunch ready, eh?"

Tom's stomach grumbled as the three set out the lunch materials.

"I heard that," said Ack. "I'm famished."

After spreading PB & J on squares of rye crisp, the boys lounged on sun-drenched granite. Crunching on crackers was a pleasant change. They raffled the last of the carrots. From the five-pound brick, Borden cut ten small rectangles of cheese that were so similar, there was no need to prioritize. Jack started distribution of the gorp with a four-finger, no thumb handful. The doling ended with a raffle for a one-finger, no thumb portion. The portion was so small, Tom didn't care that he didn't get any.

As Tom and Ack packed the wanigan, Doug asked, "GFDs, what's happening with the weather?"

"It's getting hazy," said Tom.

"Yes. As the day goes on, watch how fast the clouds thicken. The quicker the ceiling drops, the sooner the rain will begin."

"It's going to rain?" asked Chet.

"Probably," Doug said. "My guess is sometime tonight or early tomorrow."

As they gathered at the canoes, Jack said, "Gather round, sports fans. We have an exciting afternoon. We have a short paddle and then…"

He motioned to Doug.

"We have two portages to clear. We'll create two work teams. At the start of the first portage, the first work group will walk the portage, clearing as needed. About ten minutes later, the second group will begin a normal portage. Both groups should reach the end of the portage about the same time. The first group will go back to carry their stuff. The second work team will move on to the second portage and begin their work walk. If all goes perfectly, both groups will finish the second portage at the same time."

"Who's in which group?" Shaine asked.

"The first team will be my canoe and Rio's boat," said Jack.

"That means my boat and Lloyd's canoe will be the second," Doug said. "Jack, get started. We'll wait a few minutes so the landing isn't crowded."

The two canoes moved toward a yellow sign that indicated the start of the portage. The grass stood tall and showed no sign of a trail. Tom guessed they were the first group of the season. After putting the canoes and packs off to the side they discovered a leaf-covered, muddy path. Tom and the others danced from rock to rock to stay out of the muck, but after two hundred meters, the marsh expanded and it became unavoidable.

Tom sank knee deep into black goo and yelled, "Shit!"

"Let me help," Chet said. His foot slid off a partially submerged log, and he sank into the ooze. "Dammit."

"Welcome to the black bog," Shaine said. "It gets the newbies and those around them. Americans are so awkward."

"Be brotherly," Jack snapped. "Be careful. We don't want to lose a shoe. Shaine, go into the forest and bring back some branches."

While Rio took pictures, Jack extended an ax handle to Chet and Tom.

Once Tom and Chet were free, they helped Shaine collect branches. After each had deposited several loads, a wooden mat covered the mud where they had gotten stuck. While it didn't look secure, Jack announced it would be fine. He explained that as water levels fell during the summer, the ground would dry.

Beyond the swamp, the path was obvious. Periodically, someone dragged a large branch from the narrow dirt track into the woods, but overall, the trail was in fine shape. More muck appeared at the far end, and they created another mat of sticks. As they finished, Doug appeared, carrying his canoe.

"Thanks for the branches. The trail looks good."

"Good luck with the next portage," said Jack. "I hope it's as clear as this one."

With the rest of his crew arriving, Doug said, "We'll see."

After a few verbal jabs between the teams, the first group hustled back across the portage. The shady trail through the mature forest wasn't too hot or excessively buggy. Back at the start, knowing that neither Chet nor Rio wanted to haul the canoe, Tom volunteered again. He was pleased that the mat of branches supported his feet with the weight of a 16-foot boat on his back. As the carry ended, the thwart began to dig into his shoulders, and he heaved a sigh of relief. They loaded and slid out into the little lake.

With no breeze, the water reflected the trees and the clouds. The two canoes seemed to float on the sky. In front of them, very small spiders scurried away on the surface of the water.

"They're called water striders." Jack said. "The Park is the only place that I've seen these creatures. It's amazing the way that they can walk across the surface."

As they were unloading for the next portage, Borden and Ack ran toward them from the woods.

"Jack," Borden said breathlessly, "Ric and Lloyd are hurt. Doug said for you and Rio to come with us and for the others to wait."

"How badly are they injured?"

"I don't think it's too bad. Lloyd's got a cut on one of his hands. Ric fell and twisted his leg," Ack said.

Jack turned to the boys.

"Get me two longer paddles the same length."

Tom handed paddles to Jack.

"How far down the path?"

"About ten minutes."

"That's halfway." Turning to Tom and the other two boys, Jack said, "I know that it's hard to wait, but at this point, there's nothing you can do. Stay here and rest easy. Rio or I will be back as soon as we can. Eh?"

The three mumbled their agreement.

Before they started down the trail, Borden said, "Be careful. I fell. The rocks are slippery."

"Thanks for the heads-up," said Jack. "Boys, watch where you step. We don't want another injury."

Shaine and Chet sat on the wanigans. Tom paced nervously.

"Do you remember Butt Boy from Middies?" asked Shaine.

"Yes," said Chet.

On a previous Park trip, one of Shaine's cabin mates had developed a boil on his butt that became so painful, he couldn't sit down. He'd had to lie in the middle of the canoe and hobble down the portages. Once back at camp, the visiting doctor lanced the infection. The boy never really recovered, and Butt Boy went home early.

"Do you remember his real name?" asked Chet.

"Come to think of it, no. He was a wimp. He never came back."

"That's sad." said Chet. "Do you remember Johnny and his foot?"

"I wasn't on that trip, but I heard about it." Shaine asked. "What happened?"

Chet explained that one of his cabin mates had cut his foot on a discarded fishing lure while swimming and had to limp the remaining portages without carrying anything. Tom decided to keep his feet away from the bottom of the lakes.

The stories made Tom apprehensive, but he felt confident that things would work out positively. After all, they were in a park. Without any stories to share, he felt like an outsider. He felt useless and wanted to help. He walked toward the start of the trail.

"Wait," Chet said. "We were told to sit here. Someone will be back soon."

"I know, but it's driving me crazy."

"Waiting is hard, but sometimes you have to do it," said Chet. "It's nice to take a rest."

Rio walked down the path.

"Bummer, no nap time," said Chet. "How are Lloyd and Ric?"

"They're okay at the moment."

"What happened?" asked Shaine.

"Ric twisted up his knee while they were pushing a tree that had blown down onto the trail. When the tree trunk rolled at Ric, Lloyd tried to stop it and his hand had an injury. I think both will be fine."

Tom was relieved.

"Just ahead of us are many mud puddles. We will get the four canoes and everybody's packs to the other side of the muddies. Doug said it was too far long to make a brush mat, but there are enough dry rocks to step. Be careful. Once everything is on the most solid ground, we will figure out who carries what for the portage."

Dry rocks stood throughout the mud, some large, others pint-sized, some flat, and others pointed. Keeping their balance would be tricky.

After each boy had carried several smaller loads, they decided that two people should carry each canoe. As they finished carrying the final canoe, Jack, Borden, and Ack arrived.

"Doug bandaged Lloyd's hand. It'll be okay, but he can't carry or paddle. Ric's knee and ankle are sore, but he doesn't think there's any significant damage."

This news lightened the mood.

Jack took control.

"Doug is walking Lloyd and Ric to the far end of the portage. We need to get our packs and canoes over there. This means we'll all need to come back and carry a second load. Eh?"

"Great. Ric and Lloyd go get hurt," Shaine grumbled. "Now there's more work for the rest of us."

"One more thing," Jack said. "It appears that there's another blowdown beyond the one they were working on."

"Bring it on," said Borden. "A little mess won't stop us."

Tom smiled; sometimes he wished he had Borden's confidence.

"We'll walk together," said Jack. "There are seven of us, so we should get everything but the canoes on this run. We'll figure out carrying the canoes when we get back here."

Tom carried the wanigan with Rio's box on top. At the last minute, Jack stuffed a lifejacket behind his neck.

"We need to as efficient as possible." Jack smiled. "We have to fill every available space."

As the Scouts marched, Jack told them about old-time fur traders with the theme of "you think this is tough, you should have seen them do..."

At the second blowdown, everyone unloaded.

"Gentlemen, can we clear it?" asked Jack.

Having fallen together, three large trees blocked the trail.

"Not without a chain saw," said Borden. "It would take us a day or two to chop up these trees."

"I agree," said Ric. "That's a nightmare mess."

"What should we do?"

Tom had no clue, and with everyone else, was silent.

After several long seconds, Borden said, "Reroute the trail. Last summer in Temagami, we used a couple of go-around trails."

"Makes sense to me," said Jack. "Which side?"

After exploration, they decided the left looked better. Jack walked back down the trail for about five meters and turned into the forest.

"Follow me. Cut branches or the little saplings, as needed. Remember two things. This is temporary; it doesn't need to be perfect. And, two, you'll be carrying a canoe."

As Jack pushed his way through the underbrush, Tom and Borden sawed down saplings. Using the axes, Chet and Shaine trimmed branches off the larger trees. Once the new path was clear, they continued portaging the packs and wanigans.

Far more quickly than Tom thought possible, they arrived at the end of the portage. Ric was limping, and Lloyd's bandage looked like a small boxing glove. Both downplayed their injuries and said that they'd be back to normal in a day or two.

"We need to get the canoes," Doug said. "And someone needs to stay with Lloyd and Ric. Who wants to do what?"

"I'll stay," Shaine said. "I'm good at first aid."

"Thank you. We'll see," Doug said dismissively. "I'll carry one boat. Jack will do his. That leaves two canoes. Shall we have four people, each carrying half the portage?"

The Scouts nodded.

"Rio and three Scouts will go."

"Shall we raffle?" Jack asked. "The winner and the person to his right will stay."

Chet won. Shaine was on his right.

"Yes!"

Shaine pumped his fist. Tom sensed that Shaine's

display of emotion didn't create any good will.

"It's settled," said Doug. "Let's go. The canoes aren't getting any lighter."

Walking the portage path without a load was a pleasant stroll. The afternoon sun glowed in a way that softened the colors. The forest seemed calmer with fewer bird calls and no stirring creatures. Everyone seemed lost in their own thoughts.

As they walked, Tom coached Ack on the tricks of carrying a canoe. The key was finding a smooth pace. "Volunteer to take the canoe for the first half." Tom smiled. "You'll get it done and won't have to worry about maneuvering the go-around."

Rio started with their canoe. At the halfway point, Tom teepeed for Rio, who returned the favor for Tom. At the go-around, Tom discovered that the path hadn't been laid out with sixteen-foot canoes in mind. At one point, he needed to be inched forwards and backwards to move through the maze of trees.

After the portage was completed, Doug said, "Obviously, we need to change the canoe groups. I'll take Ack in my bow and Ric will sit in the middle, not paddling. Jack will have Chet in his bow and Lloyd in their middle. The third canoe will be Rio and Borden. That leaves Tom and Shaine."

"You can take the stern," said Shaine. "I'm tired."

Tom was glad to take charge but a little surprised that Shaine hadn't taken the opportunity.

During the half-hour paddle to the campsite, they passed a series of majestic outcroppings of gray moss-covered granite. The boys were quiet as they paddled through what seemed to be an enchanted realm; the rocks and trees reflected off the mirror-like water.

When the canoes approached the first campsite, Doug said, "GFDs, we're using this one. Okay?"

"Looks good to me from here," said Tom.

"I agree," said Ack.

"Without seeing it, I can't say much. You're the guide, and your decisions rule," said Borden.

"Thanks. What's happened to the sky?"

"The clouds have filled in and the ceiling has dropped," Tom said.

"What's that mean for the weather?"

"We'll probably have rain tonight or early tomorrow," Borden said.

"Pitch your tents appropriately," said Doug. "With no trenching, eh? We practice no-trace camping."

The old timers grumbled their "yes's."

The Scouts unloaded the canoes. Wanigans were stationed at the fire pit. The numerous tent sites on top of the ridge had spectacular views. Borden chose the tent site furthest from the fire pit. A dense layer of soft pine needles covered the ground.

"If we get rain, the pine needles will keep the water away from us."

Using a line between two trees, they pitched their tent and unrolled quickly.

As the three GFDs walked back into the fire pit area, Shaine was challenging the others to a competition about jumping into the water.

"No swimming yet. Given the time and the injuries, everyone except Lloyd and Ric will go get firewood," said Doug. "Follow me. This is well-used campsite, so we need to go further into the woods."

"However," said Jack. "The boy who brings in the largest load will get first choice at lunch tomorrow."

A food reward quickened the boys' energy.

Doug led the Scouts up the ridge trail toward the forest beyond the point. As they walked. Tom realized that most of the trees around the tent sites had been stripped of their lower branches. Once in the woods, Tom and Ack followed Borden. He led them a hundred meters beyond their comrades to a grove of maple trees where dead saplings greeted them.

"Ack has the longest arms. What if we worked together and set up Ack to win?" said Tom.

"Sounds good." Ack grinned.

The three pulled down the dead saplings and trimmed some of the smaller branches so they could drag them more easily. They waited until they were the last to return. Out of sight of the kitchen, Tom and Borden transferred their loads to Ack. His long arms enabled him to manage a pile over three feet across.

"Well, look at this - Ack is the winner!" said Jack.

"They cheated," said Shaine.

"How?"

"Ack's the only one carrying wood. He didn't carry it the whole way."

"That may be true. Did I say that he had to carry the load the entire way?"

"No," said Ric. "That was smart. They deserve to win."

"What does Ack win?" Chet asked.

"First choice of bannock at tomorrow's lunch. Let's get all of this wood broken up."

The Scouts created a robust pile of wood.

"That's way more than we need," grumbled Shaine.

"I doubt it," said Doug. "We need to make bannock after dinner."

Rio held up his camera.

"Who wants to take a swim quickly for a great picture as you are jumping from the rocks?"

"Hold on a minute," said Doug. "We need to examine the canoes. We have at least one tear to repair. Let's all go check."

After looking carefully at the canoes' canvas, they found two little cuts on Rio's boat in addition to the tear. Tom watched carefully as Doug used the Ambroid glue to patch the canvas.

"We need to check the canoes at the end of every day. It's easier to fix holes when they're small."

Doug checked his watch.

"We do have time for a quick swim."

After Jack checked out the depth, the boys jumped off the rock face. It amazed Tom how their enthusiastic cries echoed off the opposite shore and bounced down the narrow lake. Rio took pictures. Shaine's jumps were more sophisticated, but Tom noticed that Ack was the first to move to a higher ledge.

Quietly, Doug reminded the GFDs that it was time to start dinner.

Supper was straightforward. Ack boiled a big pot of water for the noodles. In a second pot, Borden created beef stroganoff from dried components - beef, mushrooms, onions, peas, carrots, and powdered milk.

Doug hovered as Tom began to prepare the pudding. "Making refrigerator food on a trip is an art. It can be done, but there are some tricks to it. Start by combining the pudding and milk powders," said Doug. "Add a little bit of cold water and whip it. Never add much liquid at one time. No one wants to eat chocolate soup."

Tom stirred until the pudding was the consistency of oatmeal.

"Stop. Looks good." Doug smiled. "It will harden."

At supper, everyone got large seconds of the stroganoff. Those who wished got thirds and small fourths. Tom was pleased when Jack took control of dessert distribution. He served the pudding by the spoonful, three to start and one for seconds. Ack won the raffle for the pudding pot. With a theatrical show of brotherhood, he gave it to Ric and Lloyd to soothe their booboos.

When everyone had finished, Jack suggested the rocky point with deep water on both sides might be a good fishing place. Chet rigged his pole. Borden asked to use Ric's. Watching from the rocks, an amused peanut gallery commented on their lack of success.

After the washers finished, Doug asked for bannock-making volunteers. The same three stepped forward. Tom was amazed at how simple the process was. Flour, salt, and baking powder were mixed. Cinnamon and raisins were added. The addition of a little oil and water created a dough that was put into the baking pans. Tom kept the flames burning for the reflector oven, and Ack managed the coals and twiggy fire for the Fry-Bake.

A half hour later, two browned, round loaves were set aside to cool. The pans were washed, the ovens packed away, and the breads were stored inside the lunch wanigan.

As the evening darkened, fishless Chet and Borden surrendered and stashed the fishing rods under the canoes.

A roll of thunder pealed in the distance. Everyone dashed to their tents.

Jack yelled, "Be sure to have rain gear with you."

Several boys ran to get their daypacks that had been left beside the canoes.

"GFDs, cover the wanigans with the tarp," Doug said.

The three wrapped the green canvas tarp around the wooden boxes. As they worked to protect the wanigans, Tom saw Doug tie down the canoes and tuck exposed paddles and lifejackets underneath. The next rumble of thunder was closer.

"I'm going to go put our stuff inside the tent." Borden ran up the ridge.

Jack came down the path. "The boys' tents look secure. I think they'll stay dry."

"Good. Boys, where's your rain gear?"

Ack looked at Tom. "Don't know."

"Where's your daypack?"

"I think it's back at the tent with Borden," Tom said. "Ack, head up to the tent. I'll double-check under the canoes."

As Tom was looking under one side of the overturned canoe, he discovered Doug peering from the other.

"Don't see it here," Doug said.

"I guess it's up at the tent," Tom said. "Borden's pretty good at keeping track of stuff."

"He's got lots of experience."

"Can I ask a question? Why do you tie down the canoes?"

"To be safe."

"Safe from what?"

"Being blown away."

"What do you mean?"

"One night on my Voyageur trip, we had a tremendous storm. From under the trees, at a point like this, the wind picked up one of the canoes and threw it on the rocks down the river. We had to patch a big tear in the canvas. If it had carried the canoe another ten feet into the river, we'd have had a bigger problem."

"I see." Tom smiled. "You're preventing a canoe from becoming a lemon."

"You understand."

"How did you become a guide?" asked Tom.

A clap of thunder snapped above them.

"I'll tell you later. Head for your tent. We're getting rain in a minute or so."

Seconds after Tom dove into the tent, the wind and rain began. A moment later, a bright flash illuminated everything, and a crack of thunder shook the boys.

As the wind flapped the tent, Ack asked, "Are we safe here?"

"Yes," said Borden. "Haven't you ever been in a thunderstorm in a tent?"

"No. We don't have thunderstorms in Scotland."

All three jumped at another flare and bang.

"This is sure different than being in my apartment in the city," Tom said apprehensively.

"You get used to it," said Borden. "I've been out in storms when we've been fishing and hunting since I was a little boy."

The weather was disturbing Ack, so Tom tried to change focus.

"What do you hunt for?"

Borden explained that duck, deer, and moose provided an important part of his grandparents' diet. In the late spring, summer, and early fall, they lived in a small cabin about five hours northwest of North Bay. It was accessible only by canoe or seaplane.

Ack was fascinated and asked question after question.

Suddenly, Tom noted, "The rain's stopped."

"A good time to go to sleep," said Borden. "Be careful that you don't touch the tent."

"Why?"

"It'll create a leak," Borden said. "That's the hassle with the old-style tents."

"I'm glad I'm in the middle," Ack said.

Each wiggled into his sleeping bag.

The drips bouncing on the tent kept Tom awake. He didn't want to roll into the side of the tent and get wet.

After a couple of minutes, Borden was snoring lightly. Ack was motionless.

Twisting in his sleeping bag, Tom finally found a comfortable place for his hip. The day had been eventful. Luckily, Ric and Lloyd's injuries weren't too bad, but having two hurt paddlers would mean changes and new challenges. He wondered what impact the injuries would have on the remainder of the trip. He hoped the canoe groups tomorrow would be rearranged so he wouldn't have to paddle with Shaine. His neck and back were less sore. He was adjusting to portaging, and he was pleased that his control of the canoe was better. Being a GFD had gone smoothly, and no one had complained about the food.

Above their tent, the pine boughs wheezed and moaned as the wind gusted. What would tomorrow's weather be?

Sleep came eventually.

# Chapter 12
## Sailing

"Get up, sleepy heads!" Jack shouted, sticking his head in the tent. "Oatmeal's almost ready. The staff let you sleep. We'll probably get more showers this morning, so have your rain gear handy."

Groggily, Tom asked, "Is it going to rain all day?"

"No one is going to melt," said Jack. "The rain makes you appreciate the sun."

"Remember to be careful about not touching the side of the tent," said Borden. "I'll go first."

"I'll be last." As Tom finished pulling on his clothes, the rain stopped. "Do I need my raincoat?"

"Yes, city-boy." Borden smiled. "It's going to rain again."

While the three walked to the kitchen area, a light shower began. The boys pulled on their rain gear. Tom joined everyone under the big green tarp feeling awkward in his London Fog trench coat.

"Good morning, professor," Ric said. "I do say, sir, weather has become a bit stormy, sir."

Trying to do an English accent, Tom said, "No class today, learned students."

In an equally bad accent, Chet said, "Thank you, sir. But what shall we do now, professor, sir?"

"Paddle and portage," Jack said. "It's a great day to travel."

The boys huddled together. The new brightly colored

rain gear and the dark hunting garb created a surreal picture of the new and the old. The image reminded Tom of some famous painting that he'd seen in a museum.

"Breakfast is ready," called Doug.

After lining up for their oatmeal and cheesy eggs, most boys retreated under the tarp.

"Too crowded for me." Borden walked to the rock ledge.

Tom followed.

The drizzle had become a fine mist. A loon's call echoed in the distance.

As they spooned down the hot mush, a mother duck and her line of ducklings motored across the lake, looking as though they had not a care in the world. As they cut the surface, their perfect V-shaped wake impressed Tom.

"I bet they like this weather."

"I think so. They're ducks," said Borden.

Doug came up behind them. "My guess is that it doesn't make any difference," he said. "They live here and the weather, whatever it may be, is a part of their world."

"There's a saying about duck's backs and water, isn't there?" asked Tom.

"There is. Like water off a duck's back. A duck's feathers are waterproof, so rain rolls off. For people, it means that criticism or insults don't bother you."

"Sounds good to me," said Tom.

"If you're finished, take your bowls to be washed," said Doug.

It began to rain harder as Tom walked back to the kitchen area. His intestines barked at him. He grabbed the plastic bag with the bum wad and headed for the thunder box.

The wooden cube was on the mainland, a long walk from the campsite. Raindrops splashing off his hat and coat while sitting on damp wood was not Tom's idea of a good time. A chipmunk scurried around as though he was invisible. The little creature stopped several times, once inches from his feet. It stood on its hind legs and stared at him. Tom tried not to move, but a loud hurry-up call from another Scout broke the moment. The striped animal scampered into the underbrush.

Tom thought of his mother. The idea of her pooing outside in the rain brought a smile to his face. He stepped lightly to avoid the puddles on his way back to the campsite.

Back at the tent, Tom rolled quickly.

"I hope my bedroll is waterproof."

"It looks good, but you're fine," said Borden. "I think it's going to clear up as the day goes on."

"I hope so," said Ack.

When the bulky pack was full, Tom carried it to the canoes. It was heavier with the wet tent.

Once the campers were gathered, Doug said, "Same canoe groups as yesterday afternoon. Lloyd and Ric will be the GFDs. Their injuries don't impact their brains."

"If they have any," Shaine whispered.

Chet laughed.

"They are not paddling today and will sit on bedroll packs. On the portages, they can carry light, little stuff. This means we can't do one-carry trips. We'll trade off on who goes back for a second load. Questions or comments?" Doug glared at Shaine.

"What's the day look like?" asked Borden.

"We get wickedly wet while wandering," said Chet.

"Sloppy, sucky sections of stupid streams separating soaking surfaces," said Shaine. It was impossible to tell if he was being funny or sarcastic.

"GFDs, what's the route?" asked Jack.

"We paddle through a series of narrow lakes connected by shorter portages," said Lloyd. "The carries are 175, 60, then 720 meters into Lawrence. We go up 470 meters to Rod and Gun and down 510. That puts us back on Lake Louisa, where we'll spend the afternoon."

"What's the weather going to be?" asked Ack.

"Cloudy and rain. Sometimes hard. Sometimes, not," said Lloyd.

"Are you sure?" asked Borden. "The wind's shifted to the northwest. It may clear."

"What difference does that make?" Shaine snapped. "We're going to be wet. Our feet will look like prunes tonight. Today's a slog."

"Time to load up," said Doug. "Hopefully, we can get one of the great campsites on Louisa."

As they loaded their canoe, Shaine announced that he'd take the stern. Tom decided not to argue, but he was not looking forward to a full day with Shaine behind him.

Once the boys began to paddle, heavy rain limited conversation, but eventually, the rain stopped. The breeze picked up and kept the canoes at a distance from one another.

The first portage was a well-worn path of mud. Water drops from the leaves above made it seem like it was still raining. Tom's second load, a wanigan, didn't feel bad. Maybe his neck was stronger, or he was getting used to the heavy loads.

While crossing the next lake, a steady wind swirled around the hills and knifed across the coves. Shaine cursed repeatedly as the gusts swung the canoe off course. Tom pulled silently.

Their second portage was only 60 meters, so everyone went back for a second load.

As the Scouts started back, Ack said, "This weather reminds me of the heather. It's a wonderful day to wander through the wilds."

"If you're a stupid Scot," Shaine grunted. "Let's keep slogging."

On the third lake with a strong side-wind, Shaine

continued to complain as they paddled.

The third path was longer with deeper puddles.

As the stern man, Shaine carried the canoe but whined incessantly about its weight. When Tom offered to take it, Shaine refused. When the trail became uneven, he began to curse under his breath. Tom was surprised that the canoe wasn't damaged when Shaine dumped it to the ground at the end of the portage.

When he returned to see if anything else needed to be carried on a second load, Tom met Ack and Borden halfway and finished by carrying a wanigan. The rocks were slippery, so Tom marched straight through the black pools of goo. Getting his feet wet and dirty didn't bother him anymore, and he wondered if he'd crossed some kind of wilderness threshold.

As the Scouts loaded the canoes on Lawrence Lake, Doug said, "Whitecaps on the lake. Put on your lifejackets."

"Lifejackets are a hassle with rain jackets," said Shaine. "Can we wait to see if we actually need them? It doesn't look too bad."

"No!" Doug snapped. "Put your lifejackets on. Now!"

The wind churned and Shaine continued to have difficulty keeping the canoe on course. Twice they were wildly rocked by wind and waves, and Tom was glad that he was wearing his lifejacket. When they turned up a bay towards the portage, streaks of blue began to appear in the sky.

Shaine continued to voice his irritation as he carried the canoe up the well-used trail into Rod and Gun Lake. Above them, puffy clouds surged across a clearing blue sky.

As they loaded the canoe, again Tom offered to carry the boat for the next portage.

"About time you helped," said Shaine. "I can't do everything."

Tom held his tongue.

Rod and Gun was a small pond covered with water striders. In awe, Tom watched the little spiders scamper across the mirrored surface. He wondered how each of the minute creatures stayed on top of the water.

The 510-meter portage to Louisa cut through a stand of cedar trees and moss-covered boulders. Tom was glad the downhill trail ended at a rocky beach sheltered from the wind. The sunshine was warm.

"Time for lunch." Shaine dropped his wanigan and sat on it.

"This is a great place," said Ric.

"That's what I just said," snapped Shaine. "Get out the lunch stuff! I'm hungry."

"It'll be ready in a few minutes."

"Hurry up. I'm starving."

"If you want to be one of the GFDs," Lloyd responded, "you're welcome to help."

"No. Just do your job," Shaine barked.

Despite Shaine's constant complaining on the trail, his outburst to the GFDs surprised Tom. Even more upsetting was the fact that none of the counselors said anything.

The four bow paddlers walked back up the trail together, and each did a half carry. Portaging and sharing loads had become so natural, there was no need for conversation. The breeze swirled through the trees. The big leaves created a deeper swooshing than the whispering of the pine needles.

Lunch was the cinnamon-raisin bannock with PB & J. The bakers received compliments. When Lloyd cut up the block of cheddar cheese into twelve equal portions, Tom was impressed and wondered if he'd ever develop this skill. The gorp distribution started with three-finger handfuls and then stopped after two-finger handfuls. Tom's unspoken question was answered when Doug declared they would use the remaining gorp to create dessert.

Relaxing in the sun, no one seemed to be in a rush.

"Shall we paddle this afternoon?" Doug asked. "GFDs, should we wear lifejackets?"

Ric and Lloyd counseled.

As the two talked, Doug asked loudly, "What's the white saying?"

"Don't know," Shaine muttered under his breath.

"Isn't the saying, 'Wear when you see white?'"

"Yeah, that's it," said Ric.

Doug gazed out at the lake. "Do you see white?"

"Yes. There are white caps. Lifejackets, everyone."

"Good call," said Jack.

"Before we start, let's talk about Lake Louisa," said Doug. "It's a popular lake with lots of campsites. It's Sunday. People will be paddling out. I'm hoping that one of the primo sites will be available. Well down the lake, there's a rocky point with spectacular views to both east and west. We'll need to stay close together until the campsite is in view."

"Sounds good," said Lloyd. "Let's load up."

"Shaine, let Tom have the stern," said Doug.

"He's a rookie. He doesn't know what he's doing."

"It's time to give him a chance."

"If you insist." Shaine glared at Tom. "I'll blunder in the bow."

"That's being brotherly," said Doug sharply. "Together, we trudge through tortuous torment, together, as a tranquil team."

Everyone smiled except Shaine.

After rounding the first point, the wind became pushy. Tom wrestled to keep the canoe on course, but he liked the challenge. He felt he was doing as well, probably better than Shaine had done in the morning. The churning air and the rocking white caps were exhilarating.

After a demanding half-hour, Doug pointed the canoes into the lee of one of the small islands. Glad to be out of the chop, Tom relaxed in the quiet water.

"Can we pee?" asked Borden.

"Sure," said Doug. "Be careful. There's nowhere to land, so you'll need to step into the water and figure out how to climb up onto the island."

"Can't we just pee in the lake?" asked Shaine.

"No," said Doug. "We're stewards of our environment. We take care of the land and the water, eh?"

Shaine didn't respond.

"Shaine, I asked you a question," barked Doug. "At Catamount, we take care of the natural world around us, don't we?"

With little feeling, Shaine said, "Yes, we do."

Grabbing an overhanging branch, Tom steadied the canoe and Shaine stepped into the shallow water. After he returned to the canoe, Shaine steadied the boat by grabbing a tree root. Tom found that climbing up the steep edge onto the forest floor was more challenging than it looked. The center of the island was a hidden field of delicate ferns from which the trunks of towering pines shot upward. The green was so wild and pristine that he felt like he'd stepped into a mystical place where gnomes or fairies might live.

Once everyone was back in the canoes, Doug asked, "Does anyone see signs of life at that rocky point way on the south side in the far distance?"

None of the boys did.

"Excellent. We're headed to the best campsite on Louisa. It's hard to get in the summer, but we may be lucky. If it's occupied, there are other nice ones down the lake."

Slowly and deliberately, he swiveled to Jack.

"Ready to race?"

Instantly, everyone tensed.

287

"Paddling or sailing?"

"Your choice."

After looking at the other canoes, Jack said, "The wind has dropped to a breeze. Let's sail. Any guidelines?"

"You can't use the big green tarp. No one can stand in their canoe. If anything gets blown into the water, the closest boat or boats stop racing and help retrieve what's in the water. Any questions?"

No one asked for clarification.

"Take a minute to get ready," said Jack.

Tom was clueless. For once, he was happy when Shaine took charge. Immediately, Shaine pulled their raincoats from the daypack.

"We'll use your raincoat as our sail. It's the biggest. I'll use paddles to hold it up. It'll look like a scarecrow." In a whisper, Shaine said, "Keep the canoe pointed into the middle of the lake."

"Why?"

"We don't have a centerboard. Unless we overcompensate at the beginning, the wind will push us into the shore."

"Any last-minute questions?" yelled Jack.

A chorus of "no's" answered.

"Safety first," Doug said. "Remember, we're brothers first and competitors second. If you have any problem, put down your sail and paddle, eh?"

"Yes," the Scouts chorused.

Doug and Jack lifted their paddles and looked expectantly at Rio.

After positioning his paddle, Rio shouted, "GO!"

Paddles splashed, and the canoes shot into the open lake.

Once in the wind, Shaine hoisted Tom's raincoat to form a T-shaped sail. Their spare paddle held out the arms, and Shaine's paddle ran up through the lining to hold everything aloft. Shaine kept the sail upright by pushing his feet against the blade and holding the bottom corners in his hands.

Once the sail caught the breeze, the canoe jumped ahead. Shaine's design was impressive. They rocketed down the lake in the lead. To the right, Tom saw both Rio and Jack's canoes being pushed toward the southern shore of the lake. Without significant correction, he saw the potential for both canoes to run afoul of the rocky shoreline well before the campsite. Tom leaned on his paddle, steering their canoe toward the middle of the lake.

Sailing was fast and relaxing. Directly behind them, two smaller rain-jackets pushed Doug's canoe. With a larger sail area, they were pulling away.

The breeze dropped to a whisper and the canoe slowed. A blast of air hit Tom's coat. Shaine strained to keep it upright. With a loud tear, the material split in half. Shaine scrambled to regroup, but without forward momentum, their canoe wallowed in the waves. The wind began to push the boat off course. Tom strained to keep the rocking canoe pointed in the right direction.

As Doug's canoe passed, he yelled, "Are you okay?"

"Yeah. We're fine." Tom sounded more confident than he was.

After a couple of desperate minutes, Shaine discovered that if he moved the paddles into an X-shape, the blades would hold out the arms of the coat.

While they had been rerigging, Doug's canoe had gained a hundred meters. Their new design didn't grab as much wind. The remaining race was for second place. As Shaine had predicted, the wind had pushed Jack and Rio's canoes to the shore. Both had ceased sailing. The waves tossed their canoes as the paddlers strained to make headway while staying away from the rocks on the edge of the lake.

After rounding the granite point and sliding out of the

wind, Tom relaxed. Their canoe joined Doug's in a small tranquil bay. A few minutes later, the other two canoes slid into the calm water. Earning second place felt good to Tom.

"If Tom's raincoat hadn't ripped, we would have won," Shaine said.

"But it did, and you were second," said Chet. "If Lloyd could have paddled, it would have been different."

"We beat you. I redesigned our sail, and we were catching up. If we'd had a longer race, we would have won."

"If you say so."

Tom could not figure out if Shaine and Chet's bickering was friendly or if there was tension between them.

"Well, the whole competition was rigged," said Lloyd. "With my injured hand, I couldn't do anything. It wasn't fair."

"And, Jack can't sail to save his soul." Doug grinned.

"I stayed with Rio's boat," said Jack. "If they got into trouble, I wanted to be able to help them. We were being brotherly."

"That's good, Jack." Doug smiled. "Let's go set up the campsite. We need to sting some clotheslines and dry out. We made good time and can relax."

As they unloaded the canoe, Shaine threw the ripped raincoat on the ground and stepped on it repeatedly. Under his breath, he muttered, "It's useless, like it's owner." Tom rolled his eyes. He was tired of being hassled.

The immense granite outcropping was a wonderful campsite. A stand of bushes and short pine trees protected a well-designed kitchen and fire pit area. The rocky point had an expansive view in all directions and some excellent jumping platforms. Inside the tree line, a large clearing with deep pine-needles had ample space for four tents.

Without nearby trees to sling a top rope, Borden said, "Center pole time. Follow me."

In the forest, they found a straight, dry, dead sapling. Borden broke it to the proper length and held it inside the tent while Ack and Tom staked out the sides.

As Borden emerged from under the canvas, he said, "I tried to angle the center pole so the middle person has enough space."

"I'll take it," said Ack. "I'm skinny and I need more headroom."

Tom smiled. He preferred being on the side. Sleeping between people made him uncomfortable.

"Unroll your stuff and put it in the sun on a branch, a bush, or the clothesline," said Borden. "Everything is damp because of the rain, but we need to remember to get it back in the tent sooner rather than later. I'm putting my stuff near the tent so I won't forget."

"Sounds good," said Tom. His sleeping bag did feel clammy.

Once the GFDs had organized the kitchen, Jack called everyone together.

"We're baking this afternoon, dessert for tonight and bannock for tomorrow. Let's all go gather firewood. Again, biggest load wins a prize."

The other boys scattered into the woods. Borden paused.

"We're not going in the woods today. Follow me."

Borden walked toward the bay on the lee side of the point. After pushing through a tangle of branches and hopping over several rotten logs, mounds of wood sat about three feet above the edge of the lake.

"This is good driftwood. It may be damp on the outside, but inside, it's as dry as a bone. And we've beaten the hordes to it."

"What do you mean?" asked Tom.

"I learned this from my grandfather and saw it as a Middie," said Borden. "In the late fall and after the ice melts, the wind pushes the floating wood along the lake's shores. It catches in the little bays and behind the big rocks. You can find it early in the season before the Park gets overrun by tourists."

"That's neat," said Ack.

"Let's take advantage of Ack's arms again," said Tom.

"Sounds good to me."

Each of the three managed smaller loads through the tangled underbrush. Again, using his huge grasp to carry in a massive load, Ack won the prize, first choice of the brownies.

After they broke the long pieces into a woodpile, Rio asked, "Who wants to be on the camera jumping into the lake?"

The boys appreciated the joy of leaping into the cool water and relaxing in the warm sun. When more were sitting than swimming, Doug said, "We need bakers."

Ric, Tom, and Ack volunteered.

"Ack and I are basic boneheaded bakers," said Tom. "Tell us what to do."

"Start by separating the gorp into its components," said Ric.

The raisins became part of cinnamon-raisin bannocks. The M&Ms and the nuts spiced up the evening's brownies. Mixing and baking went smoothly. When Ric struggled to start a fire, Tom remembered his pocket of birchbark. Ric smiled and mouthed a "thank you."

After the bannocks and brownies were ready, Ric and Lloyd cooked dinner. Voluminous macs and cheese with chicken satisfied the boys' appetites.

As Tom, Ack, and Borden tackled the dishes, Jack suggested that Chet and Ric should try their fishing rods.

"Ric's hurt," Shaine said. "I'll use his."

Ric looked irritated but didn't disagree.

"Anyone want to paddle in the sunset?" Doug asked.

Looking around, Tom realized that the breeze had died, and the lake was still, like a mirror.

"Sure," said Tom. "Sounds peaceful."

"And ridiculous," said Shaine. "We can't live in our canoes."

None of the other boys wanted to paddle.

"Let's both solo," said Doug.

"Sounds good," replied Tom. He hoped he wouldn't embarrass himself.

When Doug sat in the bow seat facing the stern, Tom was relieved he didn't have to lean the canoe and sit on his calves. He felt surprisingly at home gliding across the ice-like surface. Without much effort, his canoe whispered across the reflection of the sun's setting rays. A peacefulness that he hadn't felt in months relaxed him.

From the shore, Chet cried, "I got one."

Doug raised his hand to the horizon. "We have about three fingers of daylight."

Tom was mystified.

As if Doug had read Tom's mind, he continued, "You can approximate how much daylight remains if you reach your arm towards the sun and put your little finger on the horizon. For each finger, you have about fifteen minutes of daylight. Understand?"

Tom nodded.

"Time to head in," said Doug. "I do love an evening snack."

As they landed, Shaine yelled excitedly and brought in a second.

"No more," said Jack. "We only need two. The fish need to be cooked and eaten before it gets pitch dark."

"Go watch," said Doug. "I'll manage your canoe."

Never having cooked fresh fish, Tom was fascinated. He watched as Chet gutted the fish, scaled them, coated the skins with margarine, wrapped them in foil, and placed each silvery packet on the grill. Rio photographed the process as the two anglers grinned proudly.

The smell of roasting fish reawakened Tom's appetite and he discovered that he was not alone. When the fish were cooked, Chet and Shaine created ten piles. Everyone grabbed a bowl and enjoyed a second entrée followed by the brownies.

"Sorry that we made more dishes," said Chet.

"No problem," said Tom. "It was worth it."

With a smile, Tom realized that they had forgotten to empty Mean Green and Mellow Yellow, so they didn't have to get water. The washing went quickly, and the bowls were restacked to dry on the wanigan lid.

"You catch 'em and cook 'em," said Ack, "I'll gladly do dishes."

"Shaine, Chet, we still need to do something," Doug said.

"What's that?" asked Shaine.

"Do we want birds, raccoons, or bears rummaging around the fire pit tonight?"

"No."

"Wild animals love guts and bones. They need to be taken away from the campsite."

"Any volunteers?"

No one moved.

"Raffle!" Jack said.

"What about the brave fishermen?" Shaine asked. "We caught the fish."

"We're all in this, including the staff."

Shaine lost the raffle and grumbled about unfairness. Tom did not feel sorry for him and suspected the others shared his feelings.

After Shaine had plodded for a hundred meters along the darkening lake shore, Doug yelled, "That's good. Drop them and come back."

When Shaine returned, Doug called everyone

together. "Go put your dry stuff inside your tents. We're getting a heavy dew tonight."

The boys scattered. Tom was glad that his sleeping bag had a hint of warmth from the sunshine when he threw it into the tent.

After checking around the area for unclaimed clothing, Doug asked. "Anyone want tea or hot chocolate? I'll put on some water."

"Sure," said Tom.

"Sounds good to me," said Borden.

"I'm in," stated Ack.

The other boys retreated to their tents.

The three joined the counselors sitting on the rocks facing the last rays of the sunset. The wispy orange and purple clouds on the western horizon were intense but peaceful. The lake reflected and doubled the sky's colors. Across the lake, two canoes were paddling west into the darkening evening, each forming a distinct V-shaped wake. They reminded Tom of the ducks he'd seen during breakfast.

Before Tom could ask, Jack said, "It's the age-old question: Do they know what they're doing and paddling without a breeze to get a primo site? Or are they tourists doing a circle route who got wind-bound today and are trying to make up time?"

"Don't know," said Doug. "But making camp in the dark is a hassle. They'll have a great day tomorrow, though. Look at the sunset. Red sky at night."

"Does that mean we'll have good weather all day?" asked Tom.

"It'll be sunny, probably with a hefty breeze. It'll be a tail wind from here to the portage and at the start of Rock Lake. We could have a nice headwind into the river."

"How do you know that?" asked Ack.

"Experience. I've been paddling in this area since I was a boy. My family started doing this circle route when

I was about ten. When I was twelve, my grandfather let me solo the entire Louisa portage with a 17-foot wooden Chestnut Prospector. Three kilometers is a long carry."

Tom realized the longest carry of the trip was ahead of them.

With a smile, Borden said, "That's a load. My grandfather did the same thing to me when I was twelve. The canoe that I carried was so heavy, I felt like I was going to die."

"I'll bet he said that it built character." Doug grinned.

"He did."

"Now you feel great pride for doing it, don't you?"

"Yes. Not everyone can do something like that. Over the years, my grandfather has helped me build a lot of character."

Borden slapped a mosquito.

"Time for bed."

The rising hum of mosquitoes caught Tom's attention. The tent called. His questions about the portage could wait.

"I'll rinse your cups," said Doug. "Get to your tent before you get eaten."

The boys quick-stepped to their tent.

The Scouts talked tent-to-tent. The conversation focused on high school sports and became loud and lively. The talk of future schooling opened the pit in Tom's stomach. He rolled onto his side, facing the canvas. The day had been exciting. He'd enjoyed sailing, but his destroyed raincoat was a problem. He hoped the canoe groups would change. Another day with Shaine was not something he looked forward to.

After increasingly dire threats from Jack and Doug, everyone quieted and slept.

In the middle of the night, Tom awakened. Doug's prediction of a cool night had been spot-on. Tom pulled on his wool shirt and his dry shoes. He walked away from the tents to pee into the bushes.

In the distance, he heard music. A sliver of moon and the stars provided a gentle light, so he walked to the point. Up the lake, he saw a sparkling light, probably a small fire. The sounds of a guitar and laughter floated across the lake. The ranger had been right; sound carried.

Tom shivered and hurried back to his tent. Warming in his bag, he listened for man-made sounds but didn't hear any. He wondered how challenging the long portage into Rock Lake would be. The pine needles cushioned his body as he drifted off.

# Chapter 13
## Long Carry

The sound of the crackling fire opened Tom's eyes. The cold air hit his face and he retreated into the warmth of his sleeping bag until the echoing bird calls brought him fully awake. He slipped on his clothes. Both his damp socks and wet shoes had dried. He smiled at not having cold-morning-foot.

At the fire pit, Doug was brewing coffee. He offered Tom a spoon for hot chocolate. The cry of a loon echoed over the still lake. After getting their drinks, they walked to the point. The sun was already well above the sharp line of trees at the eastern end of the lake.

"Any red sky this morning?" asked Tom.

"Not a cloud in the sky. It's a glorious day for a long portage."

"Is it really three kilometers?"

"It's just under 3000 meters. I believe it's actually 2965 meters."

"How far is that in miles?"

"A little less than two. To convert, multiply the meters by .6 for distances over 1000 meters. What's 3 times .6?"

Tom thought for a minute. "1.8?"

"Yes."

"What do you do for smaller distances?" Tom asked.

"Approximate. A meter is about four inches longer than a yard, so for carries under 500 meters, the distances are about the same. It really doesn't make that much difference. I break portages into short, medium and long and define them as easy or hard. The portage into Rock Lake is long and easy, no steep uphills, no swamps, and no tricky roots or rocks. It's used a lot, so it's well-maintained."

Tom sipped his hot chocolate and watched a family of ducks swim along the shore, creating their ever-widening V. When he turned, Doug was gone.

From the woods, Tom heard Doug awaken the other Scouts. His voice was less insistent than on previous days and didn't disturb the peace of the lake.

The morning routine went smoothly. Without any of the Scouts as GFDs, the counselors took charge. They made quick work of setting out granola and cooking pancakes for breakfast. A strengthening breeze pushed puffy, round clouds across the sky.

"Lloyd and Ric, staff will do dishes," said Doug. "Go get rolled."

Rolling and loading their packs had become a natural part of their day. When everyone was ready, Doug said, "Today's briefing is simple. We paddle to the east end of Lake Louisa, carry the 2965-meter portage, and paddle north up Rock Lake to the public landing where we started five days ago. Then we wait for the van."

"Canoe groups?" asked Shaine.

"Same as yesterday," said Doug. "It's a short day. Neither Ric nor Lloyd is 100%. They are not paddling."

"Can they carry on the portage?" asked Chet.

"Light stuff," said Doug. "No canoes, no big packs, and no wanigans. Only paddles and a single daypack for each. Eh?"

Lloyd and Ric looked chagrinned.

"I can do more than that," said Lloyd. "My hand is better."

"Maybe you can, but we need you at full strength for the Dumoine. This is my decision, not yours," said Doug.

"Let's load up and go for a paddle," said Jack. "We have a lovely portage on a glorious day."

Shaine insisted on paddling in the stern.

As they headed down the lake, the breeze intensified into a strong side-wind. Shaine had difficulty holding a straight heading. When the canoes rafted in the lee of a point, Tom sensed that Shaine was glad for the break. In front of them, a headwind meant a choppy paddle.

"The portage starts at the top of this bay," Doug said. "We have two extra loads for the portage. What are we going to do?"

The first question was, should they divide the portage into two segments or three-kilometer sections? Tom said nothing. The carry would be long whatever was decided. No simple solution was apparent, and the conversation became an argument.

After a moment of silence, Chet said, "My brain doesn't work before noon. Just tell us what to do."

"Me too," said Borden. "The wanigans are light, so it's no big deal."

Doug said, "Here's my suggestion. We break the portage into three sections and rotate loads. That way, no one, including Jack, is carrying a canoe for the entire 3000 meters. We have four canoes, four wanigans, and three bedroll packs. That's eleven loads. With eight people carrying, everyone will do one additional section."

"Sounds good to me," said Chet.

"I agree," said Lloyd.

"Me too," said Borden.

"Now, who wants to start with their extra loads?" Doug asked.

"Tom and I will start," said Shaine. "If we can have bedroll packs?"

"Excellent," said Chet. "They're heavier than the wanigans."

With everyone smiling and nodding, Tom said,

"That's fine with me." He really didn't care, but he wondered about Shaine's motives.

"Now, each canoe needs to figure out who's carrying what for which section," said Doug. "No one carries a canoe for consecutive segments."

After discussion with Shaine, Tom agreed that after the extra loads, he would carry the canoe for the first and third sections.

"Tom and Shaine will start their first carry early so they're not by themselves the whole way. Now, coordinate so everyone always has a partner. No one should ever be alone, eh?"

Tom was not looking forward to walking with Shaine. He understood the logic of never being alone, but he would have preferred to walk and chat with Borden or Ack as they carried their loads.

"Lifejackets," said Doug. "We're headed into a strengthening breeze."

"Tom, do you want to take the stern? My back is sore," Shaine said.

The two exchanged places. As their canoe rounded the point, the air grabbed the bow and Tom struggled to keep the boat on course.

After a bouncy slog, the water calmed when the canoe went under the shadow of the tree line. The landing was a mix of rounded stones and medium-sized boulders.

"Out of the canoes," Doug yelled. "You'll have to get your feet wet. Keep the canoes off the rocks, or we'll have holes in our canvas. Be careful!"

Without hesitation, Tom stepped into the water. Dry socks and shoes were a short-lived luxury on a canoe trip.

As they unloaded, they carried everything up to a strip of grass. A long portage meant loads needed to be organized. As the Scouts prepared, Chet asked, "Where's the bum wad?"

"Catch."

Doug tossed it.

"Don't forget the trowel."

Doug threw it.

"Go far back into the woods. This is a well-used place that's been badly shit on."

Several laughed.

"When you're done, it's my turn," said Ric.

"Then me," said Lloyd.

"No one starts the portage until everyone's done," said Jack. "We don't want to get scattered."

Suddenly, everyone needed to answer the call of nature. After Chet returned, Tom saw Doug walk into the woods without the wad and reappear several minutes later.

To no one in particular, Doug said, "That went well."

"Didn't you use toilet paper?" Tom was amazed.

"No. I used leaves, like our ancestors did for centuries."

Several boys made faces of disgust.

Tom realized he needed to poo. His bowels became more demanding.

Quietly, he asked Doug, "Which leaves? How do you dig a hole without the trowel?"

"Walk straight back from the lake," said Doug. "Push through the little pines and you'll come to an open area. To the right, you'll see saplings with broad leaves; they're striped maples. Pick half a dozen or more leaves from several different trees,. Use your heel to scrape out a hole. Dig to the gray soil. Squat and do your business. Use two or three leaves at a time, like toilet paper. Put the used leaves in the hole and fill it with the loose dirt. Cover the disturbed earth with dead leaves. Finish by moving a branch or two to camouflage the spot. Any questions?"

"No." With his guts rumbling, Tom decided that he had to try. With a wry smile, he said, "Wish me luck."

"You'll be fine." Doug grinned. "See you soon."

Pooing in the woods without toilet paper went surprisingly smoothly. Only a few mosquitoes bit his exposed skin. Tom thought of his mother and grinned. He was sure that she'd rather die than do what he had done. As the Scouts waited for the final poopers, he felt a strange pride in his morning's accomplishment.

After the last boy headed into the woods, Doug said, "Shaine and Tom, get started with your first loads. Walk to the first canoe rack. It's a log between two trees. Leave your stuff off the trail and come back."

Tom picked up his extra bedroll while Shaine got his.

"Follow me and try to keep up." Shaine quick-stepped down the trail.

Tom trotted easily. The wind circulated under the canopy, so the bugs weren't too bad. The path was wide with few roots or rocks. After a couple of minutes, Shaine slowed to a walk. *So much for 'keep up with me,'* thought Tom.

After thinking that they'd missed the canoe rack, they saw it, a thin log tied about ten feet from the ground between two trees. Shaine dropped his pack and immediately started back.

"Doug said to put the packs off the trail," said Tom.

"It's no big deal," Shaine said. "They're not going anywhere."

Stepping off the path, Tom lowered his pack to the ground and dragged Shaine's off the trail.

"Come on!" yelled Shaine. "We don't have all day."

During their walk back, they passed everyone.

From under a canoe, Doug spoke to Shaine.

"Stay behind Tom as he carries the canoe. You're sweep."

Shaine mumbled an acknowledgement.

Back at the beginning of the portage, the view down Lake Louisa was spectacular. The crisp green of the trees along the far shore formed a bold line between the sparkling whitecaps and the puffy clouds.

"Let's get going." Shaine swung the last wanigan onto his back. "Get a move on! I hate to wait."

As Tom swung the canoe onto his shoulders, he thought, *Thanks for the teepee.*

With the canoe over his head, the trail seemed to have more rocks and roots than during his first walk. The canoe also limiting his vision, the trail seemed longer. At every rise, he hoped the canoe rack was waiting, but it continued to elude him.

"Shit."

From behind, Tom heard the crash of wood on rock.

"Are you okay?"

"Not sure. I tripped on a rock."

Tom didn't want to put down the canoe. Awkwardly he turned so he could see behind him.

Shaine pointed. "The tree rack for the canoe is just ahead. Go rest the boat on it. I'll be okay."

Tom wasn't comfortable leaving Shaine, but there wasn't a safe place to set the canoe on the ground. After a couple of minutes of moving quickly, he angled the bow over the suspended log and stepped from under the canoe. He scrambled back down the trail to Shaine.

"What's wrong?"

"I caught my foot and twisted my ankle. I'll be all right in a couple of minutes."

"You sure? I didn't see any packs. Everyone's ahead of us. We're the last two."

The forest seemed very quiet.

"I'm not sure. My ankle hurts." Shaine grimaced. "Let's rest for a minute or two."

Tom's mind froze. Should he stay with Shaine or get help as quickly as possible? He battled to stay calm. It didn't help that mosquitoes were beginning to buzz around them aggressively.

After a minute of silence, Shaine stood and stretched

cautiously.

"I think I can walk. But it's real sore."

"Can you carry the canoe?"

"The ankle feels weak. I'd hate to slip and drop the boat. Ripping the canvas would be bad for everyone."

"Okay, I'll take it. Can you carry the wanigan? It's not that heavy."

"I think so," said Shaine. "I'll have to go slowly."

Tom helped Shaine lift the wanigan on his back. It was light.

Balancing the canoe on his shoulders, Tom said, "Ready?"

"I'll try. I'll stay behind you so I'm not in your way if I slip and fall, eh?"

"Fine."

Trudging slowly along the path, the two boys went fifteen, twenty, and twenty-five minutes without seeing the next canoe rack. Whenever the path widened, Tom raised the bow of the canoe, hoping to see signs of humans. They saw no sign of the others. Tom knew they would be the last to finish.

When the pain of the thwart digging into his neck and shoulders became intense, Tom jammed the bow between two narrowly spaced trees. The canoe slid a foot and held firm. Shaine was a hundred feet behind.

The underbrush quaked beside Tom. A giant wooly animal ambled onto the trail. It had no horns, but he knew it was a moose. He froze, unsure of what to do. The animal stared at him and snorted. Its eyes seemed to say, 'It's hot and I'm tired.' Mosquitoes buzzed around its nose and ears.

"A moose!" Shaine shouted. "Don't move or it will charge."

Tom stood motionless, fascinated by its size. It didn't seem scary.

The creature shook its head and ambled away down

the path away from the boys.

When Shaine shuffled to Tom, he said, "That was close. They're dangerous. They trample people to death all the time. You were lucky. Can you help me get the wanigan down? My ankle is killing me."

Shaine limped, favoring his left leg. Tom thought Shaine had rubbed his right ankle at the time of the fall, but he wasn't sure.

"How do you feel?"

"It's sore, but I'm okay. It doesn't feel like it's going to collapse."

"That's good."

Once the bugs began swarming, Tom loaded the wanigan onto Shaine's back then hoisted the canoe and continued along the trail. Whenever the track took a downward tilt, Tom hoped they were nearing Rock Lake. But the path always angled up. His shoulders were becoming numb.

After another long ten minutes, Doug jogged up the trail.

"Were you lost?"

"No. Shaine hurt his ankle before the second section, so we stopped for a while. I've had the canoe since then. How far to the end?"

"About three minutes. Do you want me to take it?"

"No. I've come this far." Tom gritted his teeth. "I'll finish."

"You sure?"

"I'm finishing."

Doug winked.

"I like your style."

The last meters before the landing area were the worst. Determined to finish strong, Tom marched on as his muscles screamed. With sweat dripping into his eyes, he walked through his fellow Scouts and stomped into the lake. Swinging the canoe onto his thighs, gently he floated it on the water.

"Three thousand meters is a long portage."

"Did you carry it all yourself?" asked Ack.

"Yes. Shaine fell, so we rested. He said the canoe was too heavy for his twisted ankle, so I carried. It's no stroll in the woods."

"Good job." Borden smiled. "Your grandfather would be proud."

"My ankle is killing me." With a heavy sigh, Shaine lowered the wanigan and slumped onto a bedroll pack. "We saw a moose! I saved Tom from being killed. It was about to charge him."

While Shaine expounded on his efforts to save Tom from the moose, Jack evaluated the injured ankle.

"Shaine will live. He needs to be careful. What a trip! Three people hurt. Thankfully, we're almost done."

The midday sun was hot. The mosquitoes were buzzing. Tom chose not to contradict Shaine's exaggerations about the moose encounter. He had accomplished something impressive. Shaine could talk, but Tom had succeeded. In a deeply satisfying way, he felt fully alive.

When Ack handed Tom a cup of water, he smiled. It was crisp and refreshing.

Standing beside him at the landing area, four older canoers readied their canoes and packs for the portage to Lake Louisa. As they discussed who would carry what and for how long, Tom realized he had become an experienced paddler and felt a kinship with the men.

Out on the lake, several canoes were headed toward the start of the portage.

"Let's get loaded and back on the water before those paddlers get here," Doug said. "We'll do a late lunch at the public landing."

As they readied their canoe, Shaine said, "I'll take the bow. My ankle is sore."

Tom wasn't sure how Shaine's ankle related to his ability to paddle, but he was glad to be in the stern.

The beginning of the paddle up Rock Lake was easy. When the canoes rounded the point into the open lake, however, a cross wind made for strenuous paddling. Tom enjoyed the demands, both physical and mental.

In the calm of the next point, Doug said, "Break time. From here to the river, we have a headwind."

"I love finishing a trip with a breeze in my face," said Jack. "It builds character."

Most of the Scouts did not share Jack's enthusiasm. As the boys paddled into the wind, several canoes glided past in the other direction. Tom wished that he was paddling downwind on a new adventure. He had become comfortable in the Park with its daily routine of paddling and portaging. He was apprehensive about what the next few days at Catamount would bring. If things continued well, he'd stay for the Dumoine. But Shaine was becoming a big problem without an easy solution.

He was tired and eager to finish. The longer they struggled, the weaker Shaine's paddling seemed to be, but there was nothing specific that he could identify. Their canoe was the last into the calm waters of the river's mouth.

As they rested, Doug said, "It's amazing how we always have more headwinds than tailwinds. I think it's Jack's fault. He's cursed."

"No. It's the Park." Jack grinned. "It seems to know when Catamount is coming. Fifteen minutes to the landing."

"Can we eat lunch when we get there? I'm starving," said Ric.

"Let's not get ahead of ourselves," Doug said. "It's Monday. The public landing area will be packed with people, canoes, packs, and cars. We're early for our pickup. First, we'll need to carry everything to an overflow parking lot about 100 meters up the gravel road."

"Can't we pull our stuff off to the side?" asked Shaine. "My ankle is sore."

"No. We need to get out of everyone's way. When you're leaving for a trip, you have priority," said Jack. "We're returning. We're dirty, and we smell bad. We need to act like Catamen. We're known for being adventurous, being brotherly, and being courageous. This means no silliness at the landing. Eh?"

Tom joined the chorus of "yes."

"We'll land one canoe at a time," Doug said. "Jack will be first, then Rio, then Tom. My boat will be the last."

Doug's prediction proved to be true. The landing area was chaotic. Tom noted that those who were heading out seemed respectful of the boys, but also wary.

The Scouts moved efficiently through their portage procedures. Borden and Ric carried both a pack and a wanigan at the same time so they could exit the confusion as quickly as possible.

While Tom hoisted a wanigan for Ack, a young girl wearing a too-large lifejacket asked, "How long were you out on your trip?"

"Five days and four nights," Ack said.

The girl's eyes went wide.

"We're doing two nights."

"Enjoy."

Ack smiled and trotted away.

As Tom prepared to flip the canoe onto his shoulders, he had a feeling that those heading out were impressed by the Scouts' competence. He grinned, grabbed the far gunwale, and flung the boat upward. The canoe didn't seem as heavy at it had an hour ago.

After all their equipment arrived in the parking lot, Jack called, "Lunch is ready."

The boys inhaled their PB & J lunch. Ric accepted

praise for baking the bannock and acknowledged Tom and Ack as co-creators.

Once lunch was over, Jack called everyone together.

"We have a great deal to do in the next few days. Today is Monday. Tomorrow is Tuesday. What's this mean for us?"

Tom hadn't a clue and was pleased to see blank stares from his fellow Scouts.

"We leave for the Dumoine on Friday morning. That's only three full days at camp. The Circus is Wednesday evening. We need an outstanding act."

Everyone focused.

"Hopefully, we'll get picked up in time to get back to Catamount to unpack and shower before dinner. If we have a late pickup, we'll stop and eat in Pembroke."

This brought a wistful sigh from some. Tom didn't really care. He just knew that he'd be hungry.

"Tomorrow morning is the second Tuesday of the session. What happens?" Doug asked.

Tom was clueless and, again, felt like an outsider.

"Voyageur send-off. That'll be you next summer. Assuming you survive the Dumoine."

"They will. We haven't lost anyone in a few years." Jack laughed. "Tomorrow morning will be normal. Tomorrow afternoon, we start whitewater prep with on-water drills at camp. Wednesday morning, we'll do whitewater prep in moving water at the dam. On Thursday, we'll pack our food and equipment. You'll have to pull your stuff together and be ready to roll. We'll be on the water for 12 days. Any questions?"

Overwhelmed, Tom knew that he should have questions but didn't know what to ask.

"What about laundry?" asked Borden.

"It'll go out tomorrow morning and be back Wednesday afternoon or Thursday morning."

Tom felt better.

"When will we know canoe groups?" asked Shaine.

"Another good question." Doug smiled. "Initially, after our time at the dam. However, they may change. They did on this trip. On the Dumoine, your canoe group will be your bedroll pack. That will focus each canoe on keeping its things dry. We'll have GFDs again and we'll pick the initial groupings at Kipawa before we leave the landing. Any more questions about the Dumoine?"

Tom wasn't sure about canoe groups being tent mates. That could be good or bad.

"Is there a dance with the girls' camps after the Circus?" asked Shaine.

"Yes," said Jack. "It'll start after the younger campers go back to their cabins."

"Good. I need some female company."

"Me too." Ric laughed. "Not that I don't enjoy your company, my fellow Scouts, but a pretty face and some sweet smells will be delightful. You are so rough and undignified."

The idea of seeing the girls sent a wave of excitement through the boys, but it made Tom uncomfortable. While he looked forward to seeing Cecille, being in a setting with others around could be awkward. He could withstand the ribbing, but he was uneasy about what might happen in a larger group.

The old-time boys began talking about previous dances.

"Boys!" Jack struggled to get their attention. "Scouts, does anyone have any good ideas for a circus act?"

There was a resounding silence.

"Would an animal act be accepted?" Rio asked.

"Sure," Jack said. "We need to do something impressive."

"To the south of us, in Italy, sometimes, they make large animal puppets. I was thinking that we could make some elephants. Our elephants could perform tricks like

311

they do in the circus."

"Rio, that sounds wonderful. Why don't you brainstorm with the boys?" Jack seemed pleased that he didn't have to be involved. "I need to use the washroom."

"Who wants to help design and build the elephants' ears and trunk?" Rio asked.

Ack, Borden, and Lloyd expressed interest.

"We four must innovate and be planning," Rio said. "The remainder of you go do something."

Shaine, Chet, and Ric moved into the shade and started talking about girls and the dance. Sitting between the groups, Tom felt overwhelmed as he listened to both conversations. As the puppeteers brainstormed, he was fascinated by their ideas for building a large elephant puppet. But he didn't want to look like an idiot when performing. The social boys seemed so knowledgeable and sophisticated; their confidence was beyond his understanding.

There was a part of him that would prefer to stay on the water. Traveling from lake to lake and campsite to campsite had created a simple rhythm. Prepping for the Dumoine, planning for the Circus, and anticipating the dance was both thrilling and frightening. But a large part of him wished he could just paddle away from the confusion of life back at camp.

His escape deadline was the morning after the circus. He was torn. Even though he was beginning to be accepted by his fellow Scouts, he still felt like an outsider. Shaine was becoming an antagonist who was careful to publicly stay on the good side while being actively mean when no one could see. Tom was beginning to feel that he would constantly need to watch his back.

The Circus planning ended, and Borden called, "Come join us. Everybody is playing Land."

Being active and included felt good. The game ended quickly. Shaine and Chet formed an alliance and marched aggressively to victory.

"I need to pee," Ric said.

"Me too," said Chet.

Both walked toward the woods.

"Go use the washroom," Doug barked. "We're back in civilization."

"It's the brick building down the road," said Jack.

Suddenly, everyone needed to pee.

"Come back promptly," Jack said. "Remember, we're guests. Be polite. Don't hang around. Be nice. Don't do any stupid stuff."

Going inside a building without windows unexpectedly made Tom feel claustrophobic. He wondered how the other boys felt, but he didn't want to seem weird by asking about it.

Once everyone was back in the parking lot, a second game of Land began. The play became intense. Tom formed an alliance with Ack and Borden that eliminated Lloyd and Chet. They turned to battle Shaine and Ric.

In the heat of the afternoon, areas of dirt exchanged ownership. The longer the game went on, the more determined Shaine was to win, and the more Tom wanted to defeat him. In a surprise maneuver, Shaine turned on Ric. Ric's territory meant that Shaine surrounded Borden.

"I surrender," said Borden.

The momentum had changed. Shaine controlled two-thirds of the world.

Hefting the stick, Shaine smiled. "Now, I can get you."

The van pulled into the parking area, and the game ended.

Shaine, Chet, and Ric rushed at the doors.

"Wait!" Doug yelled. "After we pack everything, we'll raffle for the order of loading the van."

Behind Doug's back, Tom heard Shaine grumble under his breath to Chet and Ric.

"Wait a moment or two," said Rio. "I need to assemble

my camera."

Despite having to stop and smile for Rio's picture-taking, the loading moved quickly. Lloyd won the raffle. Tom was last.

Although they weren't the first to board, Shaine, Ric, and Chet got the prized rear seats and started talking about the dance. Tom thought their bravado about the girls was all talk. From what he could figure, the boys and the girls would be together for about four hours and almost all the time would be filled with group activities. He wondered if Cecille had sent him another letter.

Tom realized that the sun was low in the sky by the time the van reached the main road. He tried to listen as the adults discussed options for supper, but he couldn't discern anything specific.

As they approached Pembroke, Jack called for quiet.

"We will not make it back to camp for supper, so we'll have to stop and get something. We gave Henry the choice and he decided on McDonald's."

A loud cheer echoed.

"Henry and the counselors will go inside first. We'll wash up and talk with the manager. Once things are set by tent groups, you'll come in, use the washroom, and line up for food. You can get one reasonable order - burger, fries, and a drink."

"Can we super-size them?" Ric asked.

"Can we get a dessert?" asked Chet.

"Yes, and yes," said Jack. "We know that you're hungry, but you're not starving. We are in public. The camp's name is on the van. Be respectful and polite. Eh?"

The boys mumbled a chorus of "yes."

"We'll start with Borden's tent, then Lloyd, and finally Shaine's. Bring your food outside and eat on the grass near the van, eh?"

Tom suspected that Jack and Doug had followed this procedure before when Henry pulled the van and the trailer to the far end of the parking lot. Waiting in line for a single indoor washroom felt confining after the freedom of the trip. When Tom washed his hands, the soapy water was black.

The food lines were slow. By the time the last person exited with his food, Tom and most of the others had gobbled their meals.

"Can we get more?" Ric asked. "I'm still hungry."

"No," said Jack. "You ate over 2000 calories. That's an entire day's total."

"I could eat all of that, again... in a heartbeat!"

"No way," said Chet. "Your stomach would explode."

"I could do all of that in less than five minutes."

"No way."

A spirited conversation commenced about how fast people could consume McDonalds' offerings. After argument and compromise, the boys agreed on a future contest. The next time the cabin ate fast food, an eat-off would occur.

After the boys mellowed, Jack asked, "Exactly what have you decided?"

"Those interested will get a Big Mac, large fries and a shake," Chet said. "The first one to finish wins, provided he keeps the food down for half an hour."

Everyone agreed to give the winner a dollar. Having seen Chet, Ric, and Borden eat, Tom knew he couldn't win, but he found the crazy competition exciting.

Their stomachs full, several boys fell asleep during the drive. Now that he'd finished a trip, Tom wondered how he'd be seen at camp. Would he still be a new boy or be accepted as an experienced camper?

When they arrived at Catamount, twilight was deep. Henry drove the van and trailer to the canoe dock.

Before unloading, Doug said, "Put the wanigans, extra gear, and the tents inside the Boathouse. Take your bedrolls and personal stuff back to the cabin."

Earnie walked down to meet them. In an upbeat tone, he said, "Welcome back. Hope you had a good trip. I look forward to hearing about it when we talk tomorrow morning."

Then, with a quieter voice, he continued, "I want to update you on the Director. He's recovering from the accident and with time should make a full recovery. Hopefully, he'll be returning to camp before the end of the summer."

He cleared his throat.

"In the meantime, I've become the Acting Director and moved to center camp. Since we're no longer cabin mates, I'll miss getting to know you. Whenever you wish, feel free to stop by the office."

The silence was awkward. Tom was disappointed that Earnie would not be sleeping across from him. He hadn't realized how reassuring it felt to have one of his grandfather's friends in the cabin.

Shaine walked to Earnie and shook his hand.

"Congratulations on the promotion."

With the awkwardness of not-knowing-what-to-do, Chet and Ric immediately followed Shaine's lead.

"Relax. No need for formality. It's no big deal. It's temporary."

With a flourish, Earnie clamped his nostrils with his fingers.

"You smell like wood smoke, which is putrid. After I distribute your letters, paddle to the cabin and take showers. When you come to breakfast, bring your laundry."

"What about packages?" asked Chet.

"Tomorrow. Come see me after activities before lunch."

"Bummer," said Shaine. "I know my cookies will be the best."

"They always are," said Chet.

"Let's get going," said Jack. "I want a shower. You can read your mail when we get to the Point."

When Earnie distributed the mail, everyone but Tom received multiple letters. His one envelope was from his grandmother. Tom realized he hadn't thought about his grandparents in days and felt guilty.

"Let's paddle," said Rio, holding a stack of letters with strange looking stamps.

Once at the cabin, Jack raffled for the shower sequence. Tom was in the first group.

"Short showers so there'll be enough hot water for everyone. Rio and I are setting a leadership example. We'll take the last showers. We expect hot water."

The warm water and soap was refreshing and relaxing. Being squeaky clean felt wonderful. Putting on fresh clothes seemed luxurious. When Tom put his trip clothes into the laundry basket, the acrid odor bit his nose.

Sitting on his bunk, Tom opened his letter. It was handwritten, so he knew his grandmother had done it hurriedly. Deciphering her words took time.

*Dear Tom,*

*Just a quick note. I hope camp is going well. The flight back went smoothly. Grandfather pushed himself too hard and will be spending a couple of days without much activity. He doesn't seem to understand that he is lucky to be alive and that his recovery will take time. He's determined to get up to Catamount so he can see you and spend some time with Earnie. The doctor says this is questionable. However, he's already made plane reservations into Ottawa, so we'll see.*

*Hope the Algonquin trip went well. More later.*

*Love,*

*Gema*

Tom was concerned because he knew his grandfather

would move heaven and earth to come to Catamount. Tom didn't want to be the reason he was jeopardizing his health.

After the second shower rotation, Ack sat next to Tom. He whispered, "I need to tell you something."

"What?"

"Be quiet," hushed Ack. "If Shaine or Chet walk in, I'll have to stop and finish in the morning. Okay?"

"Sure."

Apprehensively, Ack watched the door.

"I heard Shaine bragging to Chet about how he tricked you into carrying the canoe for the entire Louisa portage. He didn't think I could hear them."

Tom was stunned. Before he could respond, Shaine and Chet waltzed into the cabin, talking loudly and shining their flashlights. A chorus of watch-the-lights and be-quiet came from the clean Scouts encapsulated in their sleeping bags. The two continued whispering loudly.

When Jack and Rio returned from the showers, Shaine and Chet slid into their bunks.

Outside, the darkness was complete.

"No story tonight," Jack said. "Sleep well."

In his sleeping bag, Tom wrestled with Ack's news. He had been right to question which ankle Shaine had sprained. Looking back, he realized that Shaine had shown no discomfort during Land. Should he tell anyone? If he did, what could be done? Shaine would just deny everything.

His shoulders ached. As he lay still, it seemed so quiet. No leaves rustled, no bugs hummed, no loons called. Tom's mind raced. While he tried to be silent, he knew his restlessness echoed throughout the cabin. Maybe going back to the city would be the right thing to do. But the Dumoine pulled at his core. Wrestling with pros and cons, he longed for sleep.

# Chapter 14
## Moving Water to Elephants

In the middle of the night, Tom awakened to pee. Knowing the exact steps to the bushes and what to avoid along the way was comforting. The air felt colder outside the cabin.

As Tom wormed his way back into his sleeping bag, his thoughts began to whirl again. He was angry that Shaine had conned him. His grandmother needed help but would never admit it. He was worried about his grandfather. Tom felt useless in Canada. He was confused about what to do.

Knowing that Shaine was bragging about his deviousness infuriated Tom, but he was conflicted. Shaine was outspoken and shrewd, and would deny his transgression. Tom knew that speaking against Shaine could be perilous. On the other hand, he'd been tricked because he'd tried to help a fellow Scout.

And while he didn't want to run away, the bright lights of New York City and its comforts were appealing.

His agitation deepened as he tried to relax. His breathing exercises didn't seem to be working...

"Up and at 'em!"

Jack's cry roused Tom from a deep sleep. When he sat up, his head banged against the angled roof. He cursed silently and missed sleeping in a tent. Pulling on dry socks and shoes felt delightful, and his hooded sweatshirt warmed him. The cabin rang with energy as his fellow

Scouts jostled and joked. He missed the early morning tranquility of a campsite.

As they walked to the washroom, Ack glanced around before he spoke.

"What are we going to do about Shaine?"

"Not sure. Probably nothing. He'd deny it. We're newbies, and I'm not sure that anyone would believe us."

Tom saw Ack thinking and wondered what he was contemplating.

"I guess you're right. None of the others will stand up to him. He schemes in the background and does stuff when no one can see. It sucks."

"Yes, it does. Maybe something will happen, and he'll get his."

"We can hope."

Before the Scouts paddled to breakfast, Jack called them together.

"Don't forget to check the job wheel. You won't need bathing suits until this afternoon. We'll be back at the cabin for rest hour."

Tom was scheduled for fields clean-up today, cabin sweeper tomorrow, and washroom sweeper on Thursday. He was relieved to have simple solitary tasks for the next few days.

As the Scouts paddled back to Boat Bay, Tom realized their daily canoe groups had fallen into a pattern. He was in the stern with Ack and Borden in front of him. Shaine was the stern man with Chet in front. The third camper boat had Ric paddling ahead of Lloyd. Tom was pleased they both looked fully recovered from their injuries. Jack and Rio paddled together and discussed staff things.

There were fewer boys milling around the Main Yard and Tom assumed that many of the younger boys were out on their trips. He hoped that this would mean a quieter Dining Hall.

After racking the canoes, Jack called the Scouts

together.

"First period, we have our debrief with Earnie, and then we do our post-trip cleanup. You'll be free for second period."

"Let's all practice softball," said Shaine. "We've got to be ready for the Lumberjack Roundup."

Tom was not playing softball. He did not want to be anywhere near Shaine. Rio said he'd work on their circus act. While Tom was interested, he needed time and space.

When the breakfast bell rang, the boys surged into the Dining Hall. Even with fewer campers the noise was grating. Feeling unfocused, Tom tried to make sense of conversations floating around him. Life had been simpler on the trip, although sitting at a table was definitely easier than squatting on a rock and balancing a bowl in one hand.

During announcements, he decided to canoe during second period. If he decided to stay, becoming a better paddler would be important.

After breakfast, the entire camp walked to the parking lot to send off the Voyageurs. They looked prepared and confident, ready for their five-week journey into the wilds of Quebec. Caught up in the excitement, Tom wanted to be a Voyageur next summer. After boring speeches by Earnie and George, the expeditioners climbed into the van. With a loud cheer, they drove out the gravel road, throwing up clouds of white dust.

As they walked down from the parking lot, Tom asked, "Jack, when do I clean up the fields?"

"Don't worry. I took care of it. You don't have to do it. I told the Admin-in-Charge that we had a post-trip meeting with Earnie."

While Tom was relieved to know he was excused, a part of him had looked forward to walking around by himself.

Jack ushered the Scouts into the Trip Shed, where

Earnie joined them.

"It's a tradition for the Director to talk with boys after their trips. I'd like to hear the highlights of your trip. We'll go around the circle. Ric, you start."

"I liked how everyone pitched in to help when I was hurt. My leg feels much better today."

"That's good to hear. I'm glad that your Catamount brothers were supportive. Shaine, you're next."

"I liked catching the lake trout on Louisa." Shaine smiled. "Having Chet cook it was even better."

Shaine's comment sounded positive, but Tom knew he was playing at being a good camper.

"Chet, you're next. No repeating what's already been said by people before you."

Chet was caught off-guard by not being able to repeat things. An awkward silence hung.

"I liked the way we combined loads by putting bedrolls into the wanigans. That made portaging easier."

"That was good thinking. Who suggested it?"

"It was Tom's idea."

"New perspectives are welcome. Glad to hear the American contributed." Earnie winked at Tom. "Lloyd, what did you like?"

"Being a GFD. Having the maps and making decisions made me appreciate how everybody works together."

"Excellent, more brotherhood," said Earnie. "Ack, you're next."

"I liked winning the sailing race. It's too bad Tom's coat ripped, but otherwise, we might not have won."

"That sounds exciting. I'd like to hear more about sailing at some point. Now, Tom, what was your highlight?"

"The whole trip. I'd never done anything like this before. I loved being outside all the time. I didn't mind the rain. As hard as it was, carrying the canoe for the entire Louisa portage gave me a sense of accomplishment."

All of his fellow Scouts smiled. Tom knew he had said nothing stupid. But Shaine's grin looked like a smirk.

"Sounds like you're learning to appreciate the North. I heard adventure, brotherhood, and courage. Borden, you're the last."

"I liked using the Fry Bake. I think it's easier than a reflector oven."

"Thanks for sharing," said Earnie. "I'm interested in the Fry Bake. A question for everyone - What do you think about the two baking methods?"

The comments were observant and thoughtful. The discussion, which became spirited, showed no consensus about which was better. Each device had its positives and negatives.

"Thanks for your opinions," said Earnie. "We want to try new things. While we value our Catamount traditions, we need to stay abreast of what's happening in the larger world of camping and tripping. Jack, how's clean-up organized?"

"By GFD groups. Borden, your group can hang the tents, the packs, and the big green tarp to dry in the sun. Before lunch, come back, fold them, and put them away. Remember to note any holes so we can repair them. We'll be using them on the Dumoine. Ric and Lloyd will take the pots, pans, bowls, and cutlery to the dish room for a thorough cleansing in hot, soapy water. Shaine and Chet will wash out the wanigans, refill the spice bottles, polish the reflector oven, and put away the tools. Any questions?"

There were none.

"Go to it."

The clean-up went smoothly, and all the groups finished at about the same time.

"Next period and the first period this afternoon are open. Do what you want," Jack said.

"Softball practice!" said Shaine.

"Or elephant building," said Rio. "Remember, the Circus is coming."

"Yes!" stated Jack, with emphasis. "Some of you need to help Rio, or we'll be embarrassed tomorrow."

"I'll help with elephants," said Ack.

"Me too," said Borden.

Tom saw Shaine give Borden a dirty look. The bell rang for second period.

As they exited the Trip Shed, Ack asked, "Want to come help with the elephants?"

"Thanks, but no. I'm going to work on my paddling," Tom said. "I'll get some quiet time. I need to think."

"I understand." Ack nodded. "See you later."

At the Canoe Dock, Tom saw only a few boats on the water.

"How was the Park?" George smiled.

"It was great. A good trip."

"How much did you paddle in the stern?"

"Some." Because Tom didn't want to talk about the details of the trip, he asked a question. "Are there many people who don't want to paddle in the stern?"

"Yes. Some find it hard to keep a canoe going in a straight line. Why do you ask?"

"I was surprised at how many weren't comfortable."

"The stern takes concentration and practice. Not everyone your age wants to put in the time and effort."

"Well, I do. What test is next for me?"

"Go get your paddle and lifejacket. I'll check."

When Tom returned, George said, "At the advanced intermediate level, you need one thing. That's paddling the triangular course during a windy day. Today won't work."

The weather was lovely, sunny with a gentle breeze. Tom was disappointed.

"However, you can start your solo paddling."

"Sure."

"I'll paddle beside you, so we need to get two canoes."

Tom helped George put a 16-foot wood and canvas canoe at the edge of the dock.

"Let's get a practice canoe."

From inside the Boat House, they carried a 14-foot canoe. As they placed it in the water, George said, "It's shorter and lighter, which makes it more responsive."

Once they were in the water, George said, "I know that you've done this before, but watch me carefully."

Kneeling behind the center thwart, George sat on his ankles. He shifted his weight into the rounded side of the canoe so that the right gunwale was three inches above the surface. He pulled gently with his paddle. The canoe slid forward. Tom was surprised when George's paddle remained in the water for both pull and recovery.

"Now, do the exact same thing."

Tom kneeled and shifted his weight into the canoe's tumblehome. Even though he'd done this before, Tom felt unsteady and was afraid that he was going to tip over.

"Relax. You are more stable than you think," said George. "Rock the canoe, and you'll see. It helps to have your paddle in the water so you can brace as needed."

After readying his paddle, Tom wiggled his hips. The canoe didn't capsize, but he still didn't feel secure.

"Now, take a forward stroke."

Tom pulled with power. The canoe glided forward, and its bow swung dramatically to the left.

"From the start, you need to build in your correction. Trace a shallow C with the power face of your paddle. Then recover in the water so you can correct the canoe's direction using the edge as a rudder. Watch me."

Concentrating on his hands and the paddle took an intense focus. After several attempts, Tom's canoe traveled in a straight line. He was pleased with himself, but his knees and calves began to throb. He rocked gently, trying not to groan.

"You're hurting, aren't you?"

"Yes, a lot."

"Sit up and stretch. I forget how long it takes for your body to accept the kneeling position. It's not easy or natural."

After stretching for a few minutes, Tom resumed the solo position. This time, it felt a bit better, and he relaxed. George led him through a series of exercises, turning the canoe to both the left and the right.

"You're beginning to get the hang of it. Let's try something more challenging."

George maneuvered his boat so that it was perpendicular to the dock. "Sit up and stretch your legs. Watch me side-slip."

Keeping the canoe at a right angle to the dock and its bow near the edge, George moved sideways, first away and then toward Tom.

"On your paddle-side, you scull. Going away from your paddle, you pry. For the test, the bow must stay within a foot of the dock for 15 meters in both directions."

"Sounds hard."

"Not really. It takes practice. Go ahead. Try it."

At first, Tom's canoe had a mind of its own, wanting to rotate. He shortened his strokes and gentled the power, and the boat began to respond.

"You're getting it. That's enough for today."

Tom's calves, thighs, and knees throbbed when he got out of the canoe.

"It happens to everyone." After exiting his canoe, even George's first steps looked uncomfortable. "The more you do it, the easier it becomes. But it always hurts a little."

Tom smiled as George stretched some more.

After they put the canoes away, George said, "You've got a few minutes before the period ends. If I were you, I'd go up to the office. There's a package or two for you."

Tom walked up the hill to the Lodge office. Earnie looked up from his deck. "Tom, good to see you. How can I help you?"

"Is there a package for me?"

"Matter of fact, there are two. I hope one solves your raincoat problem. It sounded like you would have beaten Doug if your coat hadn't ripped."

With a look of confusion, Tom said, "I forgot I need a new rain jacket."

"Coming back from a trip can be discombobulating."

The once empty shelves were loaded with cardboard boxes. Earnie selected two boxes with New York return addresses.

"You can open them here. Any treats will be shared with your cabin mates. We manage each cabin's sweets. Several of your fellow Scouts have boxes. They'll come open theirs after activities. Jack will take the day's offerings to the cabin after lunch."

"The day's offerings?" asked Tom.

"We don't let anyone take all of his food to the cabins. It attracts bugs and varmits. Eh?"

One box had a long letter and clothes. The other contained a large tin of cookies and two cardboard boxes of Swiss bittersweet chocolate bars.

"If you'd like, you can sit and read the letter."

"Thanks, I will."

The letter was from his grandfather. It was long, but thankfully, it was typed. Grandfather did like to talk and write.

```
Dear Tom,
    I am typing this so hopefully it will
be easier for you to read. I am writing
while you and Gema are on your way to
Catamount and will get it to the Post
Office as soon as I can. I hope that it
gets to you before your first trip. This
```

box contains some things that I think you will find helpful. As you probably know by now, Gema rushed when she packed your clothes for Catamount. I imagine that you have some outfits that are not practical for the trail. If the clothing doesn't get to you until after your first trip, then you'll really appreciate what I'm sending.

First, and probably most important, is the red-checked wool shirt. Wool keeps you warm when it gets wet. A cotton sweatshirt does not. It'll keep you warm when you get up to pee in the middle of the night. The other red thing is a wind shirt. It's finely woven Egyptian cotton, so it's both light and water resistant. It'll cut the chill of the wind and keep you warmer without making you sweaty and clammy. It took me a while to find this. I wasn't sure that anyone still made them, but I loved mine. Hopefully, it'll work for you.

The green jacket and matching pants are a rain suit. It will keep you dry in heavy rain. It's made of Gore-Tex, which is supposed to keep you dry and also breathe so you don't get overheated. I'll be fascinated to talk with you about whether it works. If you are like me, you'll begin to sweat heavily if you are doing any physical activity while wearing the rain stuff. I rarely used my rain gear when I was actually paddling or portaging. I wore it when I was in camp or at a campsite. On trips, I often just wore my lifejacket and my wool shirt. If it got really cold, I'd put on my wool pants. But I'm not sending any wool pants because you will not be in the far North, just the near North. And it's summer. I always wore shorts until October.

However, I am sending a set of cashmere

long underwear. I was able to find a set for you in gray. It's designed for older ladies in the winter. Generally, they sell it in pink or light blue. My grandmother heard me complaining about the cold at camp and told me about how she kept warm in the winter. Her house in Scarsdale was always cold. My set was so very helpful. If you are like me, being warm is nice, especially at night. To keep your roll small, the staff may make you choose between the wind shirt and the long underwear. Take the underwear. It's easier to roll.

The cookies in the tin are from my favorite bakery down the street. Share them with your cabin mates. The chocolate bars are for your next trip. We found that the Swiss bittersweet chocolate didn't melt as quickly as regular milk chocolate bars. They are a delightful treat at lunch or after the long afternoon portage. I'm sending two cases as I believe that you have two trips.

I'm getting my strength back. By the time you read this, I know I will be taking walks outside. There is nothing better for one's recovery than pushing your limits. I look forward to taking long walks in the Park.

I know camp is going well. As I said when you left with Gema, I admire your decision to go to a new place where no one knows you. Catamount was a wonderful place for me and your father. I believe you will make friends and enjoy canoe tripping.

We need to paddle together again. When you were little, we did some simple trips. I was stronger and did almost everything. Now, I'm older, and you are young and strong. It's your turn to carry the canoe and gather the firewood.

   Please give Earnie my best and tell him
I WILL make it up to Catamount at the end
of July.
Love,
Grandfather


"Grandfather says hello," said Tom. "He's coming up to Catamount."

"Thanks." Earnie smiled. "He and I talked for a while yesterday. He sends his best to you. He's beginning to walk outside and feels confident that he and your grandmother will come at the end of July. It'll be good to see him."

Tom was surprised that his grandfather talked with Earnie. They seemed to be talking quite often and wondered what they were discussing.

"He'd love to get into a canoe and said he'd love to paddle in your bow. George tells me you have promise."

With hope in his voice, Tom asked, "I'm a rookie. Do you think I could be a stern man on the Dumoine?"

"Maybe. Some stern men are made with time and practice. Others take to it almost instinctively. Doug told me you are a natural in a canoe."

"Thanks." Tom beamed.

"You got some letters in today's mail. Do you want them now, or do you want to wait until it's handled out at lunch?"

"I'll wait. Don't want the other Scouts thinking I get special privileges."

After an awkward moment, Earnie asked, "Is everything okay?"

"Yeah. I'm fine."

Tom wondered how Earnie knew he was troubled.

"I'm here if you want to talk."

"Thanks. See you later."

Tom walked to the tetherball courts to wait for lunch.

"Where were you?" Shaine demanded. "After practice, we put away the dry stuff. We did your job for you."

"Sorry. I forgot. I was talking with Earnie."

"Brown noser." Shaine turned to the other Scouts. "Who's next? I'm unbeatable."

Shaine had assumed the winner's role. Frowning, Tom watched.

Ack and Borden arrived a minute later.

"We had a great start," Ack said.

"The elephants are going to be fantastic," Borden said. "We're going to be the best ever."

"Elephants are stupid!" said Shaine. "We need to concentrate on winning the softball and basketball games."

Both Ack and Borden waited in the challenge line. The others were eager to see Ack and Shaine battle again. Their last match before the Park trip had been epic. As Ack stepped onto the court, the lunch bell rang.

"Saved by the sound," Shaine said. "Scotsmen suck sheep stomachs."

"Haggis is horrible," said Chet.

A silence fell, and Tom began to feel uncomfortable.

Breaking the tension, Lloyd said, "Let's go see what's for lunch."

Spaghetti and meatballs were better than PB & J on bannock. In the middle of lunch, Earnie distributed mail to the Scouts. Everyone received several letters. Quiet descended on the table.

Tom's letters came from his mother and his grandmother. Jack handed him a bright pink envelope from Cecille. His hands got sweaty.

Tom realized he missed his mother, so he started with her letter. Her fancy handwriting was difficult to read.

*Dear Tom,*

*I miss you and hope that camp is going well.*

*Your grandmother wrote and told me about your grandfather's accident and your decision to go to camp. Your father really enjoyed Catamount and felt that it had been good for him. I hope that you are being careful and making friends.*

*Delhi is a fascinating city. You'll love it when you visit over the holidays. Our apartment is first class with four large bedrooms and a lovely balcony. We have a maid, a driver and a cook who does all the shopping. He's a wonderful man whose meals are a treat.*

*Pierre's job means we are going to lots of parties and meeting fascinating people from all over the world. It's very exciting. I have friends from Paris, Bonn, Tokyo and Bangkok. We are exploring the city together.*

*I hope that camp goes well for you. Stay safe.*
*Love,*
*Mom*

As Tom finished, the announcement bell rang. After hearing about Ack and Borden's plans during lunch, the creation of the elephant puppets intrigued Tom. He'd agreed to help them afterwards, so he paid no attention to what was said.

As the Scouts waited on the Canoe Dock for the waiter and washer, Jack went over the schedule for the next two days.

"Second period this afternoon is paddling prep for white water. Be ready to get wet. Tomorrow morning, we'll drive to the dam for actual moving water preparation. We'll get wet. Early tomorrow afternoon is circus prep. Late afternoon tomorrow is the Circus followed by the dance. And finally, much of Thursday will be trip prep and packing for the Dumoine. Any questions?"

No one spoke. Tom suspected that everyone was tired of Jack continually repeating the schedule.

"You need to write another letter home. It's due before dinner on Thursday."

"Really?" asked Ric. "We wrote letters home less than a week ago."

"Yes. We're back in civilization. Some of your parents would like to know that you're still alive. Write about what we did in the Park. Tell them that we'll be out for two weeks on the Dumoine. Who has care-packages in the office?"

Besides Tom's, several hands went up.

"Excellent. I'll bring some from each box."

Jack walked to the office and returned to the canoes with a large shopping bag filled with cookies.

"Got some from each box." Jack smiled. "No one will go hungry."

After they landed at the cabin, Jack said, "Air out your sleeping bags. Put them on the clothesline or drape them over a bush. Then, I hand out the goodies."

From the multitude of sweet treats, Tom was pleased that his cookies were judged the best. The boys scattered around the point, enjoying the sunshine. After Tom had spread his sleeping bag over a bush, he opened his grandmother's letter. She had typed it but reading still took time and effort.

Dear Tom,
   I know camp is going well for you. Earnie told me it's still the wonderful place that

it was for Grandfather and for your dad. He told me that your counselors are the best and that the boys in your cabin are fine young men. I think that you'll find that the Canadians are no different from your friends here in the city.

I hope that your trip to Algonquin Park went well. As a girl, I did several trips in the Park.

Grandfather is slowly getting better. He is trying to push himself so he'll be able to get up to Catamount. The doctor has said that it is possible, but it will be a last-minute decision. As you know, he can be so headstrong. At times, he's driving me crazy, but what's new. He did not get where he is by being timid or listening to people when they tried to say No or IT WON'T WORK.

I have been looking at schools for you. There are a couple of options in Connecticut that would be good for you and your needs as a learner. One might mean that we would all move up to the cabin, and Grandfather or I would drive you to school each day. The other option would be a boarding school where you could come home on most weekends. The boarding school is bigger. It has a full athletic program so you can continue with your sports. It also has an outdoor program that operates all year. In the winter, they ski, both downhill and cross-country. You might really like cross-country skiing. It's like your long distance running, but on skis through the woods.

Let me know your thoughts about the two schools. Both are interested in having you attend in the fall. You will need to meet in person with whichever school you decide makes sense to you. It is your decision.

I am hoping to come up to Catamount at the end of July. It was so peaceful to be away

from the city.
Love,
Gema

Tom was pleased that his grandfather was doing better but afraid that his intense drive might cloud his judgment. He also had confidence that his grandmother would find good schools for him. His mother had been more concerned about the school's reputation than about finding a place that would help him be a more effective student. Sitting still while listening to a lecture was so hard. Tom loved to learn by doing things; He'd learned so much at Catamount. Maybe one of the schools would be more like camp.

Cecille's letter was next. There had been a few comments at lunch when Jack produced the pink envelope. With the Circus and the dance coming, he knew that there would be more catcalls. But he hoped that knowing one of the girls might make interacting with new people less awkward.

Tom,

Welcome back to camp. I hope that your trip to the Park was good. Duncan said that his work trip last summer was a nightmare, and they spent a whole day building a bridge over a swamp.

I'm working on my solo paddling skills and am getting much better at my landings. We leave for our big trip after the circus. We'll be spending almost two weeks in Algonquin Park. I wish that we were doing a whitewater river like you.

No need to write back as I'll see you at the circus.
Your paddling friend,
Cecille

Tom wondered whether Cecille was a time and practice paddler or a natural. He realized it didn't matter. She was very good in a canoe.

Ack put down his letters. Tom walked over.

"What's the news from home?"

"Not much. Mom hasn't found a job yet, but she says that there are some good prospects. She enjoys living with her parents and says that their apartment is very convenient – she can walk everywhere. And my grandfather is jealous of my being at camp. What's your news?"

"About the same. My mother loves living in Delhi, lots of parties. She's got a cook and a driver, so she's happy. My grandfather's getting better. He and my grandmother are hoping to come get me at the end of July."

"That's good."

Tom was glad that Ack hadn't asked about high school, a subject he wished to avoid.

"Time for sleeping bags to come in," Jack yelled. "Get ready for the afternoon."

As they loaded into their canoes, Jack asked, "Does everyone have his bathing suit?"

Both Ric and Shaine had forgotten and the other Scouts waited impatiently for them to return to the boats.

The paddle to the Canoe Dock was almost silent. Tom wondered if it was the intensity of the sunshine on a cloudless afternoon, or each Scout being caught up in the news from home.

Ack and Borden were eager to show Tom the results of their efforts. A variety of small pieces of lumber and various cloths were strewn around a corner of the Trip Shed. With Rio's guidance, they had engineered a three-person elephant that used pulleys and stretchy cords to curl the trunk. One boy stood as the front legs and manipulated the trunk. The second boy bent at the waist to become the elephant's rear legs. The third boy sat on

336

the front boy's shoulders and used his arms to flap the ears. Old, wrinkled tent cloth had become the elephant's skin.

"What needs to be done?" Tom asked.

"We need to finish sewing the skin," said Borden.

"Then we need to work on one or two more elephants," said Ack. "But I'm not sure we have enough time. Any ideas?"

Making another three-person elephant would be difficult and time consuming.

"What if the three-person elephant is the mom and we have two babies," said Tom. "They could be two-person puppets. The standing person maneuvers the ears, and the back person could use one of his arms to swing the trunk. That way, there's no pulley to build."

"Outstanding," said Borden.

"Makes perfect sense," said Ack. "But do we have enough time? The sewing is slow."

Ack was right. The elephant skin had to be more than cloth draped over a person. It had to have some shape.

"What about using staples and duct tape?" Tom asked. "The costumes aren't going to be permanent."

"Tom, you're a genius," said Ack.

After Rio acquired two staplers and several rolls of tape, construction moved rapidly.

The mother elephant was ready first. Sitting on Borden's shoulders, Tom became its head and flapped the ears. Borden manipulated the trunk. Bending at the waist, Ack became the hind legs. Rio was delighted and snapped photos.

With the three working together, construction sped up. When the bell rang for the second afternoon period, they were excited to have completed two of the three elephants. They were hopeful that finishing the third would take only a few minutes.

The Scouts met at the Swim Shed and changed into

water clothes. They found Doug waiting for them on the Canoe Dock.

"Good to see you again, my faithful Scouts. I will be your guide on the Dumoine."

Tom was pleased and sensed that most of his cabin mates were happy. Shaine didn't seem excited.

"Let's get canoes in the water. Lifejackets on. We'll start with two people to each boat. Jack and I are paddling together. Tom, start in Rio's bow."

Tom was disappointed.

"Ric, you're in my bow," Shaine said. "Lloyd, Chet can go in your bow. Borden teach Ack what to do in the bow."

Tom saw Jack frown and look at Doug. Doug shook his head and mouthed "no."

Once the canoes were away from the dock, Doug said, "This afternoon, we're reviewing canoe-over-canoe and some simple paddling skills. But we'll throw in some tricks."

Tom saw eyes rolls. The Scouts had done numerous boat rescues in the previous summers.

"Pay attention. Rio and Tom will capsize first."

Rio immediately rolled their canoe, catching Tom off guard. Sputtering to the surface, Tom saw Jack and Doug flip.

From behind him, Shaine shouted, "Shit! What are you doing?"

Rio was capsizing his canoe.

Tom heard a yell from Chet, followed by splashes. Someone had overturned Chet and Lloyd's boat.

Four canoes were upside down.

"Quickly!" yelled Doug. "Get us out of the water and into our canoes."

Swimming away, pushing a water-filled canoe, Jack shouted, "We're floating towards a waterfall!"

From the only upright canoe, Borden took control.

First, he and Ack righted Doug's boat and then Rio's. Then, Doug and Jack quickly emptied Shaine's canoe. At the same time, Borden and Ack helped Tom and Rio into their boat. The two experienced counselors moved quickly to Lloyd's boat, righted it, and helped both boys out of the water. Tom was impressed how smoothly the confusion was cleared.

Once the canoes were upright and the paddlers ready, Doug said, "Borden, you did a good job getting things started, but the whole process took too long. On the river, we need to be ready for anything. You always need to be ready to rescue someone or something and do it quickly. We try to be safe, but rivers are tricky places. Understand?"

Heads nodded. Doug had made his point.

"Now, we're going to play follow the leader. Expect some new commands, eh?"

The Scouts tensed.

"Follow Jack and me. Stay as close together as possible."

The canoes completed a diamond drill without any of the canoes hitting one another.

"That went well," Doug said. "On to the slalom course."

"This is where my whitewater paddle will shine." Shaine held his new paddle aloft.

Even though he had paddled the course with George, Tom welcomed Doug's explanations. To the right of a small floating dock, the starting line stretched between two poles suspended about two meters apart. After the start, three gates - pairs of identically colored poles - guided the canoes right, left, right. At the far end of the course, the canoe circled completely around a buoy. On the way back to the finish line, the canoe angled through three more gates going left, right, left.

"Jack and I will start. Shaine and Ric, you're second.

Rio and Tom, third. Then, Borden and Ack. Lloyd and Chet's boat will be last."

As Tom watched the two canoes in front of them paddle the course, the sequence of strokes seemed obvious. For a change, Rio grasped how to snake the canoe through the hanging poles. Tom hoped that Rio was beginning to absorb the finer points of canoeing.

Everyone's teamwork was smooth until Doug yelled, "Your canoe hit a rock. It's turned around. Reverse positions and finish paddling the course."

Tom spun quickly. Rio turned around slowly. His strokes became awkward and ineffective.

"Faster!" Doug barked. "Waterfall ahead!"

At first, Tom struggled but quickly gained control. When he realized that many of the others had been flustered, he didn't feel as bad.

After all the canoes finished, Doug rearranged the boats. Tom was partnered with Chet.

"Take the stern," Chet said. "I'm no good there."

This time, the new pairings ran the course, timed from start to finish. Tom and Chet were third.

"We'll do another timed run with the same groupings," said Doug. "We expect improved times. Talk with your partner."

"What can I do better?" Chet asked.

"Reach further and pull harder," Tom said. "If we tilt too far, I'll brace so we don't flip."

"You sure?"

Smiling, Tom projected a confidence that he didn't have.

"I've got you. We're a team."

During their second run, Chet leaned and twisted with more agility. Their time improved by nine seconds, the best improvement of the Scout canoes.

"New partners. Tom, go into Lloyd's bow."

Tom was disheartened. He'd hoped to continue in the

stern.

"New partner, new challenge." Doug stood on the floating dock. "Each canoe will paddle towards me. I'll point left or right. Turn in that direction and paddle past the floating dock."

Shaine and Ack were first. Doug didn't point until their canoe was close to the dock. They reacted slowly, and the canoe almost hit the dock.

"Tom and Lloyd, you're next."

Having already seen the drill, their canoe was more responsive. After two runs for all canoes, Doug had the paddlers switch ends and repeat the exercise. Both in the bow and in the stern, Tom felt he worked well with Lloyd.

"That's all for today," Doug called. "Tomorrow morning will be exciting. Head to the Canoe Dock."

After changing into dry clothes, the Scouts played tetherball. Tom won several matches, but never more than three in a row. Being included in the give and take of the challenger's line made him feel good. For a change, Shaine didn't dominate everyone. Ack seemed to anticipate his moves and beat him a couple of times.

When the dinner bell rang, Shaine was defending the winner's place and shouted, "I'm the King! Let's get inside."

The Scouts were surprised and followed.

The conversation at supper was animated. Initially, the boys speculated about canoe groupings. On the river, they knew three counselors would be in the stern. Shaine had strong ideas about who should paddle with whom; he would be the camper stern man. Eventually, talk turned to the Circus. Tom, Borden, and Ack tried to convince the others that the elephants would be a great act. Shaine and Ric thought otherwise.

At Shaine's insistence, they discussed the line-up of the softball team. Shaine felt that the starting team should include all the Scouts. Succumbing to the pressure, Tom agreed to play. But he stated clearly that he hadn't played much softball in the past. As the meal ended, Jack told the boys that they would spend the evening finishing the elephants and practicing their act.

In the Trip Shed, Borden, Ack, and Tom displayed the completed elephant to the others. "They look ridiculous." Shaine said under his breath. "We're going to be laughingstocks."

"I heard that," Jack said.

A deep silence fell over the boys. Tom felt awkward and guessed that the others felt the same way.

"Let's talk it out," said Jack. "We need to clear the air. We're not being brotherly. Shaine, what do you want to do?"

"The Circus is stupid. We need to practice for the softball game. No one cares about what kind of act we do."

Tom sensed agreement from Ric and Chet.

"Okay, Shaine. With the Voyageurs on their trip, we're the oldest. This is our first time to be the camp leaders. The Scouts are the final Circus act. We have to do something impressive. What do you think our act should be? Does anyone remember what the Scouts did last year?"

"They were clowns," said Lloyd. "They burned the Boat House with cardboard flames. They rescued George with hoses and buckets of water. Remember?"

"Yeah. It was kind of silly, but it was funny when they carried George out in the canoe and threw him in the lake," said Chet.

Tom saw the old-time campers smile.

"Yeah. That was pretty creative," said Ric.

"Well, I thought it was stupid," said Shaine.

"Okay, Shaine." Jack paused and continued in a conversational voice. "You're in charge. You tell us what to do. You tell Borden, Ack, Tom, and Rio that their work has been a waste of time. You are the King of the Scouts."

Tom heard a sharp intake of breath. Jack had called out Shaine for being a jerk. Tom knew Shaine was trapped.

After a tense few seconds, Shaine said, "I'm sorry. I'm worried about winning the Lumberjack Roundup. The elephant act could be good. I know Borden is excited about it."

"Thanks, Shaine," said Jack. "Now, let's find out how we become elephants. Rio, you're the designer. What do we do?"

Turning to Borden, Ack, and Tom, Rio said, "Boys, go put on the elephant suit."

Once in costume, the three waddled across the floor. Tom flapped the ears. While lifting the trunk, Borden 'honked.'

"That's neat," said Ric.

"Very impressive," said Chet. "I've never seen anything like that."

"Me neither," said Lloyd. "It's pretty cool."

Borden explained how the ropes operated for maneuvering the mother's trunk. Ack described how the baby elephants would work. For one baby, Ric became front legs and ears with Shaine being the hind legs and managing the trunk. The other little elephant had Lloyd in front and Chet behind.

With additional hands, finishing the remaining skin took only a few minutes. Then, the three elephants practiced individually, learning to walk in costume, wiggle the ears, and manipulate the trunks.

When the boys felt comfortable, Rio became the ringmaster and orchestrated the elephants' group movements. They marched out, turned to their right, and put their right feet forward. They circled to the left, and, with a group 'honk,' they wiggled their trunks in unison. To end the act, the elephants circled and marched off stage. The entire performance took about a minute and a half.

"Excellent. Well done." From the door, Earnie clapped loudly.

The elephants came apart. Standing half-in and half-out of their costumes, the boys were embarrassed and self-conscious.

"From what I saw, your act looks very creative. However, I have one question," said Earnie. "What's Jack's role?"

Jack was sitting in a corner.

"He needs one," said Earnie. "Jack, come here. Rio as well. I have an idea."

The three conferred. A big smile spread on their faces. Jack headed outside. Earnie walked to the supply room and came out with a small pot.

"Ack, come here."

Earnie handed the pot to Ack. Earnie whispered to Ack, who nodded and smiled.

"We will do the act one more time," said Rio, "to see how much time we need for getting ready. We will be the last act, so we must be smart to not be in costume any much longer than we must. Go stand next to your costume."

Each elephant talked about how to dress most efficiently.

"What's in the pot?" Tom asked.

Ack smiled. "You'll see. It's a surprise."

"We're ready," Chet said.

"Just a minute," said Rio.

Jack popped his head inside the door. "I'm ready."

"Earnie, can you time the length of our acting for us?" said Rio.

"Sure."

"Everyone ready. Get into costume."

It took longer than expected. Finally, the three

elephants were in starting position. Rio walked onto the pretend stage.

"Ladies and gentlemen," Rio's introduction began.

The pachyderms executed their routine. Earnie clapped. In a new finish, Rio ordered the elephants to take a bow.

"Stand tall," whispered Ack. "This is my cue."

From under the costume, Tom saw the baby elephants trying to bend. He felt Ack move and heard something scatter onto the floor. From the corner of his eye, Tom saw Jack, wearing a silly cap, jump through the doorway pushing a wheelbarrow. He shuffled to the pile, held his nose, and swept up whatever was on the floor. When finished, he bowed to the imaginary crowd and trotted off. Rio ordered the elephants to exit.

"Bravo!" Earnie clapped. "A superb performance. An Academy Award!"

The elephants tumbled apart. Laughter exploded when Ack revealed that the pot contained peanuts. "That's neat," said Shaine. "Jack performed pushing putrid poo."

The tension of performing dissipated as the Scouts realized the final focus would be on Jack and not on them.

After two more run-throughs, the Scouts left feeling good about their act.

On the paddle to the cabin, Tom was surprised to see Ric join Shaine and Chet as a three-man canoe. Borden stayed in his bow. Ack paddled with Lloyd. As the Scouts paddled, the western sky turned gold. Tom wondered what weather the glow forecast.

On the way back to the cabin from the washhouse, Ack stopped, looked around, and whispered.

"Tom, tomorrow at the dam, be careful if you have Ric or Chet in your boat."

"Why?"

"I'm not sure. During the paddle back to the cabin, I

heard Shaine lambasting Chet for his slalom paddling with you. I think he was trying to get both of them to sabotage you in the white water."

"Thanks for the heads-up. Go ahead so no one will think we were talking."

Tom was beginning to feel that he couldn't succeed in spite of trying to get out of Shaine's way. But he wanted to be the best paddler possible. In some way, he felt that by working hard, he could connect with his grandfather and honor his father's memory.

Back at the cabin, the boys anticipated the next day with bubbling excitement. Both white water at the dam and the dance after the circus were electrifying. Tom listened.

"In honor of the dance, I'll start a new Jack London story," Jack said. "He wrote *Call of the Wild*."

"He's one of my favorites," Shaine said. "Everyone be quiet."

"Thank you," said Jack. "It's called *A Daughter of the Snows*. It's about a girl in the Yukon during the gold rush."

Eventually, everyone settled into their bunks. Jack began reading. The cabin was quiet.

At first, the story held Tom's interest, but not for long. Whitewater and acting were new challenges. He tossed and turned in his sleeping bag. The thought of paddling in moving water was thrilling and scary. He wasn't sure that he was ready. Ack's news had added a new level of concern. Being on stage in front of a crowd made him anxious. He wondered what the girls would think of a pooing elephant. Cecille kept creeping to the front of his thoughts. While he'd seen her only for part of a day, her letter had been encouraging. He hoped that she'd be happy to see him.

"Ric, be quiet or you'll be sleeping on the floor next to me," Jack barked.

Ric had been whispering with Shaine.

"Yeah, be quiet," Shaine whispered, loud enough for all to hear.

There were no more sounds. Jack continued reading.

The night was cooling, so Tom wormed into his sleeping bag. Tomorrow, he would try to keep a low profile and watch his back.

Jack's slow reading about snowstorms and dog sleds became monotonous. Tom lost interest. Eventually, the warmth of his sleeping bag relaxed him.

# Chapter 15
# Whitewater Circus Dance

Once Tom fell asleep, he'd slept like a rotting tree. Jack's "Up and at 'em. Whitewater today" awakened him and sent sparks running throughout the cabin. The Scouts moved quickly, preparing for their big day. Tom was both scared and excited. He'd never been in white water and wondered if he was up to the challenge. The thought of seeing Cecille was making him nervous. He hoped that they would become more than pen pals.

Jack yelled over the turmoil.

"Remember, we're not coming back to the cabin after breakfast. Wear your bathing suit and your wet shoes. Don't forget a towel and a warm shirt. You may get chilled being in and out of the water. Bring dry clothes in a daypack."

As Tom finished packing his daypack, Jack walked over. "Tom, you're sweeping the cabin. Ack, you've got the washroom. Don't forget!"

The simplicity of sweeping required just enough focus to keep Tom from fretting.

Before the Scouts loaded the canoes, Jack gathered the boys. Tom was thankful that, for once, everyone was prepared.

"When we get to the Canoe Dock, rack the canoes. Then take your paddles, lifejackets, and daypacks to the back porch. We're doing a bacon-biscuit breakfast. Eat quickly. We need to get moving as soon as possible. There are a bunch of pickups today so all the campers can get back for the Circus. Questions?"

There were none. The canoes returned to their regular groups. As they pulled away from the Scout Point dock, Tom appreciated how smoothly Ack and Borden paddled in front of him. The three of them were a good team. He wondered with whom and where in the canoe he'd be on the Dumoine trip. He hoped their threesome would be together. The thought that the reality might be different worried him.

The biscuits were tasty. Immediately after eating, the Scouts packed into the van. The trailer was loaded with aluminum canoes.

Even though the energy was high, the conversation was subdued during the half hour drive. Tom was eager and apprehensive. He continued to be amazed at Shaine and Ric's fixation on the dance.

"Unload all five canoes. We're starting with two-man boats."

Only Tom and Borden moved. Doug had to shout again to be heard above the rushing water.

"Carry the boats down to the grass at the landing ramp. Make a pile of your daypacks. They're safe here."

Except for the dam, the area looked remote. At the edge of the river, the water jumped up between the rocks and swirled back down into the suck of the current. Tom felt both excited and unnerved.

"We're walking up the road to the top of the dam. Leave your gear with the canoes," Doug said. "Be aware of cars on the highway. Walk in single file."

As they walked, Tom stared at the river. It was wide, and the dam was massive. They stopped at an overlook. In front of them, a wide tongue of surging water shot from a spillway. Its power was hypnotizing.

Doug launched into a lecture.

"Welcome to moving water. I use the term 'moving

water' as opposed to white water because, most of the time on a river, you want to be in the moving water and not in the white stuff."

"Why?" Rio asked the question that Tom had been unwilling to ask.

"The white water is turbulent. You can't tell where it's going. It might be a hole that won't support your canoe."

Doug had everyone's undivided attention as he talked about the difference between white water and smooth downstream current. As he pointed out the river's features, Tom recognized the train of standing waves and the eddies that swirled behind the boulders and below submerged rocks. The swift water ended at a rocky island.

"The big eddy behind that rocky island would be an excellent place to station a rescue canoe. It would also be a good place for rescuers to stand with throw ropes. Now, what can I clarify?"

Rio asked a series of questions and seemed apprehensive. As Tom listened, it was apparent that Rio wasn't seeing the river as clearly as he did. The interplay of the currents, the rocks, and the eddies seemed obvious to him.

Suddenly, Tom remembered spending hours playing with his father at the stream near his grandparents' cabin. They'd analyzed the water's flow and raced sticks down the currents. He smiled at the feeling generated by those memories.

"Those were excellent questions," said Doug. "Anyone else have any concerns?"

It didn't surprise Tom that there were none. He had a feeling that the boys were eager to get on the river, but a little afraid of the complexities of the moving water.

On the walk back along the road, Ric and Shaine started fooling around.

"Single file," shouted Doug. "Pay attention. You're

acting like children."

"This is serious stuff," yelled Jack. "If you can't behave on dry land, how can we trust you on the river? Do you want to sit and watch?"

"No," said Shaine.

Tom saw Shaine mutter something to Ric, who waited and walked sheepishly at the end of the line.

At the canoes, Doug reviewed safety protocols. Tom listened carefully. He was bothered that some of his fellow Scouts were paying little attention.

"What are our paddling groups?" Shaine asked.

"Same as we started yesterday," said Doug. "We'll see how everyone does in two-man boats. Then, people will shift around. We'll end the morning with two three-man canoes."

"That's good by me. I'm a natural stern man," Shaine said. "Me and my whitewater paddle. It's so much better than that old piece of wood."

Shaine kicked at Tom's paddle.

Tom was tired of being harassed but didn't react. He was trying to understand Doug's thinking. Rio had his strengths, but paddling didn't seem to be one of them. Rio was snapping photos and seemed happy as the photographer. Tom wished he would concentrate more on paddling.

"We'll start by capsizing the canoes in the current. Moving water is powerful. Stay upstream of your canoe. Don't stand up unless you're in knee-deep water. Hold on to your paddle. We don't want to spend time retrieving paddles as they drift downstream. Any questions?"

The Scouts were silent.

"Let's load up. We'll meet in the big eddy on the other side."

As they paddled across the current, the power of the moving water pulled their canoe off course.

"Pull harder," yelled Rio. "The water is strong."

Once all the canoes rafted up in the eddy, Doug said, "Jack and I will be the safety canoe. Tom and Rio will be the first to paddle up into the current and capsize. Once they're back in their canoe and functional, they'll become a second rescue canoe. Then, we'll have two canoes dump in the current and do two rescues at the same time."

While Tom appreciated the honor of being first, it was scary.

Tom turned and looked at Rio.

"Ready?"

Rio nodded. "Let us turn over to the right."

They powered into the current, grabbed the gunwales, and flipped the canoe. The water yanked Tom downward. It felt much colder than at camp. As he fought to the surface, he remembered to hold on to his paddle. When Jack and Doug paddled to rescue them, he tried to push the canoe toward them. Influencing a water-filled canoe in swirling water was difficult.

Doug hauled the water-filled canoe out of the river, emptied it, and slid it back onto the surface. Climbing back into the canoe took more energy than Tom expected; the water wanted to keep him. As the canoes scraped and bumped in the turbulence, he saw why they were using aluminum boats. If they subjected their wood and canvas boats to this turmoil, it might result in a long evening session with the Ambroid, if they survived at all.

Once Tom and Rio were ready, Doug yelled "Shaine and Ric, you're next. Once they're over and in the water, Lloyd and Chet, you flip. Rio and Tom will be your rescue boat."

After Shaine and Ric upended their canoe, both boys came up sputtering. In desperation, they immediately grabbed on to the overturned canoe. Jack and Doug reached them quickly.

"Shaine, move to the upstream side," Doug shouted.

Doug's skill was impressive. Moving as if it was one continuous action, he pulled, flipped, and shoved the boat into the water. Before Shaine and Ric were ready, their canoe was waiting.

"Where are your paddles?" yelled Doug.

Their paddles had floated downstream. Tom was glad that he'd held on to his.

"We'll have to get their paddles," Doug shouted. "Lloyd, Chet, come out and flip. Rio and Tom will rescue you."

By the time all the canoes had capsized, Tom appreciated how moving water complicated the rescue process. The river pushed the boats wherever it wanted, and often not to the safest places. High spirits and adrenaline kept things exciting.

After the rescues, he understood both paddlers' parts of a rescue. Getting the capsized canoe emptied and back in the water as quickly as possible was the stern man's job. Holding the canoe perpendicular to the water-filled boat was the bowman's responsibility. Rio moved slowly, which made Tom uneasy.

When all the canoes were resting in the big eddy, Doug said, "Remember that you want to be on the upstream side of a water-filled canoe. It weighs the same as a small car."

"You don't want to be between a full boat and a rock. You'll get squished." Jack clapped his hands and rubbed them together. "You don't want to become applesauce."

"Time to change partners," Doug said.

"Lloyd, you're coming into my bow," said Shaine. "Ric, go with Chet."

"STOP!" Doug glared at Shaine. "Who put you in charge?"

"I was trying to be helpful."

"I don't need your help, nor do I want your input. I am the GUIDE. I make the decisions. When I speak, IT IS

A COMAND!"

Shaine stared over Doug's head.

"If necessary, I'll make every single decision for the entire trip! Understand?"

"Yes. I just thought..."

"I don't want your ideas, unless I ask for them. UNDERSTAND?" yelled Doug.

"Yes." Shaine lowered his gaze.

"Thank you! Anyone have any questions?"

No one said anything. Looking around, Tom saw Doug had made his point.

"Tom, move in front of Borden. Lloyd, go into Shaine's bow. Ric, go in front of Rio. Jack will be in the stern with Ack in the bow. I'll have Chet with me."

Paddling with Borden gave Tom a sense of confidence. Hopefully, in a little while, they would exchange front and back.

"We're going to ferry across the river," Doug said. "The bowman provides the power. The stern man sets and holds the angle. Let the current slide the canoe. I'll go first. Jack will be second. Watch. Then, do. Let's go!"

Borden was a strong paddler, but Tom sensed he had difficulty finding and maintaining the appropriate slant. He felt like they were straining to hold their place rather than have the surging water drive the canoe across the river.

After everyone had ferried both across and back two times, Doug called, "Tom and Borden, Lloyd and Shaine, change positions. Bow to stern, stern to bow."

"Thank God," said Borden.

"You did well," Tom said.

"If you think so. I felt like we were a second away from disaster. It was tense."

Paddling in the stern, the geometry of the canoe and the currents made sense to Tom. Borden's powerful strokes in the bow enhanced their precision and their boat danced over the flowing river.

"Time to change partners again," shouted Doug. "Ack, you're going to Tom's bow. Shaine will be in Jack's bow. Ric, you're in front of Lloyd. Chet, you go in front of Rio. That leaves Borden to suffer with me."

Staying in the stern made Tom feel good. His concentration on paddling at camp was paying off.

After ferrying across the current and back, Ack turned to Tom. "You seem to know what you're doing. This canoe is as steady as it was when I was with Jack."

Tom smiled. "Thanks."

"Raft up. We're doing well. Time to make things more exciting. We'll head upstream for S turns. We'll sneak up the river from eddy to eddy. Then we'll peel out into the current and head downstream." Doug pointed across the river. "Catch the big eddy behind that large rock on the far side. Your canoe should move in the shape of an S."

Immediately, Tom understood the maneuvering. Rio asked for more detail. Doug explained the sequence of each step. After a third step-by-step analysis, Rio said that he understood.

"I'll lead. Shaine and Jack will be the initial safety boat. They'll stay down here. Shaine, you've got an important place as the bowman of the rescue canoe."

Tom thought that Shaine's salute and nod looked disingenuous.

When Doug's canoe moved forward, Tom said, "Ack, ease off. We're fourth, so we can watch the others and learn."

Sliding from eddy to eddy, the three boats ahead of them moved upstream. As they watched, Tom explained the paddlers' strokes to Ack. Some needed to be as strong as possible while others needed to be precise.

Well upstream of them, Doug's canoe popped into the river. When the current caught the bow, the boat snapped downstream. Both Borden and Doug looked excited as their canoe rushed down the river. A minute later, Ric and Lloyd were grinning ear to ear as their canoe did the same. In front of Tom and Ack, Chet and Rio's boat inched into the fast water and was rocked sideways into the flow. Neither looked comfortable.

As Tom positioned their canoe, he said, "Paddle on the left side. You'll be leaning downstream. The canoe will be more stable."

"Sounds good," said Ack. "The water's moving fast."

"Take one strong forward stroke and lean out on a draw," said Tom. "Let's go."

Their canoe popped into the fast water and spun downstream. Being caught by the current was exhilarating, and they flew down the fast water.

After a couple of strokes, Tom aimed the bow toward the big eddy.

"Cross draw!"

Ack jammed his paddle deep into the water.

The canoe twisted precisely into the eddy.

"That was cool. I did nothing. You're a magician," said Ack.

"Not really. It's all in the timing. Without your cross draw, we'd have missed it. Good job."

Shortly after, Tom was surprised when Shaine and Jack slid into the eddy behind them. He'd thought they were the safety canoe. Doug answered his unspoken question.

"Once Borden and I were in this big eddy, we became the safety canoe. Then, Shaine and Jack followed Ack and Tom. As we travel down the Dumoine, we'll always designate a safety canoe but know that it may change."

Immediately, Rio asked for an explanation. While Tom was mildly upset with himself that he hadn't seen Shaine and Jack behind them, he accepted the fact that there was still a lot to learn. When Rio questioned the changing of the designated safety canoe for a third time,

Tom was pleased to see that he was not the only one who was struggling.

Finally, Doug said, "Now, we'll do this again. Same order, but this time, when your boat gets into the big eddy, it becomes the safety canoe. The other boat paddles to the landing for a break."

Ack turned to Tom.

"I'm glad we're not first. I like watching them."

"Me too."

As other canoes worked upstream, they watched. Borden and Doug were smooth again, but Ric and Lloyd got rocked into a wave. They looked tense. Chet and Rio inched into the current and spun slowly, but they appeared to have more control than last time.

"Ready?"

"Yeah," said Ack. "This is exciting."

"Remember we become the safety canoe when we get into the big eddy."

Over his shoulder, Ack grinned at Tom. "Yes, Captain."

"Ready?" Tom said. "Pull hard."

Their canoe stabbed into the river.

"Draw!"

Ack's stroke caught the current and smoothly their canoe snapped downstream. As they rode the waves, Tom smiled. Moving water was fun. They entered the eddy smoothly.

Looking upstream, Tom saw Shaine and Jack beginning their S turn. When their boat hit the current, Tom saw a problem. Its angle was wrong. The canoe teetered. Jack tried to brace, but the canoe capsized and flung the paddlers into the raging waters.

"Get ready to rescue," yelled Tom. "Ack, paddle hard, now."

As Shaine drifted past, Tom swung the canoe into the current.

"Ack, grab Shaine and pull him in."

"Shaine, we've got you!" Ack shouted.

After a couple of pulls, their canoe caught up with Shaine. While Tom maneuvered, Ack helped Shaine climb in.

"I don't know what happened. The river grabbed us, and we went over."

"Where's your paddle?" asked Tom.

"Don't know."

Looking upstream, Tom saw that, from the other side, Borden and Doug had rescued both Jack and the canoe.

"Ack, we're going downstream to get Shaine's paddle. Keep your eyes open."

The paddle was floating below the big eddy. Its glossy finish made it sparkle. Ack handed it to Shaine.

"The shine must make it hard to hold." Ack smiled.

"It's the best money can buy!" Shaine snapped.

Doug stood in his boat and signaled for them to paddle to the landing.

As they pulled to the shore, Earnie was waiting. Tom wondered how much of the morning Earnie had seen.

"Tom, Ack, you did a nice job getting Shaine."

Proudly, Tom stood taller.

"I've been watching from the parking lot. I've seen some impressive paddling. It's time for the staff to talk. Relax for a few minutes. I brought some cookies."

Sitting in the sun, Tom dried off and warmed up with the energy of the cookies radiating through his body. Maneuvering in the swirling water had been electrifying and all-encompassing; he hadn't realized how cold he'd gotten.

The Scouts were uncharacteristically quiet as they chewed on their cookies. The anticipation was tangible. Tom's stomach felt like someone was squeezing Playdough into snakes. Shaine, Chet, and Ric seemed preoccupied, chatting about the dance and girls. Tom and the others listened with minimal interest. Tom wondered what the adults would decide.

After a few minutes, the staff rejoined the boys.

When Earnie started speaking, Tom knew that he'd say that it had been a difficult decision. As Earnie droned on about teamwork, camaraderie and cooperation, he tried to look attentive.

"Now, the tentative canoe groups."

The boys sprang to high alert.

"The first boat is Ric with Jack in the stern. The second is Chet, Lloyd, and Rio."

Tom was calm on the outside, but his guts were gnashing.

"The third canoe is Shaine and Doug."

Had Tom heard accurately?

"And the last group is Ack and Borden with Tom in the stern."

The three high-fived their jubilation. But suddenly, Tom was terrified. He was the stern man. He was in control of the canoe and, in many ways, responsible for the other two. As the three celebrated, Tom felt a few daggers of hurt feelings from a couple of the others. He had expected Shaine to argue and was surprised when he said nothing.

"It's time to go back on the water and test these groupings. Remember, they're not final." Earnie pulled on a lifejacket. "Now that you are four canoes, I'll paddle solo in the extra one. Let's play follow-the-leader."

Once the canoes were ready, Earnie led them in ferries and simple S turns. Tom's boat jelled quickly as a team. After each task, Ack and Bordon exchanged bow and middle positions several times. Both said they were comfortable in either location. Ack's long arms and Borden's strength enhanced Tom's control. Their boat glided across the water, hopping from eddy to eddy with precision and grace.

The other three canoes also worked well together. Earnie led them upstream into faster, more turbulent water.

With all five canoes tucked together in a small eddy close to the dam, Earnie issued a challenge.

"This is the last task of the morning. Each canoe will peel out into the tongue. Once you're headed downstream, try to catch the little eddy behind that almost submerged rock."

Earnie pointed to the place where the main current divided into two streams.

"Then, you'll ferry across to the long eddy on the other side, below the white angled boulder. Finally, peel out and catch the big eddy below the island. There are three maneuvers. I'll demonstrate."

"What happens if we miss the little eddy?" asked Rio.

"You'll get swept downstream. If that happens, paddle into the big eddy. This is a demanding sequence. Any more questions?"

No one asked anything.

"I'll start," said Earnie. "Then, Doug's boat. Rio's canoe will follow. Tom, you'll be fourth. Because they are the furthest downstream at the beginning, Ric and Jack will be the initial safety boat. Once I'm sitting in the big eddy, then I'll be the safety boat. Take a minute and plan things with your canoe mates."

Ack and Borden turned to Tom. He shrugged his shoulders.

"The worst that can happen is we'll flip over and float through the wave train."

Saying this out loud made Tom feel better. Without much discussion, the three agreed on their sequence of paddle strokes.

Earnie's canoe popped into the rushing current. He caught the faint eddy perfectly, and for a moment, his boat sat peacefully surrounded by raging water. He knifed across into the narrow eddy and paused. Skating back into the current, he ended the run in the big eddy.

"He makes it look so simple," said Ack.

"It's harder than it looks," said Tom.

As they watched, Doug's boat struggled to catch the first eddy and, with Shaine pulling like a madman, made it. They glided through the remaining maneuvers.

"That was impressive," said Borden.

"Hopefully, it'll be easier with three of us," Tom replied.

When Rio's canoe hit the tongue, it rocked wildly and threw its paddlers off balance. They were shaken and missed both the small and long eddies. They slipped into the big eddy, joining the first two boats.

"Our plan won't work!" Tom shouted. "We need to do the second sequence on opposite sides. Got it?"

Ack and Borden nodded.

"Let's go! Paddle hard."

Their canoe shot into the billowing water and twisted downstream. As the bow of the canoe touched the little eddy, Ack planted a deep cross draw; Borden surged a forward stroke; and Tom jammed a pry. Their canoe spun and caught the eddy. They took a deep breath.

"Outstanding!" Tom shouted. "Shall we keep going?"

Ack's fist pumped, thumb up. Borden saluted.

"Okay. Pull hard!"

Their boat popped into the current. As Ack and Borden strained against the driving current, Tom held the canoe on a steep angle. Their canoe slid smoothly into the long eddy.

"Excellent teamwork. Let's take a breath."

"You did a great job, skipper," said Ack.

"Thanks," said Borden. "You nailed it."

"We make a good team." Tom grinned. "Ready to continue?"

"Yeah," shouted Ack. "Let's go."

Ack's cross draw pulled the boat into the main flow. The canoe bounced through the waves and joined the three boats in the big eddy.

All eyes turned upstream.

As Jack's canoe swung into the tongue, Ric seemed to lose his balance, and the upstream gunwale dipped into the current. Instantly, the boat capsized and catapulted the paddlers into the swirling water.

One swam toward the far shore. The current pushed the other toward the island. The overturned canoe floated down in the center of the current.

Doug shouted commands.

"Tom, get the canoe. Rio, ferry across and get the swimmer on the far shore. My boat people sit tight. I'll get the one coming to the island."

"What about me?" Earnie yelled.

"You're the safety canoe!"

Doug grabbed a throw line and ran up the rocky shore.

Doug's first toss was perfect. Ric grabbed the rope and was pulled to shore. On the other side, Jack crawled out of the river and met Rio's canoe.

Near the end of the standing waves, Tom's canoe caught the submerged boat. Ack and Borden completed the canoe-over-canoe smoothly.

"Borden, can you solo the canoe into the quiet water?" Tom asked. "We'll safety."

"Okay."

Once Borden was ready to paddle, Doug signaled for everybody to move to the landing below the parking lot.

As the Scouts regrouped on dry land, several seemed shaken. Rio tried to be calm, but it was clear the rescue had rattled him.

"Get your towels and warm up," said Doug. "We're finished for the day. The van should be here soon."

Once people were dry, they seemed calmer. Doug

debriefed the Scouts. Tom paid attention. When the talk droned on, it frustrated him that some of his fellows lost interest.

Earnie spoke up, and everyone focused.

"To echo what Doug said. Things happen on a river and that's why you can never relax in moving water. As a group, everyone stayed calm and responded quickly. Your teamwork says a lot about your trust in each other. That's what Catamount is all about - adventure, brotherhood, and courage."

Tom wished that Earnie had ended on another note. He was tired of hearing about the ABCs. He could only imagine how boring the same speech felt to the old timers.

"The van will be here any minute. See you back at camp."

Earnie walked to the parking lot and drove off.

"Get your daypacks," said Jack. "If you want to change, there's an outhouse on the far side of the parking lot."

Tom sat on the grass to relax. Large white clouds filled the blue sky. The morning had gone well. With the paddling completed, he began to feel apprehension about the Circus and the dance.

Looking for something to do, a couple of Scouts began to skip stones. Shaine walked over and shook Tom's hand.

"Congratulations," Shaine said loudly.

Outwardly friendly, he smiled and sat. Whispering, he said, "I hope you follow your escape plan tomorrow. You're a rookie. You shouldn't be a stern man. You ruined my chances. If you don't get sick and go to hospital, I'll make you sorry. The Dumoine will be the worst time of your life. I promise."

Shaine stood and walked to the edge of the river.

Tom was stunned. How did Shaine know about his

option to leave?

The Scouts started competing for the most bounces and the farthest distance. But, for Tom, time stopped. He stared at the river. The current churned, in/out, up/down, this way/that way. Caught by an eddy, a stick twisted, unable to escape. He felt kinship.

Doug walked over and sat.

"You okay?"

Smiling a brave face, Tom said, "I'm fine, just tired. Didn't sleep well last night."

"I understand. Your first time in moving water is the scariest."

The two sat silently.

"Thanks," said Tom.

"For what?"

"For putting me in the stern."

"You earned it."

"But this is my first river trip. Shouldn't it be someone with more experience?"

"You're a natural. You sense the canoe and know what it's going to do. For most people, that understanding comes with time and experience. For some, it's intuitive, like you were born with it."

"I guess so."

"I'll bet that there's a part of you that's scared. It's a lot of responsibility."

"Yeah." Tom sighed. "I hope I can do it."

"You can. You'll be tested. But you'll learn and become more comfortable."

"How'd you learn about rivers?"

Before Doug could answer, a cheer erupted. The van and trailer had pulled into the parking lot. The boys loaded the canoes quickly. Inside the warm van, the conversation focused on the Circus and the dance. Both topics made Tom uncomfortable. But sitting between Borden and Ack, he felt safe and dozed.

The Scouts arrived at camp as lunch was being dismissed. Food had been saved, and they gobbled it on the back porch.

After they ate, Jack said, "No rest hour today. We're helping with Circus setup. And remember, we're the carnies during intermission."

Tom turned to Borden.

"What does that mean?"

"At the halfway point in the Circus acts, there's an intermission. It's like a carnival. We sell drinks, candy, and popcorn to the younger campers."

"How do they get money? I thought we weren't allowed to have money at camp?"

"While we were out in the Park, the younger campers earned Circus Bucks doing chores. It's pretend money."

"Sounds like slave labor," Ack said.

"It was a blast," Lloyd said.

"We did some silly stuff when we were little," Chet said. "I remember sweeping the path to the washroom."

"As a Middie, I built shelves for our foreign counselor," Ric said. "Boy, I over-charged him. He was a sucker. Now, as Scouts, we sell the goodies. We're partnered with the same ages at the other camps."

Smiling, Shaine smoothed his hair. "Working with the ladies will be fun."

"Enough small talk," Jack said. "Time to work."

Moving tables, assembling the sales booths, and carrying boxes of treats took several hours. Tom was glad because it kept his mind focused on the immediate. While carrying a large box, something caught Tom's ankle. He tumbled to the ground.

"Let me help you." Shaine smiled. "The big boxes are so awkward. You can't see where you're going. You could get hurt."

Tom saw nothing that would have caused him to stumble.

"Hope nothing got broken." Shaine grinned. "I mean, in the box."

By mid-afternoon, they had transformed the Main Yard behind the amphitheater into two rows of stands. When Jack held a raffle for the choice of assigned tasks, Tom and Ack chose popcorn.

At Rio's insistence, they went to the Trip Shed for a final run-through of their act. The performance went smoothly. Tom was confident that the sweeping finale would be a scene stealer. Jack had a knack for acting silly.

Wanting their act to be a surprise, the Scouts carried the elephant costumes to the Boat House and stored them out of sight.

As they paddled to the cabin, Shaine made several low comments about Jack becoming a clown and Ack being a shitter. He got some laughs, but his remarks had an edge.

Jack hustled them to shower and change clothes. After the customary raffle, Tom was in the last trio. While waiting, he had a panic attack about what to wear. Jack resolved the dilemma by handing out dark blue Camp Catamount t-shirts.

As Tom dressed and combed his hair, his cabin mates hurried him with jokes and barbs about Cecille. As the ribbing continued, he became numb to it and relaxed a little.

After paddling back at the Main Yard, the boys helped carry the food and utensils for the cookout. As they finished, a Camp Caribou van drove up, and a group of girls disembarked. When Tom recognized Cecille, his mouth became dry. Led by their counselor, a tall dark-haired young woman, the girls walked toward the Scouts.

Jack broke the ice.

"Mary Rose, welcome to Camp Catamount. You're a little early, aren't you?"

"No, Jack, we're right on time. No one told you we were coming over early to decorate for the dance?"

"No, but that's fine with us. Can we help?"

"Absolutely. Let me introduce the girls."

Turning to the boys, she said, "At Caribou, we're called Martens. Martens are cousins to Wolverines and are one of the fiercest creatures in the northern forests. If you respect them, they are friendly. But, if you're not polite, they'll bite you, very badly."

Tom wasn't sure exactly what Mary Rose was saying, but he got the polite or else message. Introductions started with Cecille. Her blonde hair sparkled. He didn't catch the names of the other girls.

After Jack introduced the Scouts, Mary Rose asked for volunteers. Tom and Ack joined Cecille and another girl as they walked to the van.

"Ack is new like me and he's from Scotland," said Tom.

Cecille stuck out her hand.

"I'm Cecille. This is Rhomae. She's new as well. She's from Paris."

"That's cool," Ack said. "How did you get from Paris to Camp Caribou?"

"My dad's a diplomat. He'd gone to Catamount as a boy. We're moving to Ottawa in the middle of the summer, and he suggested I go to camp. My mom goes nuts when we move, so I agreed to get out of the way."

"How's camp been treating you?"

"It's been good. We start our big trip in a couple of days," said Rhomae.

"So do we. We're doing the Dumoine. It's a whitewater river." Ack stood taller.

"My brother did the Dumoine last summer." Cecille shrugged and let out a sigh. "We'll be in the Park, going all the way across it and doing some fish research on a couple of remote lakes."

"That sounds cool," said Ack.

There were four boxes in the back of the van. Ack

picked up one of the bigger boxes. Before Tom could do the same, Cecille grabbed the second large one. Smiling at Tom, she said, "You know that girls can do anything that boys can do."

Tom grinned awkwardly. "I know."

"Follow me," said Ack. He led them to the back entrance of the Lodge and into the dining hall.

The Martens and Scouts strung lights and dangled strands of crepe paper between the beams. The energy was high. Several times, Chet and Ric had to be reminded that throwing rolls of crepe paper was not decorating.

While stretching to run an electrical cord, Tom stood on a chair. Ric stumbled into him. Losing his balance, he tumbled onto the floor.

"Sorry," Ric said. "Shaine, watch out. I knocked Tom off the chair."

"Standing on chairs is so dangerous." As Shaine walked away, he said, "We wouldn't want our new stern man to get hurt."

"No harm, no foul," said Tom. He was angry but knew that making a stink was useless.

When they were finished, the dining room had been transformed. Tom wondered how long everything would stay up. If his school dances were an indication, their efforts would be demolished in the first half hour.

The group exited onto the porch. Tom noted the clouds had darkened and the ceiling was falling.

Below them, the Main Yard was filled with colors. The dark blue of Catamount contrasted with the bright yellow of Timberland. The forest green of Caribou clashed with the powder blue of Pine Bluff. Tom wondered if the oppositions were intentional. The younger boys and girls stood in separate cabin groups, while the older campers intermingled. Waiting in two long lines, everyone inched toward two large grills from which the aroma of charbroil wafted.

Jack extended his arm to Mary Rose.

"Mademoiselle, may I escort you to the culinary delights of the Catamount kitchen?"

Tom gulped, "Cecille, shall we follow them?"

"Sure." Turning to Rhomae, she said, "You and Ack should join us."

After securing their food and drinks, Tom led them down to the Canoe Dock. He was uneasy when the rest of the Scouts and the Martens followed them but found an empty rack away from the rest of the group.

As they ate, Tom asked, "How is your paddling going?"

"Really well. I hope to complete the final parts of the master solo exam in the middle of August," said Cecille.

"That's great."

"How's your paddling?"

"I'll be sterning the camper canoe on the Dumoine."

"That's impressive. You did seem natural in canoe."

"Thanks."

Tom couldn't think of anything else to say.

As the silence was becoming awkward, Cecille said, "Tell me more about New York City. I'd love to see it one day."

Tom's use of the subways and busses amazed Cecille. After Rhomae described the Paris Metro, Ack talked about his recent wandering around London. Tom saw that Cecille felt left out.

"What are the Martens doing for the Circus?"

With hesitancy, Cecille said, "We're going to be clowns. I hope we're funny. What are you doing?"

"An animal act," said Tom. "Rio, our counselor from Switzerland, helped us make some costumes. I hope it goes okay." Not wanting to divulge more, he asked, "How's the fire season up north?"

"So far, it's not bad. But generally, it doesn't heat up until later in July and August. How's your grandfather?"

"He's better."

Tom felt a stab of guilt. He felt pressure to continue the conversation and babbled the first thing that came to him.

"My grandparents are planning to come to Catamount to get me at the end of July. He'll love being back at camp. I wish he could do a short trip, get back on the water again."

Cecille cocked her head.

"I have a crazy idea. Do you know Treasure Island?"

"No, what's that?"

"It's an island in the middle of the Ottawa about 10 kilometers upstream from here and 10 kilometers downstream from Caribou. It's where the youngest campers go for their first overnight trips. We're going there for our change-over outing."

"What's a change-over outing?"

"Most of the campers only stay for a month, and new campers come for August. Rhomae and I are two of a handful who stay for the whole summer. Over that weekend, we're acting as junior guides on a trip to Treasure Island. Maybe you could take your grandparents on an overnight trip and join us. What do you think?"

Before he could say anything, Ack jumped in, "I'm at camp all summer. I'd love to join you." He turned to Tom. "Wouldn't it be neat? That way, I wouldn't have to hang around with the little kids at camp."

Tom's mind overflowed. It sounded like a great idea. But everything about it was beyond his control. He mumbled a response.

"I'll write them about the idea. And I'll ask Earnie about it."

While the other three chatted excitedly about the trip, Tom was engulfed with the enormity of what he'd said. The clang of the Lodge bell broke his paralysis.

From the Scout-Marten crowd, they heard Jack shout, "Don't forget to throw away your trash. We'll regroup in the rear of the amphitheater."

"Martens, do the same," Mary Rose said. "Leave no trash. Sit up top with the Scouts. That way, we'll be near the tables for intermission."

The Scouts and Martens sat intermixed with the same-age campers from Timberland and Pine Bluff. Borden and Lloyd had connected with two Caribou girls. Tom was not surprised that Shaine, Ric, and Chet had connected with Timberland boys and Pine Bluff girls. Shaine knew how to work a crowd.

The Circus began with Earnie and the other three directors making brief speeches. Tom was delighted when Borden whispered that the acts from the younger cabins were short. While the performances were cute, Tom felt as though he'd seen them multiple times before at school assemblies.

"Get up quietly and move to your tables," said Jack.

Tom and Ack went to the popcorn stand. Cecille and Rhomae joined them.

"How did you know we were doing popcorn?" asked Ack.

Rhomae smiled and winked at Cecille.

"We have ways."

The kernels began to pop just as the intermission began. By the time the end-of-intermission bell rang, they were exhausted by shoving bags of popcorn at the crowd of youngsters who were shoving red Circus Bucks at them.

"Shut down quickly," Jack said. "We have to get ready for our act. Boys, once you're finished, go to the Boat House."

"Girls, we're gathering behind the Boat House," said Mary Rose. "There are only a few acts before us."

As the Scouts gathered, Shaine, Ric, and Chet were

missing. As the second act ended, they arrived.

"Where have you been?" barked Borden. "We go on soon."

"The ladies," said Shaine.

"The ladies, my ass," said Borden. "We're getting ready, and you've been goofing around."

"No big deal. All I do is walk hunched over; no one knows who I am or what I do."

Outside, applause rang loudly.

"You're part of the team. We depend on each other," Borden growled. "Get ready."

"Or what!" snapped Shaine. Defiantly, he stepped toward Borden.

"Or I'll send you home," Jack said quietly. "We go on in a minute or two. Get ready!"

Tom climbed onto Borden's shoulders, filling out the elephant's head and ears. Ack shuffled into his place behind Borden under the elephant's skin. They ambled to their ready-to-go position. The crowd clapped and became quiet. Tom heard wheels squeaking, horns honking, and loud guffaws. He guessed the Martens were performing. The audience erupted in cheers.

After the audience silenced, the Scouts heard Rio begin his ringmaster's introduction.

The next few minutes were some of the scariest of Tom's life. What happened was a blur. Borden walked from dark into light. Hopefully, on cue, Tom twisted and wiggled. Below him, Borden marched and bowed. He heard the peanuts fall. The audience gasped, giggled, and exploded with cheers. Finally, Borden ambled back into the shadows.

"You can get down now," said Borden.

Tom slid down Borden's back, relieved to be in the safety of the Boat House.

Outside, the crowd was roaring its applause. Rio rushed them a back onto the stage to take a bow. Jack got a standing ovation.

Back inside the Boat House, smiles broke out, followed by shouts of triumph. Earnie and George rushed in, gushing with compliments. Tom was just overjoyed that the act was behind them.

"Gentlemen," Jack yelled. "You did a wonderful job, but no time to celebrate; we have to help clean up. Leave your costumes here and go up to the tables. We need to pack up the stalls and the goodies."

As the Scouts walked up the hill, the younger campers treated them like rock stars. Then reality struck and they were carrying half-full boxes and bags of trash. Navigating through the crowd of animated boys and girls was maddening.

More quickly than Tom had expected, they finished and headed into the dance. Apparently, Canadian kids listened to the same music they listened to in New York City. This was comforting because he knew the songs.

Dancing was not one of his talents, so he stood with his back to a wall. The darkness was intense, the sound harsh, and the moving bodies felt like an alien force. He had felt this isolation before at school events and sometimes in the crowds of the city. Tom's refuge was outside. A couple of steps at a time so it didn't look like he was actually moving, he maneuvered to the front porch.

The dusk turned to darkness. Tom sat on the top step and looked out over the river. He tried to relax, but his mind whirled with everything that had happened in the last few hours.

A girl's voice asked, "Can I join you?"

Seeing Cecille, Tom smiled. "Sure. It's noisy in there."

"That it is."

In the reflected light, her hair shone and her eyes sparkled.

"It's peaceful out here," she said.

"Yes, it is." Tom knew he should say more, but what?

After a long moment, Cecille said, "The elephant act was amazing. How did you create those costumes?"

"It was Rio's idea. At first, he worked with Ack and Borden. I joined them after lunch yesterday, and together we figured out how to make the ears flap and the trunks wiggle."

Cecille looked interested.

"Rio is an engineering student and figured out how to rig the pulleys to make the mom's trunk go up and down. There were three of us as the mother elephant. I sat on Borden's shoulders with the ears connected to my arms. Ack was the hind legs and the body."

"It was so unique. They'll be talking about it for years." Cecille smiled.

"No way."

"Yes. And Jack was so funny. What a way to end it. I thought Mary Rose was going to die laughing. You know they're dating seriously, don't you?"

"I guess so."

"Well, how do you think our letters got back and forth so quickly?"

"Makes sense." Tom paused, unsure of what to say. "With Rhomae, you sounded pretty excited about your Park trip. I thought you felt that it was pretty lame."

"I do, but she and the other girls need to be excited. Mary Rose and I have talked, and we have a plan for August."

"What kind of plan?"

"A parallel trip!"

Tom had never heard of such a thing, but he knew he had to look interested.

Cecille's words flew.

"Enrollment is down at both Caribou and Catamount, so things need to change. You agree, don't you?"

Tom nodded.

374

"Many people feel it's because the programs haven't changed in years. Girls are as capable as boys. Mary Rose has pressed the Caribou people, so our July trip is girls-only. This means no male staff as canoe carriers. Showing we can thrive without men will appeal to strong-minded girls."

Again, Tom nodded. So far, Cecille was making sense. She took a deep took a breath and raced on.

"So, in August, our idea is to do a parallel trip with the Scouts on a white-water river. The groups paddle together but camp separately. Having girls nearby would appeal to boys, wouldn't it?"

Tom wasn't sure, but he didn't want to dampen Cecille's enthusiasm. He nodded and said, "I think so."

Cecille looked into Tom's eyes. "You know this kind of trip will generate lots of enthusiasm. Future campers will be excited, and more will come. What do you think?"

"Sure," said Tom, wondering where she was going with this idea.

"So, after a successful whitewater trip, the excitement will mean that in the future Caribou and Catamount will have full enrollment, eh?"

"That would be good."

"Unfortunately," Cecille lowered her voice. "All of this is possible because the Director was hurt in the car accident last week and might not be able to return this summer. This means more liberal people are in charge. This is an opportunity, right?"

Tom nodded again.

"This is a big secret. You can't say anything." Cecille stopped abruptly.

Sitting quietly, they stared at the river. Tom tried to connect all the dots. He liked Cecille and didn't want to disappoint her.

"The trip idea sounds pretty exciting," Tom said hesitantly.

She smiled and cocked her head waiting. He knew he had to ask the question that frightened him.

Trying to sound positive, he asked, "Is there anything that I can do to help?"

"Yes."

Tom's heart stopped.

"What's that?"

Cecille looked around and leaned in.

"You need to get Jack and Doug on board."

This dumbfounded him.

"What does that mean?"

Even more quietly, Cecille whispered, "On the Dumoine trip, when the time is right, you need to share this idea with them. Will you do this, please?"

Tom knew what he had to say.

"Yes. But why me?"

"Because you're the new boy. You see things differently. We paddled well together at the start of camp, didn't we?"

"Yes."

"You were comfortable with me paddling. You know I can handle a canoe as well as anyone. You had confidence in me in the stern, didn't you?"

"I did."

"You can say that. You can talk about how unpopular the single-sex schools were with your classmates. I think you said no one wanted to go to an all-boys or all-girls school, didn't you?"

"Maybe I did. It's true."

"Well, on a parallel trip, it would be the best of traditional single-sex and the modern coed. We'd have independent campsites, but paddle together."

"Yes, but I wouldn't be on the trip..."

"That makes your observations so much stronger."

"I guess so." Tom felt trapped. "But won't they be surprised?"

"What do you think Mary Rose is telling Jack right now? I didn't come up with this plan on my own. Will you do it?"

"I'll try."

"Promise?" Cecille looked intently into his eyes.

Tom knew she had trapped him.

"Yes."

"Thank you! This means so much to me. It could be good for both camps. Don't you think so?"

"Of course."

Tom knew he had to respond positively. He'd been set up. His piece was a small part in a larger plot.

"You're wonderful." Cecille stood and smiled. "Now, do you think we should go dance? We don't want people talking about us, do we?"

"Not any more than they already are."

Trying to be a gentleman, he held out his hand. He was happy when Cecille took it.

They danced together for several songs, but when a slow ballad came on, they fled to the porch. Ack and Rhomae joined them.

Cecille led the conversation and talked about the change-over trip. She seemed so confident. Tom was glad that she didn't mind that he was quiet. As the four planned, Ack explained their baking experiences. Both girls wanted to see Ack and Tom in action. In the distance, lightning flashed. There was no rumble of thunder.

"It's miles away," said Cecille. "I hope we get back to Caribou before we get dumped on."

Quicker music began. Ack and Rhomae went inside. After a silent minute, Cecille pulled Tom into the Lodge. He would have preferred to sit and talk. The last dance was slow. While he felt awkward with his arms around Cecille, he enjoyed the experience.

When the lights popped on, the crowd surged into the Main Yard. As goodbyes were exchanged, the counselors from the visiting camps hustled their campers to the buses.

"It was good to see you again," said Tom.

"Yes. It was nice to see you."

"Have a good trip in the Park."

"We will."

As Rhomae and Ack walked away, loud enough to be heard, Cecille said, "Remember, you promised to do it. You will, won't you?"

"I will," said Tom, uncomfortable at being heard.

"Thank you. You are so kind and so courageous."

Cecille smiled.

"Martens, up to the bus," commanded Mary Rose. "We don't want to get wet."

"Scouts, time to help clean up the Dining Room. Let's go!" Jack yelled. "Now!"

Mary Rose forced the girls toward the parking lot. Jack drove the boys back into the Dining Room.

As Tom swept up the shreds of colored paper on the floor, he wondered why anyone would want to decorate when they knew it would be destroyed. Maybe it was a girl thing. Somehow this realization made him feel better about Cecille's plot and his agreement to take part in it. If Mary Rose had talked to Jack about it, the worst that could happen was Doug and Jack would say no.

Once finished, the boys walked to the Canoe Dock, chatting excitedly about who had done what with whom.

"We need to be quiet," Jack said. "The younger campers are in bed, so we have special permission to paddle. Don't mess this up, or they will never let us do this again."

As the Scouts paddled, they struggled to be silent. They were abuzz with energy and whispered stories. The intermittent flashes of light in the distance seemed to echo their excitement.

From the bow, Ack whispered, "What did you

promise to do?"

"I'll tell you later. It's complicated."

"If Cecille made you promise to do something, you're in trouble. She's a smart one."

Tom swallowed. In a conspiratorial tone, he whispered, "You have a role in this, if you want."

"Sounds intriguing."

Suddenly, in a loud, pretend whisper, Jack said, "First canoe around Voyageur Island and back to Scout Point wins extra cookies. But be quiet! Ready. GO!"

Jack and Rio jumped to the lead. Ack strained, and Tom paddled as hard as he could. Their canoe was the first camper boat around the island, right behind the two counselors. Tom began to tire and saw that Ack was fading. He realized another canoe was right behind them.

"Harder!" Tom muttered. "Switch sides. They're going to pass us."

Their burst of energy worked for a few strokes. However, Chet, Ric, and Shaine charged ahead to win.

As the canoeists drifted to cool down, Jack whispered, "Who wants to take a dip?"

This got everyone's attention. Cooling off sounded delightful.

In a conspiratorial voice, Jack said, "Be quiet. It's late. We're not supposed to do this. We don't wake up the younger boys. No jumping. Once the canoes are racked, take off your clothes and slide off the dock. No swimming. Just stand in the water. Eh?"

The water was delightful. It relaxed Tom and calmed the others. After a silent minute, Shaine whispered to Chet, who laughed.

"Be quiet," whispered Jack. "If we get caught, we'll be in big trouble."

A flash of light was followed by a crack of thunder.

"Out of the water," Jack said. "It's going to storm."

Grabbing their clothes, the boys scrambled to the

cabin.

"If you need to pee, go use the washroom, now," Jack said.

Tom was last in the urinal line. Finally, when he stood at the basin, one of his knees was jammed from behind. As he tumbled to the floor, his urine sprayed wildly. The light switch snapped, and the darkness enveloped him.

"Got to watch your back," Shaine hissed. "Have a long night. Get sick."

The door slammed.

Tom's T-shirt and gym shorts were too wet to sleep in. How was he going to explain changing his clothes? The dampness permeated his core.

The flare and the boom were simultaneous. The wind howled. The rain pelted down, almost blinding Tom. By the time he had inched to the cabin, he was drenched.

"You okay?" Jack asked.

"Yeah. Just waited too long."

"Too bad. Get changed and have a good night."

As Tom tried to change silently, Ack whispered, "What happened? You were right behind me."

Above the drum of the rain, Jack barked, "If I hear another voice, someone is sleeping on the floor next to me!"

"Tell you in the morning."

Tom slid into his sleeping bag. His mind buzzed with all that had happened. He knew that sleep would not come easily.

The storm raged. Tom was glad that he was not in a tent. Becoming a stern man had been exciting, but now he was responsible for Borden and Ack. The elephants had been a success. The dance had been okay, but now he was involved in Cecille's wild plan. Shaine had shown that his threats were real.

Tom's brain whirled. Paddling a wilderness river had been a childhood dream. What should he do? Was he ready? Or was he setting himself up for disaster?

A gust rocked the cabin's screens. A fine mist nipped at his face. He tried to be silent as he turned over, but his bunk creaked. Then, he realized that the cabin was filled with squeaking and squirming. It would be a long night.

# Chapter 16
# Decision

Blazing sunlight awakened Tom and his brain began firing on all cylinders. Why was it sunny? It had been storming last night. Everything was in flux. What should he do about Shaine's threats, his promises to Cecille, the responsibilities of being a stern man, the remoteness of the Dumoine, the comforts of the city, the unknowns of his school future, his grandfather's recovery, the strain on his grandmother? If a Treasure Island trip could happen, it would make his grandparents happy. If he left, he would disappoint them. But hopefully, they would understand. Maybe, or maybe not. If he stayed, he'd be facing everything alone. His stomach churned.

The angle of the sunlight told him it was early. Cursing silently, he reversed his position with his feet facing toward the outside of the cabin so those first intense sunbeams wouldn't hit his face. What else was he not learning? Was he ready? What would he do after breakfast?

As Tom squirmed, he tried to be silent. How much sleep had he gotten? Hoping it would quell his twisting guts, he tried his breathing exercises. Slow and deep. In and out. Gradual and prolonged. Lungs full and empty. Again, and again.

A hand shook Tom's shoulder. His mind leaped to full consciousness. But his eyes were heavy.

"Up and at 'em! The sun's out!" Jack shouted.

Tom rolled over. His shoulders ached. Had he injured something yesterday?

At Jack's second yell, "Rise and shine," Tom bolted upright. He didn't hit his head, thankfully. His fatigue made his muscles feel lame. His mind buzzed. The choice he had ahead of him attacked, and he lay down.

Jack's third shout, "We'll be late for breakfast," created movement throughout the cabin. His "Do-your-jobs-before-we-leave" produced panicked activity.

While pulling on clothes, Ack asked, "What happened last night?"

"I'll tell you in the washhouse. I've got to pee," said Tom.

"Go ahead. I'll be there in a sec."

Tom grabbed his kit. What was he going to say?

When Ack walked in, Tom was washing his hands.

"So, what's up with the girls?" asked Ack.

Relieved at Ack's choice of topic, Tom looked around. They were alone.

"We've got to be quiet about this."

Tom explained Cecille's parallel trip plan as Ack washed up.

"That girl's a schemer," Ack said. "It sounds like she's thought of everything."

Shaine was leading a loud group toward the washhouse.

"We need to keep this between the two of us. At least for now. I'll tell Borden later. But please, no talk until we know what we're going to do."

"I agree."

"I'll meet you at the canoes. I've got to sweep out this pigsty."

"It wasn't this bad yesterday. Getting ready for the dance made everyone lose their minds. I'll go check the firewood."

Ack walked toward the cabin, and Tom grabbed a

broom.

"Tom, you look like you're sick," said Shaine.

"Didn't sleep well."

"Maybe you're lovesick." Ric grinned wickedly.

"Tommy's got a girlfriend." Chet smirked.

"Americans can't handle Canada, the wilds or the women." Shaine laughed. "You look awful. Maybe you need to go to the nurse."

From the dock, Jack yelled, "Let's go! Time to eat."

As Ack and Borden loaded into the canoe, Tom knew his front paddlers were two of the strongest. He thought they'd be fine if they did the trip without him.

While paddling, the Scouts' conversation featured tales of new girlfriends and plans for the Lumberjack Roundup. Tom was overjoyed when no one mentioned Cecille. Listening to the wild plans for their clandestine meetings was a welcome distraction. Caribou was about 20 kilometers from Catamount, which at full speed was a three-hour paddle. He thought Pine Bluff was farther away. Shaine and Ric's romantic rendezvous plans could never be completed between lights out and sunrise.

After they racked the canoes, Jack called the Scouts together. Tom groaned internally at the thought of another review of their daily schedule.

"Gentlemen, working together last night, you did a great job. This morning, we'll continue our brotherhood and all go to softball practice during first period. Then, everyone is free for second period. After rest hour, we'll be in the Trip Shed preparing for the Dumoine trip. Remember that letters home are due at supper, so I need them at the end of rest hour."

There was a collective groan. Tom was silent. Maybe the easiest thing to do would be to go to the nurse. His stomach did hurt. If he stayed, he'd have to struggle through two letters.

The bell rang and the Scouts hurried to breakfast.

Sitting at the end of the table, Tom played with his food. Next to him, Borden talked softball with the others. Across from him, Ack sat silently. Tom was grateful to hide in the crowd.

At breakfast announcements, a rousing cheer saluted the Scouts for their Circus performance. As they stood to receive their adulation, Tom noted Borden and Lloyd were like him, uncomfortable in the spotlight. The others loved the attention. After they sat down, Earnie recognized the four trips that were leaving and spotlighted tomorrow's dawn departure for the Scouts' Dumoine trip.

The dining room sizzled with excitement. A part of him wanted nothing to do with the energy. Another part looked forward to the adventure of the Dumoine. A third part yearned for the familiarity of New York. And a fourth wondered about what Earnie might say. His stomach groaned.

At dismissal, Borden said, "We've got things figured out. There's a good place for you on the softball field."

"Got to go to the washroom," Tom said. "My guts are squirmy."

"A good dump will make you feel like a new man. See you in a minute."

"Sure. Start without me."

"We'll wait."

Tom fled to a washroom stall. His intestines emptied in a foul flood. His cramping intensified. Someone walked in. He stifled a groan. He couldn't take it. He was going to the nurse.

For a couple of minutes, the person shuffled around before exiting. Glad to be alone, Tom snuck out of the bathroom and used the Lodge's back entrance. He walked slowly, not wanting to be seen. At the path to the nurse's cabin, he stepped off the road. He was going back to New York; the city was his home.

"What are you doing here?"

Tom's eyes jerked upwards. Ack stood on a joining path.

Both stared, still as scarecrows.

"What are you doing?" Tom asked.

"Going to the nurse. My stomach hurts, really bad. I might need to see a doctor."

"Me too." Tom froze. "Wait a minute! Do you have an escape plan?"

Ack's eyes widened. Tom's heart raced.

"Yes. Do you?" Ack asked.

"I do." Something inside Tom snapped. Anger surged. "Is it because of Shaine?"

Ack lowered his head.

"Yes. He threatened to make me miserable on the Dumoine. He's been after me ever since I almost beat him at tetherball the other day. He's been relentless."

Tom's blood boiled. Ack was a good guy. He'd do well on the Dumoine. He could become a real Cataman. He couldn't let Shaine take this away. Ack needed a place to belong.

"Has he been at you?" Ack asked.

"Yes. Same kind of thing. He said that he'd hurt me on the river."

"Me too. That's scary." Ack stood taller. "But you have so much potential. You're a really good paddler. You've earned the trip. It means so much to you, considering your dad and Grandfather."

Tom stiffened. Ack was saying the same thing about him that Tom had thought about Ack.

The two stared at each other like gunfighters waiting for the other to make the first move.

"Maybe we could each have the other's back?" Tom asked.

Cocking his head, Ack said, "We can't let Shaine do this. He's a jerk."

"An asshole."

"A shithead."

They stood, awkwardly. Tom grinned, and Ack smiled. They stepped together and shook hands. Tom felt energized. He had to protect Ack.

"Shall we go play softball?" Ack asked.

"Yeah. We need to tell Borden."

"You're right. We can be the Three Musketeers."

"Maybe. How about being the BAT boat, B-A-T?" Tom questioned.

"Not so sure. That puts me in the middle."

"That way, I have your back."

Ack stood tall and winked.

"I can't wait to see Shaine's face when we walk up together."

"I feel a lot better," said Tom. "I guess my stomach problems were just nerves."

"Me, too," said Ack.

The two were welcomed at softball practice. Tom became the right fielder. Jack had recruited several Cadets to fill out the roster.

Tom discovered he could run and catch. But hitting a ball with precision would be a long-term learning experience. Ack was the opposite. His shinty skills made him a fearsome batter. But his hand and ball interaction left much to be desired.

During a water break, Borden asked, "Where were you? I started to wonder what was going on."

"Earnie grabbed us as we were coming out of the washroom in the Lodge," Ack said, loudly. "He wanted to know how things were going for the two new boys from different countries. He's a good guy. It was an interesting conversation."

Tom saw Shaine stiffen.

"He's very understanding," Tom added. "He wants all of us to have a good trip."

"Stop the chit-chat," Jack yelled. "Batters out in the field. Fielders, your turn to hit."

When the bell rang to end the period, Jack gathered the boys.

"Good practice. Now, I suggest we focus on other parts of the Lumberjack Roundup. Some of you should go to campcraft to practice your lumber jacking. Cutting with the two-man saw and rolling logs with the peeves take some practice. Some water events have also been added. Obviously, some will be canoeing; others will be those silly kinds of races. Somebody may want to go practice on the slalom course."

Walking down from the fields, Shaine said, "Adding canoeing and those silly water races is stupid. If I'd wanted to do that shit, I'd have come in August for the Regatta."

"No, you wouldn't," said Chet. "You have football practice, Mr. QB."

Shaine smiled. "It's going to be a good year on the gridiron."

The boys divided themselves. Shaine led Chet and Ric to campcraft. Tom and the other three headed toward the waterfront.

"Gentleman, what brings you to the Canoe Dock today?" George said.

"Jack sent us," said Tom. "He said that they've added some canoeing events to the Lumberjack Roundup."

"Yes. The directors wanted to have more campers competing, so they asked for more events."

"What's for us?"

"Not sure. We'll know more after a meeting next week. When you get back from the Dumoine, we'll know what's going on."

"What can we do to prepare?"

"I'd suggest that you work on the slalom course. Who's paddling with who?"

"I'm in the bow," Borden said.

"I'm in your stern," Lloyd said.

"I guess that means we're together." Tom nodded to Ack.

"Sounds good to me, partner." Ack smiled.

Paddling solo, George joined them as they headed to the starting dock.

"I suggest that each team paddle the course slowly. Then, you can do it for time."

Ack and Tom watched Borden and Lloyd paddle to the halfway point and then started their slow run. As they paddled, they planned.

After they finished, Ack announced, "We're ready. Can we go first?"

"Be our guest." Lloyd smiled.

Ack and Tom glided to the starting line.

George held up his stopwatch. "3, 2, 1, GO!"

Ack and Tom sprinted into the course. Ack's impressive draws and cross-draws allowed Tom to slide the canoe smoothly between the poles. The pair tired during the final gates, and the canoe slowed. When they crossed the finish line, both were gasping.

"One minute and fifty-three seconds, pretty good. We forgot to tell you that there's a penalty for touching the poles." George smiled. "You touched the poles in four of the gates, so that's twenty seconds added to your time. Your scored time is two, thirteen."

Lloyd grinned. "Shall we show them how it's done?"

"Gotcha," responded Borden.

Their canoe moved into position. George voiced the count-down. The canoe leaped forward.

As Tom watched, their canoe seemed to glide through its maneuvers. Borden and Lloyd's strokes grabbed the water with grace.

"One forty-five, forty-six, forty-SEVEN," bellowed George.

"Well done," Tom said. "But now that we know about the penalty, can we try it again?"

The waiters' bell rang.

"Time for lunch," said George.

"Maybe later?" asked Ack.

"Maybe," said George. "I believe that you're packing for a trip this afternoon. We'll see if there's time after that."

As the boys walked to lunch, Lloyd smiled. "You two did well for beginners. We didn't tell you that Borden and I were partners in the tandem slalom in last July's Cadet regatta. We practiced for a week before we raced."

"Did you win?" Ack asked.

"No. Shaine did, but his partner's not back."

Ack turned to Tom. "We need to find time to practice."

Lunch discussion focused on the morning's practices, the softball team, the lumberjack events, and the slalom course. Tom listened. He was not surprised when Shaine wanted more softball time.

When Jack asked about lumberjacking, Shaine mentioned that Chet and Ric excelled in the two-man saw. No one had practiced log rolling with the peeves, but Jack was happy to hear that Ric and Borden had won the event for their cabin the summer before and were looking forward to doing it again.

Lloyd reported that he and Borden had beaten Ack and Tom on the slalom course. Tom heard Shaine mumble something disparaging about newbies but was glad when it got no reaction. Assuming there was a solo slalom, the big question was who would paddle it. Shaine said he was clearly the best solo paddler and issued a challenge to everyone.

As lunch ended, Jack said, "Our laundry is done. Pick up the bags on the side porch and head back to the cabin. You need to get your clothing ready for the trip. And don't forget your letters."

On purpose, Tom and Ack moved slowly. The three were the last boat to leave the Canoe Dock.

From the bow, Borden twisted backwards. "Okay, what really happened this morning?"

Ack looked at Tom, who nodded.

"We decided to stay."

"What?"

"Shaine threatened both of us. We were each about to get sick and go to hospital."

"Going forward, we have each other's back," Tom said.

"Thank God," said Borden. "I was worried, and Shaine was almost dancing. He's a clever S.O.B."

"He is," Tom said. "Ack, did you see him when you said we'd talked with Earnie? He looked like someone had jammed a bat up his butt."

"When you added your 'all of us' comment, he blinked hard."

"That was nicely played," said Borden. "We'll need to watch him. I always suspected that he drove out Butt Boy. I've got both of you covered. If needed, we can be a three-man wrecking crew."

"Thanks," Tom said. "I appreciate it."

"Me too," said Ack. "However, we need to keep this quiet. It could get ugly very quickly."

"I agree," Borden said.

"Yes." Tom put his paddle in the water. "We don't say anything to anyone, and we don't talk about it unless we're sure no can hear us."

"Agreed," Ack said.

"Let's get to the cabin. We've got things to do."

Pulling on his paddle, Tom smiled. "The Dumoine awaits."

# THE END

Made in the USA
Monee, IL
25 October 2022

16533608R00229